# ENGLISH MEDIEVAL MISERICORDS
## The Margins of Meaning

BOYDELL STUDIES IN MEDIEVAL ART AND ARCHITECTURE

ISSN 2045–4902

This series aims to provide a forum for debate on the art and architecture of the Middle Ages. It will cover all media, from manuscript illuminations to maps, tapestries, carvings, wall-paintings and stained glass, and all periods and regions, including Byzantine art. Both traditional and more theoretical approaches to the subject are welcome.

Proposals or queries should be sent in the first instance to the editors or to the publisher, at the addresses given below.

Dr Julian Luxford, School of Art History, University of St Andrews, 79 North Street, St Andrews, Fife, KY16 9AL, UK

Dr Asa Simon Mittman, Department of Art and Art History, California State University at Chico, Chico, CA 95929–0820, USA

Boydell & Brewer, PO Box 9, Woodbridge, Suffolk, IP12 3DF, UK

ALREADY PUBLISHED

*The Art of Anglo-Saxon England*
Catherine E. Karkov

*English Medieval Misericords: The Margins of Meaning*
Paul Hardwick

*English Medieval Shrines*
John Crook

*Thresholds of Medieval Visual Culture: Liminal Spaces*
edited by Elina Gertsman and Jill Stevenson

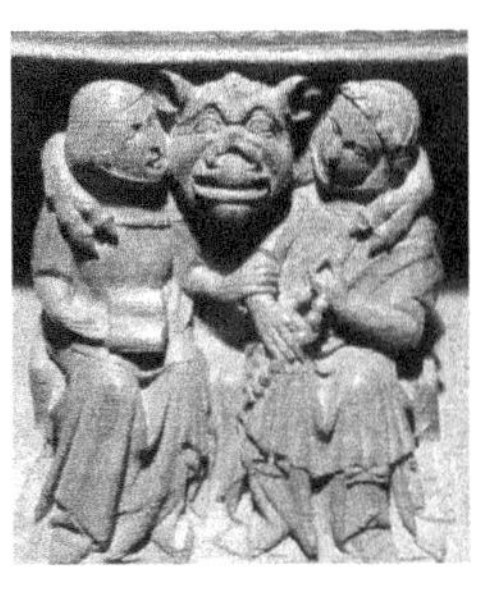

# ENGLISH MEDIEVAL MISERICORDS

## The Margins of Meaning

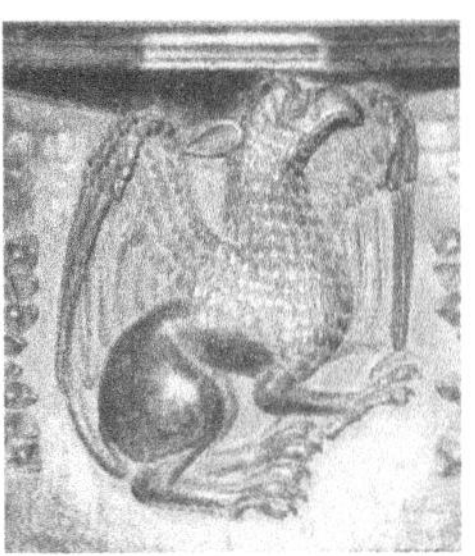

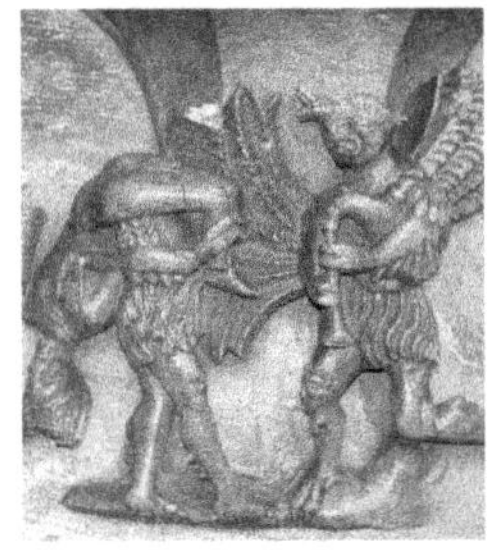

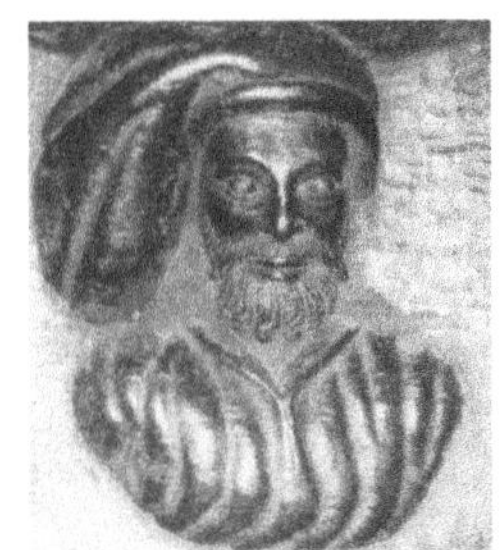

Paul Hardwick

THE BOYDELL PRESS

First published 2011
The Boydell Press, Woodbridge
Reprinted in paperback 2013

ISBN 978 1 84383 659 9 hardback
ISBN 978 1 84383 827 2 paperback

The Boydell Press is an imprint of Boydell & Brewer Ltd
PO Box 9, Woodbridge, Suffolk, IP12 3DF, UK
and of Boydell & Brewer Inc.
668 Mount Hope Ave, Rochester, NY 14620–2731, USA
website: www.boydellandbrewer.com



A CIP catalogue record for this book is available
from the British Library

Designed and typeset by Tina Ranft, Woodbridge, Suffolk

# CONTENTS

# LIST OF FIGURES

# ACKNOWLEDGEMENTS

It is customary to conclude the acknowledgements to books such as this by thanking the countless vicars, vergers, key-holders, caretakers and cleaners who have facilitated access to the material under discussion. Bucking this trend, I would like to place these people at the top of my list. However this present book may fare in contributing to the study of English misericords, it is the often voluntary custodians of our medieval churches who, through their dedication and willingness to share their time, knowledge and, on occasions, bafflement, will both preserve these fragile wonders and continue to connect the curious to this direct line to the world of our ancestors. Very many thanks.

The road from my unimpressive and best forgotten encounter with Chaucer at school to this present book has been long, winding and largely unmapped. The guides have been many, but I should single out a number from my extended association with the University of York for particular thanks: Erica Davies and Karen Hodder, along with The Lords of Misrule, for revealing the beauty and vigour of medieval literature; Philip Lindley, Christopher Norton and Richard Marks for converting my enthusiasm for the medieval visual arts into something like scholarship (and managing to increase that enthusiasm on the way); and Nick Havely for exemplary postgraduate supervision. My own teaching is always approached in hope that I may be able to inspire my students in the same way.

Particular thanks are owed to the late Elaine C. Block, whose expressions of enthusiasm for my early forays into the study of misericords amounted to a particularly charming form of press-ganging. The unstinting nature of this enthusiasm and support was such that it remains undimmed by her passing. Under her captaincy, I have certainly seen the world – or, at least, the undersides of its choir stalls – for which I am immeasurably grateful. Fellow crew members (to stretch the metaphor) have been a constant inspiration, always stimulating in conversation and unfailingly generous with their knowledge. Whilst the roll-call of shipmates is too long for rehearsal here, special thanks go to Sylvie Bethmont-Gallerand, Frédéric

Billiet, Luuk Houwen, Naomi Kline, Adrian Tudor and Kenneth Varty, although countless colleagues encountered through the colloquia of Misericordia International and the International Reynard Society could extend this list. I know that I am far from alone in owing a great debt to the late Christa Grössinger and Brian J. Levy: along with Elaine, they were both inspiring scholars and wonderful people who are very much missed. My thanks go both to Elaine for allowing me to use her photographs, and to Welleda Muller for scouring Elaine's archives for errant images. In preparing the final draft of this book, I am particularly grateful to Katie Lister, whose assistance has been invaluable.

Away from the close-knit though far-flung community of misericordians, that I have been able to keep this book more or less on track is due in no small part to both the scholarship and friendship of Meredith Clermont-Ferrand, which has helped to keep *me* on track. At Leeds Trinity University College, the support of colleagues, in particular Joyce Simpson, has been invaluable in so many ways. The institution has also provided a period of Research Leave and a number of travel grants without which this book could not have been written. I have also benefited from a British Academy Overseas Conference Grant. At Boydell & Brewer I would like to thank Caroline Palmer for her enthusiasm for this project and her support during periods of temporary derailment.

I am extremely fortunate in being blessed with an exceptionally supportive family. Thanks to Fred and Joan Hardwick, without whom …, and to Ruth, Roger and their ever-expanding dynasty. Finally, although she doesn't exactly share my enthusiasm for crawling on the floors of ancient buildings, I would like to thank the most recent recruit to the clan – my wife, Sue – for displaying a reasonable degree of magnanimity regarding the lengthy periods I have spent locked away finishing this off.

Part of chapter 1 has previously appeared in *La Nature, rythme et danse des saisons dans les stalles médiévales*, ed. Frédéric Billiet and Welleda Muller (Turnhout: Brepols, 2009); part of chapter 2 in *Bible de bois du Moyen-Age: Bible et liturgie dans les stalles médiévales*, ed. Frédéric Billiet (Angers: UCO, 2003); part of chapter 3 in *Profane Images in Marginal Arts of the Middle Ages*, ed. Elaine C. Block with Frédéric Billiet, Sylvie Bethmont-Gallerand and Paul Hardwick (Turnhout: Brepols, 2008); and parts of chapter 5 in *Reinardus* 15 (2002) and 17 (2004).

# INTRODUCTION: WHAT LIES BENEATH

Early in the twentieth century, Francis Bond devoted the first of his volumes on English ecclesiastical wood carvings to misericords, recognising their value in illuminating 'a History of Social Life in England in the fourteenth, fifteenth and sixteenth centuries as it was lived by common folk'.[1] Whilst, as we shall see in the course of the present volume, this is one valuable aspect of misericord carvings for the modern viewer, Bond's analysis – seminal though it is for subsequent studies – is restricted by the then current view of misericords which placed them very much in the category of 'folk art'.[2] In consequence, Bond's chapter dealing with the symbolism to be found on misericord carvings begins with the assertion that '[s]ymbolism is conspicuously rare on the misericords; they were carved by simple folk for simple folk', and concludes its discussion a mere twenty-one lines later.[3] This view has gradually been superseded, particularly in the past twenty years. Books by Michael Camille, Christa Grössinger and Malcolm Jones, along with the journal *Profane Arts of the Middle Ages*, have been supplemented by a growing number of essay collections and discrete articles to reveal the rich symbolism to be found on choir stalls and, indeed, across the marginal arts of the later Middle Ages.[4] The present book inevitably owes an immense debt to these studies. Where this study differs, however, is that rather than seeing the vigorous carvings to be found

[1] Francis Bond, *Wood Carvings in English Churches 1: Misericords* (London: Oxford University Press, 1910), p. vii.

[2] What constitutes folk art – or, indeed, folk anything – has itself become a contentious issue in recent years. For an interesting synoptic study of the debates on contemporary folk practices, which nonetheless has implications for the discussion of historical folk art and culture, see Bob Trubshaw, *Explore Folklore* (Loughborough: Heart of Albion Press, 2002).

[3] Bond, *Wood Carvings in English Churches 1*, pp. 157–8.

[4] Michael Camille, *Image on the Edge: The Margins of Medieval Art* (London: Reaktion Books, 1992); Christa Grössinger, *The World Upside-Down: English Misericords* (London: Harvey Miller Publishers, 1997); Malcolm Jones, *The Secret Middle Ages: Discovering the Real Medieval World* (Stroud: Sutton Publishing, 2002). *Profane Arts of the Middle Ages*, under the editorship of Elaine C. Block, was first published in 1993 by Misericordia International, details of which may be found at web.leedstrinity.ac.uk/english/misericordia_international/index.htm.

populating the shadowy underside of choir stalls largely as sites of profane exuberance, it places these lively, sometimes surprising (or even shocking) scenes more firmly within the doctrinal and devotional culture of the period. This is not to suggest that recent authors have not taken this into account: far from it. Nonetheless, the contention at the heart of my discussion will be that English late medieval Christianity should provide the primary lens through which we view even the more 'marginal' ecclesiastical arts of the period. After all, in late medieval western thought, the variety of worldly existence – sacred or profane, perfect or monstrous – was primarily held to be evidence of the infinite variety of God's creation.[5] In addition to this we must remember that these objects were commissioned by the clergy for installation in the devotional heart of the church, where they would be viewed by an exclusively clerical audience. Consequently, in direct contrast to Bond's view, my central thesis is that symbolism is in fact the guiding principle of misericord decoration, and may be found everywhere if we immerse ourselves in the devotional discourses at play in their design. Before we begin to explore the representations of this prodigious realm of creation and their symbolic resonance, however, it will be useful first to address the function, form and construction of misericords themselves.

## PURPOSE AND CONSTRUCTION

The offices of the medieval Church were, to say the least, demanding for participants.[6] The eight services of Matins, Lauds, Prime, Terce, Sext, None, Vespers and Compline were said daily, each followed by the recitation of four psalms, canticles and hymns. In addition to this were the High Mass, attended by the whole community, and – for all but the celebrant – an additional private mass. Further masses for benefactors brought with them still greater physical demands on participants, for each of these rituals required standing for a considerable amount of time – frequently with arms raised – with the only concession being that the aged or infirm were permitted to support themselves on crutches. However, at some point around the close of the twelfth century came what was quite literally an act of mercy (*misericordia*): the introduction of seats – initially amounting merely to simple arrangements supported by sticks – into the choir stalls.[7]

[5] Whilst acknowledging the oversimplification of such nebulous classifications, I trust that the reader will accept that a general broad consensus may be held to have prevailed on this point.

[6] For an excellent, concise account of the development of liturgical practices and of the architectural spaces in which they were carried out, up to and including the late medieval period, see Paulette E. Barton, *Mercy and Misericord in Late Medieval England: Cathedral Theology and Architecture* (Lewiston: Edwin Mellen Press, 2009), pp. 89–170.

[7] Elaine C. Block, *Corpus of Medieval Misericords in France: XIII–XVI Century* (Turnhout: Brepols, 2003), p. 1.

This functional development within the choir was coincidental with a growth in the use of decorative carpentry in the construction of church furnishings, a realm in which stone had hitherto been the material of choice, whilst woodwork had been used purely for structural purposes.[8] Consequently, these simple seats were soon developed into the misericords which are still to be found today in churches throughout western Europe: hinged seats not dissimilar in basic design to those which we may now find in cinemas, although balanced to remain either up or down as desired.[9] These seats, when raised, left space for standing, but also provided a small projecting upper ledge upon which the occupant could rest while remaining upright during the long hours of prayer: a mercy indeed in the frequently cold and draughty choir.

Throughout England – as, indeed, throughout the rest of Europe – by far the most common material used for misericords, and church furnishings in general, was oak. A robust tree, it could be obtained in the large sections necessary for the construction of unbroken rails and pillars. Furthermore, oak is a hard wood, enabling the skilled craftsman to produce work of remarkably fine detail which was, as is eloquently attested by those furnishings which survive into the twenty-first century, durable enough to weather most of the vicissitudes of daily wear and tear to which it was subject, short of acts of nature or deliberate human agency. Once the timber had been selected and acquired, and after due seasoning – a process which could take several years[10] – it was then up to the carver's skill to render the required design(s) in three dimensions. Whilst we may note similarities in motifs carved in both wood and stone in ecclesiastical buildings, it is important to remember that working the two materials requires very different skills and that, as the professional carver Hugh Harrison explains,

> [c]arving wood is in many ways more complex than carving stone. Every stroke is determined by the direction of the grain of the timber. The carver therefore has to be ambidextrous. The grain is at its least problematic when the cutting stroke is at right-angles to it. However, any stroke made within, say, 30° of the direction of the grain, must cut through it, otherwise the tool

[8] On the development of the structure of wooden choir stalls in the thirteenth and fourteenth centuries, see Charles Tracy, *English Gothic Choir-Stalls 1200–1400* (Woodbridge: The Boydell Press, 1987), pp. 62–9.

[9] The manner in which the seats are affixed to the body of the stall work varies. Some misericords are carved in order to leave integral projecting pivots which fit into holes bored into the partitions between seats, whilst at Lincoln Cathedral separate dowels are used to fulfil the same function. Elsewhere, the somewhat easier method of hinges joining the seat to the back rail is employed. This latter construction method has the advantage that it does not require the seats to be manoeuvred into position at the same time as the larger stall work is being carried out; instead they may be added later. In all cases, a recessed quadrant is let into the partitions to facilitate the raising and lowering of the seat.

[10] On seasoning, see Tracy, *English Gothic Choir-Stalls 1200–1400*, p. 63.

> will be diverted by the grain of the wood. When carving veins of leaves almost parallel with the grain, it is very difficult to avoid this happening.[11]

The fine quality of much of the surviving carving, whether in the details of the armour and individual faces of the crowded figures in a scene depicting the meeting of Edward IV and Louis XI on the bridge at Picquigny in August 1475 (St George's Chapel, Windsor Castle), or in the elegant lines of humans and animals throughout the stalls of Lincoln Cathedral, offers ample evidence to show that patrons were eager to employ the finest craftsmen available and/or affordable. The material chosen, then, along with the care with which it was prepared and carved, reflects the concern with both structure and surface of those commissioning the furniture for the church, even down to the decoration of partially hidden elements thereof. The deterioration of the misericords on account of careless preparation and the poor quality of the wood used at St Botolph, Boston, where the subsequent opening of the medullary rays – the fine strata of hard tissue radiating from the core of the trunk – has led to ragged cracks across the surfaces, very much acts as 'the exception which proves the rule', bringing into sharp focus the insistence upon top quality materials which is evident elsewhere around the country.[12]

Throughout the fourteenth, fifteenth and sixteenth centuries, misericord designs, along with other motifs populating canopies, rails and other elements of the stalls, became more elaborate, attesting to the importance both of the choir itself and also of its furnishings. As Charles Tracy has summarised:

> The liturgical choir was at the centre of the institution's corporate devotional life ... The choir furniture was not only an opportunity for conspicuous display. It offered a slight but valued amelioration to each and every member of the community from the tedium of the long service and the icy draughts which circulated unchecked around the building. As an institutional priority, choir-stalls are likely, therefore, to have been important on the grounds of liturgical need, comfort and display.[13]

Structurally, the furnishing of the choir is a major undertaking in terms of materials, labour and, consequently, cost. Because of the functional requirement of facilitating antiphonal singing, stalls are arranged along the

[11] Hugh Harrison, 'Technical Aspects of the Misericord', in *Profane Images in Marginal Arts of the Middle Ages*, ed. Elaine C. Block with Frédéric Billiet, Sylvie Bethmont-Gallerand and Paul Hardwick (Turnhout: Brepols, 2008), p. xxxiv. Harrison's paper is based upon a demonstration given at the 6th Biennial Colloquium of Misericordia International, held at the University of Sheffield, 18–21 July 2003, for which he had been commissioned to carve a misericord. The insight into the process of construction by a practising craftsman offers a unique perspective to misericord scholarship.

[12] On the nature of the wood and how it was prepared prior to carving, see ibid., pp. xx–xxiv. Harrison notes that, in the case of Boston, 'it seems likely ... that either the work was done "on a shoestring", or that whoever commissioned the stalls and paid for the timber was duped' (p. xxii).

[13] Tracy, *English Gothic Choir-Stalls 1200–1400*, p. xix.

north and south sides of the choir in single, double or even triple rows, depending on the size of the church and its community, with many foundations, such as Beverley Minster, Cartmel Priory and Carlisle Cathedral, having additional return stalls, that is, adjoining stalls flanking the entrance to the choir at the west end. Each seat is separated by an arm rest – itself frequently elaborately carved – with the end of the row terminated by a panel, or *jouee*, offering the patron and carver yet another surface for further decoration. Before each row of stalls would be a range of desking, the purely functional elements of which could again be elaborated upon by the addition of decorative carvings to front and end panels.[14] The rows of stalls would additionally have had dorsal panels, though these are now often lost, which acted as both sounding boards for the singing of the divine office and, as a fortuitous attendant comfort, at least something of a barrier to the chill draughts which would blow through the unheated church. These panels were, in turn, frequently surmounted by canopies of greater or lesser elaboration. All elements of this wooden construction provided areas in which the carver's art could be employed, with floral, figural, architectural and geometric designs proliferating upon all surfaces. In the present volume, however, we shall be concentrating primarily upon the carvings on the *consoles*, the substantial load-bearing blocks which support the ledges of the misericords and which carry the most fascinating array of scenes. From the quite simple, generally foliate decoration on the few surviving thirteenth-century examples, such as St Mary the Virgin, Kidlington, up to the more elaborate designs from the eve of the Reformation, such as may be found in Beverley Minster, the consoles become increasingly inhabited by either individual figures or historiated scenes.[15] Sometimes these are single scenes which cover the whole of the console, but frequently on British examples there is a tripartite scheme, with the larger central carving being flanked to left and right by smaller scenes or motifs known as *supporters*, which are often clearly thematically linked to the main carving, although at other times less so.[16] Across the stalls of individual buildings there are sometimes clearly developed narratives, as in the sequences which recount the exploits of Reynard the Fox, most vigorously portrayed in Bristol Cathedral,[17] or the hunt and capture of the bear in Beverley Minster,

[14] See ibid., pp. 68–9 and related plates, for examples of various degrees of elaboration.
[15] This is not to say, however, that purely foliate decoration does not continue. There are fifteenth-century examples throughout Britain, ranging from the boldly stylised carvings of the 'Ochiltree stalls' at Dunblane Cathedral in Scotland down to the reused misericords in the lectern of St Petroc with St Leon at Bodmin in Cornwall.
[16] Such an arrangement is uncommon elsewhere in Europe, where single console carvings are the norm. Rare exceptions may be found at Barcelona, and on the one remaining stall from Gerona. In contrast to the pattern found in the British Isles, however, the Barcelona misericords have supporters which are larger than the central carvings.
[17] For a comprehensive catalogue and discussion of Reynardian misericord scenes, see Elaine C. Block and Kenneth Varty, 'Choir-Stall Carvings of Reynard and Other Foxes', in *Reynard the Fox: Social Engagement and Cultural Metamorphoses in the Beast Epic from the Middle Ages to the Present*, ed. Kenneth Varty (New York and Oxford: Berghahn Books, 2000), pp. 125–62. We shall look more closely at foxes in Chapter 5.

although the 'labours of the months' sequence in St Mary, Ripple, offers a rare example of a clearly unified iconographic scheme which extends across all of the misericords.[18] Elsewhere, as we shall see in chapter 6, other sets of misericords appear to be related in a more thematic manner. By far the majority of stalls, however, display no obvious overall iconographic scheme across the misericords; yet we must remember that, however diverse, all the images depicted are aspects of God's rich creation and, as Paulette E. Barton has observed, '[t]he contemplation of the divine understands God's creations in this world as part of the divine plan'.[19] Within this rich plenitude, we may occasionally find a slightly greater richness in the decoration of the stalls reserved for the dean or abbot and precentor or prior at the west ends of the ranges and the chancellor and treasurer at the east, the implicit message seeming to be that whilst all men are part of the same created world, God has nonetheless ordained some to occupy stations higher than those of others.

As Tracy observes, '[i]t is important to remember that the seats were up most of the time so that the existence of elaborate carving underneath as a constituent of the display of sculpture on the furniture is perfectly logical',[20] although it should be kept in mind that for much of the time that the choir was occupied the stalls would have been in use, the occupants thereby blocking clear sight of any design. Consequently, whilst Barton's assertion that 'the images were on virtually constant display' may be overstating the matter,[21] for much of the time these carvings were nonetheless, contrary to frequently repeated assertions, far from hidden.[22] They were at least partially visible, a partial visibility which is unique in ecclesiastical decoration and which offered – as it still does today – a tantalising attraction to the viewer, enticing him to stoop to look more closely whenever the rare opportunity to do so arose. The images thus discovered may indeed, as they are often characterised, be 'marginal', but their tantalising, semi-hidden location nevertheless has the almost paradoxical effect of drawing particular attention to the contents of these margins.

Bond began his seminal study of English medieval wood carvings with a quotation from the oft-cited letter of St Bernard of Clairvaux to William, Abbot of St Thierry:

> What mean those ridiculous monstrosities in the courts of cloisters; those filthy apes, those fierce lions, those monstrous centaurs, those half-men, those spotted tigers, those fighting

[18] In addition to the twelve months, further surviving misericords show the sun and moon, along with the Zodiac sign for Aquarius (it has been speculated that other signs have been lost), motifs clearly allied to the passage of the agricultural year. We shall return to the 'labours of the months' in the next chapter.

[19] Barton, *Mercy and the Misericord*, p. 145.

[20] Tracy, *English Gothic Choir-Stalls 1200–1400*, p. xx.

[21] Barton, *Mercy and the Misericord*, p. 220.

[22] The title of Dorothy and Henry Kraus's book, *The Hidden World of Misericords* (London: Michael Joseph Ltd, 1976), makes explicit an assumption which informs most discussions of misericords.

> soldiers and horn-blowing hunters; many bodies under one head, or many heads on one body; here a serpent's tail attached to a quadruped, there a quadruped's head on a fish; here a beast presenting the foreparts of a horse, and dragging after it the rear of a goat; there a horned animal with the hind parts of a horse?[23]

St Bernard's clearly exasperated question remains a pertinent starting point when looking at the decorative margins of the medieval church, for although the implication is that the prodigies and profanities found therein are merely the products of inappropriate frivolity, it is nonetheless founded upon the hope – however vain it may be – that there is some useful, if obscure, meaning to be discovered. This, in short, is the contention of this book: if we know where to look, we may find the answers to the enigmas that greet the eyes of the curious beneath the choir stalls and thus discern meaning within the jumble of figures, beasts and other designs which conspire to perplex the viewer.

No less elusive than the meanings of some of the images to be found on the choir stalls, of course, are those craftsmen who were responsible for their design and construction. For whilst records may occasionally reveal the names of master carpenters such as the renowned William Hurley and his successor Hugh Herland, both of whom worked on projects for Edward III, or John Strode at Wells, we do not know how 'hands on' these masters would have been. Certainly, subtle – and sometimes not so subtle – variations in technique reveal that, not surprisingly, several carvers were simultaneously at work on any given large commission, and Charles Tracy's studies have revealed likely sequences of the employment of individual carvers at Ripon and Wells.[24] Whilst Tracy puts forward the persuasive suggestion that the second identified carver at Wells may have been the aforementioned John Strode,[25] it is generally impossible to identify particular individual details as being the work of one of the few known 'masters', and the other craftsmen involved in the work must forever remain anonymous. Similarly, the precise nature of the instructions which were given to these craftsmen by their patrons has long since been lost.

## DOCTRINE AND DECORATION ON 'ENGLISH' MISERICORDS

We shall return to the generally anonymous craftsmen and their patrons in chapter 3 but now, having looked briefly at the purpose, development and construction of misericords in the choir, we should consider their location and the implications for interpretation therein. The choir is the heart of the devotional life of the church. Situated at the east end of the building, focused

[23] Bond, *Wood Carvings in English Churches 1*, p. vii.
[24] Charles Tracy, 'Misericords as an Interpretative Tool in the Study of Choir Stalls', in *Profane Images in Marginal Arts of the Middle Ages*, ed. Block *et al.*, pp. 5–8.
[25] Ibid., p. 7.

towards Jerusalem and the Holy Sepulchre, it is a discrete area which would originally have been even more marked in its isolation from the rest of the building than it is today, by virtue of a frequently elaborate screen at the west end, beyond which the laity, unlike today, were not permitted to pass. Furthermore, this sense of separateness in the choir would have been increased by its insulation from the world beyond the church building by an ambulatory on the three remaining sides. As noted above, its primary function was to serve as a place in which the offices of the Church were to be carried out undisturbed as part of the all-encompassing work of a body of educated, initiated clergy: that is, the contemplation and celebration of the divine. Putting aside for the moment issues of clerical competence – a source of much consternation and debate throughout the later Middle Ages – we can, therefore, posit a clearly defined audience for whom the decoration within the choir was intended: namely, a generally male, educated audience whose contemplative focus was God's work within the world.

Such considerations of audience lend weight to Barton's assertion that, '[t]he misericord exists in and takes meaning from the quire'.[26] Whether explicitly devotional or didactic, or apparently subversive or shocking, each misericord carving is a product of the shared ideology of those for whom the choir was the centre of their devotional life, performing a function defined by a shared purpose applied to individual, community and ecclesiastical space. In approaching these carvings, then, we should ask: how do they relate to the devotional culture, and the clergy's participation in and leadership of that culture, in the period in which they were commissioned? And in asking this question we must of course bear in mind that the period in which medieval English misericords were carved, from the end of the thirteenth century to the eve of the Reformation in the second quarter of the sixteenth century, was a particularly turbulent era in England for both the Church and society at large.

It is this turbulence which, indeed, dictates the geographical scope of the present volume; for whilst misericords, as with all the arts of the Middle Ages, owe much of their vigour to a thriving cross-Channel traffic in both ideas and labour, they were nonetheless informed by specifically English – or at least British – concerns. The toll taken by the first incursion of bubonic plague into the country in 1348–9, compounded by subsequent outbreaks throughout the latter half of the century, affected not just the size of the population, with mortality rates very possibly reaching upwards of thirty per cent, but also the attitudes to both life and afterlife of that population. As recorded by the contemporary chronicler Henry Knighton of St Mary's Abbey, Leicester, the initial economic effect of the plague was that, '[t]here was great cheapness of all things, owing to the general fear of death; for there were very few people who took any account of riches or property of any

[26] Paulette E. Barton, 'Sacred Space and the Profane Image', *Fourteenth Century England* 2 (2002), 107.

kind'.[27] However, as he goes on to relate, it was not long before this widespread lack of concern with matters of the world gave way to a decidedly more pragmatic spirit as the lucrative opportunities for both material and social advancement provided by the sudden decline in population were recognised and exploited. The shortage of agricultural labour, to cite one prominent example, led to greater bargaining power for workers. This, in turn, occasioned the government response of the first Statute of Labourers of 1351, setting in train the growing mood of popular discontent and unrest which led ultimately to the so-called Peasants' Revolt of 1381. Perhaps more pertinent to the present discussion, however, although distinctions between the political and religious spheres are inevitably problematic when considering the medieval period, is the impact of the plague upon the Church. As Knighton goes on to record:

> A chaplain was scarcely to be had to serve any church for less than £10 or 10 marks; and whereas when there was an abundance of priests before the pestilence a chaplain could be had for 4, 5 or even 2 marks with his board, at this time there was scarcely one willing to accept any vicarage at £20 or 20 marks. Within a little time, however, vast numbers of men whose wives had died in the pestilence flocked to take orders, many of whom were illiterate, and as it were mere laymen, save in so far as they could read a little, although without understanding.[28]

Whilst the heightened awareness of one's own mortality engendered by the plague would undoubtedly have sharpened lay devotion – already nurtured by the emphasis on lay piety fostered in the wake of the Fourth Lateran Council of 1215[29] – there was at the same time a growing lay scepticism about the efficacy of those in the employ of the Church, mirroring the concerns over motive and suitability voiced within the institution of the Church by Knighton and others. This is evinced by the spread of vernacular anticlerical literature in the second half of the fourteenth century and, ultimately, in the rise and suppression of Lollardy, the so-called 'English heresy', in the late fourteenth and early fifteenth centuries.[30] The later Middle Ages in England, then, were a period in which the fate of the individual's

[27] *Chronicon Henrici Knighton*, cited in R. B. Dobson (ed), *The Peasants' Revolt of 1381*, 2nd edn (Basingstoke: Macmillan, 1983), p. 59.
[28] Ibid., pp. 61–2.
[29] On the impact of the Fourth Lateran Council upon the English Church, see Marion Gibbs and Jane Lang, *Bishops and Reform 1215–1272: with Special Reference to the Lateran Council of 1215* (London: Oxford University Press, 1934), pp. 94–179.
[30] Whilst the effects of the depredations of the Black Death cannot be overstated, it should be noted that concern over uneducated clergy had been voiced – at least within the Church – long before the first outbreak. This may be seen, for example, in the surviving letters of Bishop Grosseteste, who found it necessary to instruct illiterate clerics to ask for assistance from literate neighbours, and on several occasions had to reject the institution of a candidate into a vacant living on account of his being insufficiently lettered (*literaturæ minus sufficientis*), even against the will of powerful patrons. See Roberti Grosseteste, *Epistolae*, ed. Henry Richards Luard (London: Longman, 1861), p. 63 and pp. 50–4, 68–9 and 203–4.

soul, and the earthly mechanisms by which this fate could be shaped, were prominent concerns of both clergy and laity, and it is in the light of this that we should consider the religious art produced at the time, whether it be a cathedral window, a layman's psalter or, indeed, a carved misericord.

This perspective coincidentally begins to account for one of the questions which the reader may ask of the present book: namely, why the geographical focus upon England? Elaine C. Block's ongoing *Corpus of Medieval Misericords*, which will primarily act as a catalogue of surviving items throughout Europe, with analysis kept to a minimum, will itself run to five substantial volumes.[31] Considering this abundance of material, it is clear that a single-volume, pan-European study would, of necessity, lack the depth available to one covering a smaller geographical area. England, as suggested above, commends itself to such a study by virtue of its distinct devotional climate during the period throughout which most of its choir stalls were constructed, witnessing academic discussions of the role of the Church itself – and those ordained to serve therein – which spread outward to the lay population and escalated into full-blown Lollardy and, in turn, its consequent suppression. This is not to say that the British Isles were culturally isolated: quite the opposite was true. In relation to misericords and other ecclesiastical art, European craftsmen were crossing the Channel and, later, mass-produced prints made that same journey, in the process of which they provided models for a number of English carvings.[32] Consequently, many motifs which appear in England may be found throughout Europe, and in the present study we shall have cause on a number of occasions to look beyond geographical borders in order to illuminate our understanding of English material. Nevertheless, the concerns of patrons on this side of the water had a distinct complexion which must surely have affected iconographic interpretation and, thus, the choices that they made pertaining to decorative requirements. The other aspect of the 'why England?' question which needs to be addressed is, of course, 'why not *Britain*'? The simple answer is that we shall be considering artefacts which exist within the context of the English Church, which were created during a period in which the notion of an English identity was becoming stronger, and most of which are located within the borders of England. The dozen or so remaining sets of stalls scattered between Ireland, Scotland and Wales do not ostensibly show any different concerns to those found in England, and will for the most part be considered as belonging to

[31] At the time of writing, volumes on France and Spain have been published, whilst the further three books are being completed by Block's colleagues under the direction of her academic executor, Frédéric Billiet.

[32] For the trade in prints, to which we will return throughout the present study, see Christa Grössinger, *Humour and Folly in Secular and Profane Prints of Northern Europe: 1430–1540* (London: Harvey Miller Publishers, 2002). Perhaps the logical end of this cross-Channel trade would come much later in the nineteenth century, with the importation of whole sets of medieval and renaissance stalls and other furnishings from Europe to 'replace' those which were lost to Reformation iconoclasm: see Charles Tracy, *Continental Church Furniture in England: A Traffic in Piety* (Woodbridge: Antique Collectors' Club, 2001), pp. 222–68.

the same unified corpus. That being said, where specific concerns relating to cultural identities in distinct opposition to a dominant Englishness can be identified, these will be taken into account. For example, the possible implications for interpretation which are suggested by the location of the misericords in St Mary's Cathedral, Limerick – the only remaining Irish set, effectively marking the westernmost boundary of Britain, Europe and, indeed, Christendom – will need to be considered in our final chapter.

## MISERICORD MOTIFS

The present study does not attempt to offer a complete survey of the country's misericord carvings, for which the interested reader should turn to G. L. Remnant's *A Catalogue of Misericords in Great Britain* or Elaine C. Block's forthcoming *Corpus of Medieval Misericords: Great Britain*.[33] Instead, it offers a thematic approach which begins with the things of the world before moving on to things of the spirit, an admittedly problematic distinction that will be closely interrogated throughout the book. We will then, in turn, address matters of artistic influence and originality, the gendered power structure of the Church and the perceived threat of destabilisation, the allegorical roles occupied by beasts and, finally, the ambiguous implications of the imaginary. As we explore these themes, a 'case study' approach will be taken, with the bulk of the discussion centring upon a few specific carvings in each category, with further examples cited in order to illuminate and develop the theme. As we shall see, however, although suggesting convenient perspectives from which to approach the iconography of misericords, the distinctions between these categories soon break down, for as soon as we begin to scratch the surface, we find that all these diverse scenes – many of which may inspire amusement, surprise or even shock in the modern viewer – are interrelated and imbued with the devotional culture of the English Church of the later Middle Ages which, as noted above, was itself undergoing many changes. One of the most significant of these changes in terms of the present study is to be found in differing attitudes towards images themselves. For whilst figures continued to proliferate across church walls, stalls, windows and elsewhere – the so-called 'books of the unlearned'[34] – as well as in books themselves, in many quarters their appropriateness was being called into question, a position which became a key tenet of Lollardy at the close of the fourteenth century and beyond. Indeed, whilst no documentary evidence survives to confirm such a supposition, we may perhaps consider the growing proliferation of images which occurred in English churches throughout the

[33] G. L. Remnant, *A Catalogue of Misericords in Great Britain* (London: Oxford University Press, 1969). Whilst this volume contains a number of errors, it remains the most useful field guide currently available and a very good starting point for discovering British misericords. The misericords of the British Isles will be the subject of the fourth volume of Elaine C. Block's *Corpus of Medieval Misericords*. Although incomplete at the time of her death in 2008, it was in a sufficiently advanced state to be finished by colleagues and will be published by Brepols (Turnhout) in due course.

[34] A designation which we shall have cause to question throughout the present study.

period as evidence of a defensive ideological bulwark built against such criticisms, a suggestion which will be explored further in chapter 3.

Adopting a thematic approach means there will, inevitably, be some subjects which, although significant, will fall outside the main body of discussion and which, therefore, it is appropriate to address here. Like all previous major studies, the main focus of the present volume is upon figural carvings of humans and beasts, whether as portraits or as elements of illustrative or narrative scenes. Consequently, almost half of the surviving carvings on misericords – those which depict flora, whether naturalistic or stylised – will not be discussed at length.[35] Whilst most generally considered as little more than useful stylistic aids to dating particular carvings,[36] it should also not be forgotten that flowers and foliage, like all aspects of the created world, carried with them a wide range of possible meanings in late medieval culture. Matthew 6:28, for example, famously offers the lilies of the field as a sign that God will provide for all his creation. On the other hand, Michael Camille has suggested that we should consider representations of abundant nature as a reminder that we are 'part of the fallen world ... implicated in its beautiful growth and also in its decay and death'.[37] The two perspectives, of course, are not mutually exclusive, merely different – and even complementary – aspects of God's one truth; and, after all, the decay of autumn and death of winter are sure to be followed by the rebirth of spring. In addition to these more general concerns of mortality and eternity which may be inherent in the depiction of flora, individual species were endowed with their own particular associations, as is vividly illustrated in the concluding lines of Chaucer's catalogue of trees in his *Parliament of Fowls*:

> The shetere ew; the asp for shaftes playne;
> The olive of pes, and eke the dronke vyne;
> The victor palm, the laurer to devyne.[38]

[The yew for shooting; the ash for smooth shafts; the olive of peace, and also the drunken vine; the victorious palm, the laurel for divination.]

[35] Marshall Laird, *English Misericords* (London: John Murray, 1986), p. 10, estimates that plants account for around forty-eight per cent of subjects carved across consoles and supporters, with more than four thousand examples surviving. Particularly well-observed and realistic carvings of plant life may be found on the early fourteenth-century misericords in Winchester and Wells cathedrals.

[36] See Remnant, *Catalogue of Misericords*, pp. xxi–xxii. In spite of a general usefulness in terms of dating, the transition from one style of foliage carving to another was not necessarily instantaneously all-encompassing, and more than one style may sometimes be observed on the same set of choir stalls, as noted in the case of Exeter Cathedral by Charles Tracy: see Tracy, 'Misericords as an Interpretative Tool', p. 5.

[37] Michael Camille, *Gothic Art: Glorious Visions* (New York: Harry N. Abrams, 1996), p. 133. John Dickinson, *Misericords of North West England: Their Nature and Significance* (Lancaster: Centre for North-West Regional Studies, 2008), pp. 81–9, discusses this in relation to the choir stalls of Cartmel Priory.

[38] Geoffrey Chaucer, *The Parliament of Fowls*, in *The Riverside Chaucer*, ed. Larry D. Benson (Oxford: Oxford University Press, 1988), ll. 180–3.

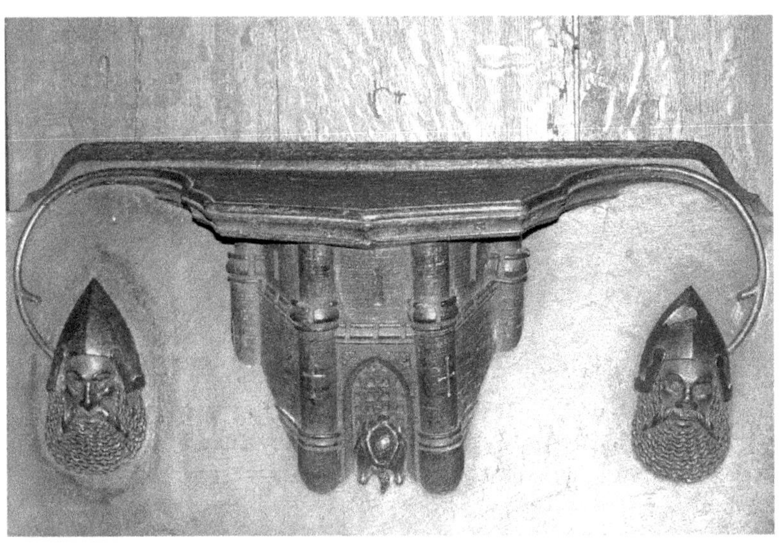

FIG. 1. LINCOLN CATHEDRAL MISERICORD

In just this short extract, Chaucer offers us an insight into the complex web of practical, symbolic and superstitious associations which was attached to plants in the late Middle Ages. Yet we should beware of taking such catalogues as definitive, for we need only look to his *Knight's Tale*, in which we find Theseus '[w]ith laurer crowned as conquerour'[39] – an association which has been recorded from classical times and which remains familiar to this day – to see that more than one meaning could pertain to a particular plant. If we add to this the complication of heraldic or livery devices – without pigmentation a rose, of which a score of examples remain on misericords around the country, could as easily be that of York or Lancaster as the Rose of Guillaume de Lorris and Jean de Meun – it becomes clear both that we should be wary of the attribution of definitive meanings to even the most innocuous-appearing image, and that the depiction of flora on medieval misericords would provide a sufficiently broad topic for a book in its own right.

At what we may consider to be the opposite end of the iconographic spectrum from the apparently simple details of the natural world are the few remaining scenes which can be identified as pertaining to what is arguably the most highly wrought literary artifice of the period, namely those illustrations of popular chivalric romance. The most famous episode from these narratives thus depicted (fig. 1), perhaps because of both the popularity of the narrative and the striking – some may even say amusing – visual image that it inspires, is the story in which the Arthurian knight Ywain (or Yvain) enters the castle of his enemy, Esclados, with such recklessness that he not only triggers the trap that has been set but flies

[39] Chaucer, *The Canterbury Tales*, in *The Riverside Chaucer*, I (A) 1027.

through it without suffering injury, although the same cannot be said of his unfortunate horse:

> He was very lucky to be leaning forward … Down comes the gate like a devil out of Hell, catching the saddle and the horse behind it, slicing it clean through the middle. But, thank God, it did not touch my lord Yvain except that it grazed so closely down his back that it cut off both spurs level with his heels.[40]

Another scene which may be found carved in several locations is derived from the *Romance of Alexander*, which tells of the legendary emperor's desire to ascend into the sky beyond the edge of the world. As a mid fifteenth-century Middle English alliterative version of the popular story tells us:

> Þan made he smythis to gaa smert · & smethe him a chaire
> Of blake iren & of bigge · & bynde it with cheynes,
> A sekir sege in to sitt · & sett him on-loft.
> And foure Griffons full grym · he in þat graythe festes;
> He makis to hinge ouir þaire hede · in hokis of iren
> Flesch on ferrom þaim fra · at þai miȝt noȝt to reches,
> To make þaim freke to þe fliȝt · þat fode for to wyn,
> For þai ware fastand be-fore · halden for þe nanes.
> Now is he won þurȝe þar wingis · vp to þe wale cloudis …[41]

> [Then he caused smiths to act promptly and forge him a great chair of black iron and bind it with chains, a secure seat in which to sit and set him on high. And four fierce griffins he fixed there; he hung meat high over their heads on iron hooks so that they may not reach it, to make them eager to fly in order to gain the food, for they had been kept hungry for this time. Now he has reached, through their wings, up to the very clouds …]

The visually dramatic nature of Alexander's flight no doubt accounts for its popularity on misericords, not to mention its subsequent ease of identification.[42] Other identifiable romance scenes include King Mark spying from the tree upon the tryst of Tristan and Iseult,[43] and the Swan Knight,[44]

[40] Chrétien de Troyes, Yvain, in *Arthurian Romances*, trans. D. D. R. Owen (London: J. M. Dent, 1987), p. 293. The scene survives on five misericords: St Botolph, Boston; Chester Cathedral; St Mary, Enville; Lincoln Cathedral; and New College, Oxford. Whilst these generally depict just the horse's rump protruding from the portcullis, the Enville misericord also shows Ywain's trailing leg, presumably being pulled clear, although it must be conceded that the carving does make his plight appear hopeless.

[41] *The Wars of Alexander: an Alliterative Romance, Translated Chiefly from the Historia Alexandri Magni De Preliis*, ed. Walter W. Skeat, EETS e.s. 47 (London: N. Trübner and Co., 1886), ll. 5515–23.

[42] Examples of carvings which have been interpreted as showing the flight of Alexander may be found at: St Mary, Beverley; Chester Cathedral; St Cuthbert, Darlington; Gloucester Cathedral; Lincoln Cathedral; Wells Cathedral; St Mary, Whalley; and St George's Chapel, Windsor.

[43] Found at Chester Cathedral and Lincoln Cathedral.

[44] A unique example in Exeter Cathedral.

whilst Jennifer Fellows has recently offered persuasive arguments for the identification of two hitherto unrecognised misericords as scenes from the popular romance *Sir Bevis of Hampton*, amongst other possible narrative sources.[45] Although undoubtedly secular in their derivation, and apparently secular in their concerns, these narrative entertainments readily lay themselves open to moralisation in an ecclesiastical setting. However, as with the plants discussed above, the symbolism is far from rigid: should we, for example, read Alexander's flight as an exemplar of worthy ambition to be emulated, or as an illustration of overweening pride which should be shunned?[46] It may be suspected that the perspective taken on the narrative would be altered by the priest or monk in order to accord with the didactic needs of the moment. Or, indeed, we may recall the famous anecdote of the thirteenth-century abbot Caesarius of Heisterbach, who roused his audience's flagging attention with the promise: 'My brothers! Listen carefully, because I am going to tell you a story all about King Arthur!'[47] Once he had thus regained their rapt attention, he went on to berate them for their preference for romance over righteous words which could guide them to salvation; yet this anecdote serves to confirm both that romances were known to the clergy and that they could thus be employed as a means to draw in an audience for more weighty matters, which may perhaps even involve a moralised reading of the story itself.

In briefly addressing the very different worlds of botany and romance, then, we have seen that they have one important factor in common: they mean – or can be interpreted as meaning – much more than first appearances suggest. These two distinct worlds may be said to meet in the figure of the Wild Man or Wodehouse, a curious figure who straddles the worlds of both romance and the wild wood, and whom we shall consider in detail in chapter 6. A distant cousin to the Wild Man, though lacking his robust vigour and frequent good humour, is that curious, ubiquitous presence, the foliate head or, as it is more popularly known, the Green Man. Invariably serious, often threatening and occasionally even pained in demeanour, the Green Man's challenging glare – which stares unflinchingly from more than fifty misericords throughout the country – has given rise to shelves of 'New Age' speculation in an abundance which, unfortunately,

[45] See Jennifer Fellows, 'Romance among the Choir Stalls: Middle English Romance Motifs on English Misericords', in *Profane Images in Marginal Arts of the Middle Ages*, ed. Block *et al.*, pp. 123–41. The misericords identified as being from *Sir Bevis of Hampton* are of a knight fighting with a giant (possibly Bevis's combat with the Saracen giant Ascopart) in Gloucester Cathedral, and of a knight battling a giant boar (as in Bevis's reported encounter with such a beast at Cologne) in St Mary, Beverley. Whilst it should be noted that other romance heroes may lay claims to these images, Fellows persuasively argues for Bevis being the most likely candidate.

[46] The question in this case is further complicated by ambiguous associations attached to griffins, to whom we shall return in due course.

[47] Caesarius of Heisterbach, *De domino Gevardo Abbate, qui monachos in sermone dormitantes per fabulam Arcturi excitavit*, in *Dialogus Miraculorum*, ed. Joseph Strange (Cologne and Bonn: Hebeele, 1851), p. 205.

appears to be inversely proportionate to available verifiable fact. That antecedents of the motif appear in Roman art as early as the late first or early second century AD is certain, but why such an image enjoyed widespread popularity throughout medieval Christendom remains an intriguing puzzle with which scholars continue to wrestle. Fran and Geoff Doel's designation of the Green Man as 'the most prolific non-Christian symbol to be found in or on British medieval religious buildings and their counterparts in parts of France and Germany'[48] assuredly attests to the importance of the image throughout the period but, in casually describing it as 'non-Christian', this assessment somewhat pre-emptively limits the possibilities for interpretation. Whilst notions of widespread pagan survivals in Christian Britain may be attractive, the Doels' 'selective gazetteer' of over two hundred sites, most of them medieval ecclesiastical buildings, encompassing close to a thousand carvings (including a great many on misericords), may stand as more than convincing circumstantial evidence that, whatever its origins, by the later Middle Ages the Green Man had become fully incorporated into the repertoire of Christian symbolism. As Kathleen Basford persuasively argues, however, the precise nature of this symbolism could vary: 'Some are demons; some probably represent lost souls or sinners', or, more generally, 'the darkness of unredeemed nature ... [or] man's fallen and concupiscent nature'.[49] The combination of the human face with verdant foliage is certainly suggestive of man's place in nature, but the hybridity of the image surely implies that within this shared existence man is clearly lowering himself to a state beneath that to which he has been divinely ordained. Consequently, the proliferation of Green Men on misericords and across all carved surfaces of the medieval Church may encompass all of Basford's suggestions, their solemn gaze unflinchingly scrutinising the conduct of the viewer, unceasingly warning him of the ever-present threat of temptation and sin. However the Green Man may have been understood in the late Middle Ages, what is certain is that, as with symbolism drawn from the natural world, medieval Christians could appropriate the art of past ages which they found around them and employ it in the service of God.

From the foregoing examples we may see that, as John Dickinson has succinctly expressed it, '[the] understanding that symbolism must imbue everything was fundamental to the medieval imagination'.[50] He goes on to note that:

> However, by 1430 the medieval mindset was shifting to early modern; the world was becoming more scientific, defined through observation and the rational consideration of objects in their autonomous and disengaged state. No longer was the symbolic, God-centric world the only option.[51]

[48] Fran and Geoff Doel, *The Green Man in Britain* (Stroud: Tempus, 2001), p. 17.
[49] Kathleen Basford, *The Green Man* (Cambridge: D. S. Brewer, 1978), pp. 20–1.
[50] Dickinson, *Misericords of North West England*, p. 85.
[51] Ibid., p.85.

If we take this to be the case, in the years following the institution of *De haeretico comburendo* in 1401 and Arundel's *Constitutions* in 1409,[52] both forceful assertions of the inflexible authority of the English Church and, at the same time, tacit acknowledgements of the extent to which the institution felt itself to be increasingly under threat from a literate and doctrinally questioning laity, we may suppose that there would be a greater rather than lesser recourse to a 'God-centric' symbolic order when it came to the matter of ecclesiastical decoration. That such symbolism is often initially baffling to the modern viewer is undeniable; indeed, given the educated and theologically aware primary audience by whom and for whom it was created, it may well have been baffling to any medieval layperson – even including, perhaps, the carver following his patron's instructions – who may by some circumstance have found himself confronted by the 'merry company' of images gathered in the very heart of the church building. It is with this company that we shall begin our investigations: the broad sweep of medieval laymen and women whom we may still find going about their daily business across the panorama carved beneath the choir stalls.

[52] For Arundel's *Constitutions*, see *Concilia Magnae Britanniae et Hiberniae*, 4 vols, ed. David Wilkins (1373: repr. Brussels, 1964), vol. 3, pp. 314–19.

# 1 A FAIR FIELD OF FOLK

> A fair feeld ful of folk fond I ther bitwene–
> Of alle manere of men, the meene and the riche,
> Worchynge and wandrynge as the world asketh.[1]
>
> [A fair field full of folk I discovered in between – of all kinds of men, the humble and the rich, working and wandering as the world demands]

So writes William Langland in his late fourteenth-century allegory *Piers Plowman.* Falling asleep one May morning on the Malvern Hills, Langland's narrator, Will, finds himself in an unknown wilderness, separated from the world yet able to look upon it from a privileged vantage point. He is distant from all that he sees but, in consequence, he is able to see clearly the intricate workings of society – the winners and wasters, the pious and pernicious – bounded on one side by the finely wrought tower of Heaven, on the other by the dreadful defile of Hell. Will's position may in some respects be likened to that of the modern viewer of misericords, party to a rich spectrum of flourishing medieval life which is consciously balanced between salvation and damnation, yet nonetheless separated from that life. Like Will, as we survey these scenes we may frequently find ourselves asking, 'what may this be to mene?'[2] And, again like Will, it is to Holy Church that we must turn in order to find the answers to our perplexed questions. Before we engage with the matter of how meaning may be illuminated by Holy Church, however, it will be useful first to find our bearings by surveying the range of everyday activities, pastimes, trades and occupations to be found carved on misericords, '[o]f alle manere of men, the meene and the riche, / Werchynge and wandrynge as the world asketh'.[3] Later in this chapter we shall focus upon the ploughman as a particularly striking example of the

[1] William Langland, *The Vision of Piers Plowman: a Complete Edition of the B-Text*, ed. A. V. C. Schmidt (London: Dent, 1995), B Prologue 17–19.
[2] Ibid., B I 11.
[3] Ibid., B Prologue 18–19.

significance of representations of labour, but we shall begin by looking at depictions of more leisurely activities.

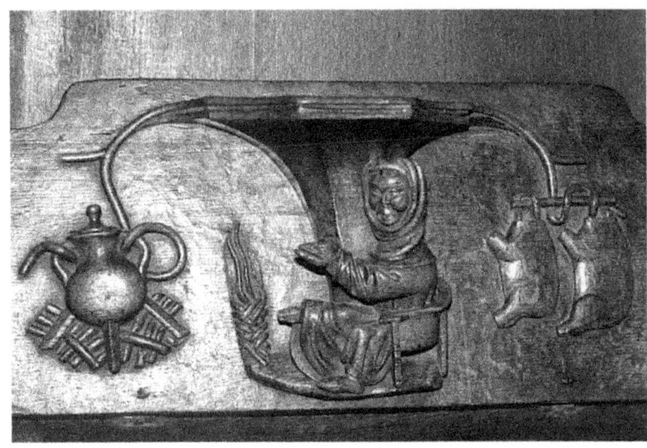

FIG. 2. ST LAWRENCE, LUDLOW MISERICORD

In surveying the types of subjects and activities represented on English misericord carvings, Francis Bond refers to 'a large and interesting class in which there is no ulterior intent other than to portray faithfully the daily life of humble folk'.[4] Such is the way in which we may perceive these lively scenes which depict the work and play undertaken by, in general, the less elevated classes of late medieval society. There are many carvings that show domestic interiors, with food and fireside being particularly popular features, suggesting homely comforts and security. One such example of this domestic felicity may be found at St Lawrence, Ludlow, where we see a man contentedly warming himself by the fire, seated in a sturdy chair which is placed between his ample cooking pot and well-stocked larder with two hanging flitches of bacon (fig. 2). These scenes of figures resting by the fireside very possibly relate to the activities ascribed to winter in the common trope of the 'labours of the months', in which 'each season has its own special character and concerns' which, in turn, form the basis of countless visual representations in all media throughout the late medieval period.[5] A unique survival of a complete cycle of misericords representing monthly activities may be found in St Mary, Ripple, in which for December or January a man and woman, warmly dressed against the cold, sit together in front of the fire.[6] Other common seasonal tropes depicted in Ripple include scenes of sowing, harvesting, and slaughtering livestock – in this case pigs – which, taken together, remind the viewer that, in the words of Ecclesiastes 3:3, 'To every thing there is a season'.[7] Bridget Ann Henisch points to the proliferation of cooking implements in winter fireside scenes

[4] Francis Bond, *Wood Carvings in English Churches 1: Misericords* (London: Oxford University Press, 1910), p. 87.

[5] Bridget Ann Henisch, *The Medieval Calendar Year* (University Park, PA: Pennsylvania State University Press, 1999), p. 2. On scenes representing the winter months in medieval art, see pp. 29–49.

[6] G. L. Remnant, *A Catalogue of Misericords in Great Britain* (London: Oxford University Press, 1969), p. 169 suggests December, whilst Christa Grössinger, *The World Upside-Down: English Misericords* (London: Harvey Miller Publishers, 1997), p. 162 suggests January. For a full discussion of the fireside motif, see Henisch, *The Medieval Calendar Year*, pp. 29–49.

[7] Common in all artistic media throughout the later Middle Ages, scenes of sowing may also be found in Great Malvern Priory and Worcester Cathedral; harvesting in St Mary Magdalene, Brampton, St Mary, Fairford, Great Malvern Priory, the Victoria & Albert Museum, London, and Worcester Cathedral; slaughtering livestock in Bristol Cathedral (pigs) and Great Malvern Priory (cattle).

as 'one means by which the twin terrors of winter and of death's approach were tamed',[8] and there is certainly an air of contentment about the comfortable figure depicted in Ludlow, mentioned above, as he takes pleasant solitary refuge from the elements at home. The Ripple couple aside, however, it is notable that when a man and a woman are depicted sharing the domestic interior – as on a pair of misericords showing fireside chaos in Beverley Minster – such comfort is generally lacking. Conjugal harmony is rarely to be found for, as we shall see in chapter 3 when we consider, amongst other things, the aforementioned carvings from Beverley, the woman is generally portrayed as more of a threat to a man than his helpmeet when she finds her way into the carvings in the all-male preserve of the church choir.

Alongside these scenes of domestic comfort and conflict may be found many other apparently secular activities taking place both indoors and outdoors, with a particular emphasis upon activities pertaining to the lower classes. In her overview of village life as it is depicted on English misericords, M. G. Challis opines that, '[i]t is clear that those who were responsible for the wood carvings in our churches were not prepared to accept any strait jacket of strict Christian beliefs'.[9] This view of the village craftsman being allowed free rein happily to carve what he observes around him is initially seductive, and vivid scenes of recreation – both outdoor and indoor – may be seen everywhere. One of the most famous of the former is the spirited game played at Gloucester Cathedral, in which two vigorous youths in short tunics and liripiped hats race for possession of a bouncing ball. Although they are frequently referred to as 'footballers',[10] we should not be led astray by the term into thinking of the rigidly codified game as it has been played since the eighteenth century. That the Gloucester players are clearly making use of their hands to bounce the ball identifies the activity as one of the more riotous rural sports recorded – generally in disapproving terms – as early as the twelfth century, and surviving in traditions such as the Shrove Tuesday ball games at Alnwick, Ashbourne, Atherstone and Sedgefield.[11] Elsewhere, in Sherborne Abbey, a supporter showing a youth riding a fine hobby-horse and fleeing from a young archer who occupies the centre of the console may depict either a childish game or some kind of dramatic performance.[12]

[8] Henisch, *The Medieval Calendar Year*, p. 48.

[9] M. G. Challis, *Life in Medieval England as portrayed on Church Misericords and Bench Ends* (Nettlebed, Oxfordshire: Teamband, 1998), p. 45.

[10] See, for example, Marshall Laird, *English Misericords* (London: John Murray, 1986), p. 24.

[11] For these and related customs, see Jennifer Westwood and Jacqueline Simpson, *The Lore of the Land: A Guide to England's Legends, from Spring-Heeled Jack to the Witches of Warboys* (London: Penguin Books, 2005), pp. 53–5.

[12] The scene is rendered more ambiguous by the depiction of a further youth who is riding, or perhaps wrestling, a lion on the opposite supporter. For suggested interpretations ranging from calendar customs to the Book of Revelation, see Laird, *English Misericords*, p. 23. Laird suggests that both this carving and that of the ball game referred to previously may represent 'Youth' in an 'Ages of Man' schema. Whilst it is hard to find a coherent development of the life cycle in either set of misericords, we may well suspect that either carving could be pressed into service to illustrate the moralising theme of the 'Follies of Youth'.

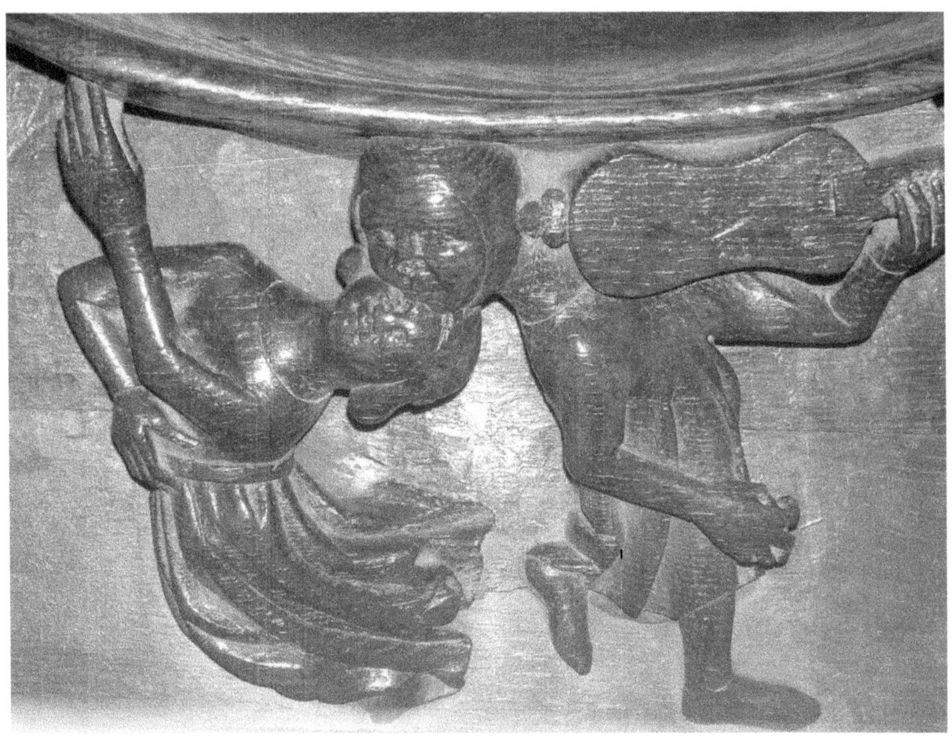

FIG. 3. CHICHESTER CATHEDRAL MISERICORD

In contrast to these energetic outdoor revels, in Chichester Cathedral we may see an example of indoor entertainment, as a fiddle-playing minstrel steals a kiss from a beautifully rendered dancer as she sweeps sinuously past him (fig. 3). In the same choir, though rather more sedate in tone, a harpist and a piper seated in high-backed chairs face each other with expressions of rapt concentration as they perform. These are just two of a great number of scenes depicting musicians which are to be found under choir stalls and, indeed, throughout church decoration of the period – an omnipresence that is hardly surprising in view of the 'intrinsic part of cultural life [music formed] throughout the Middle Ages'.[13] Yet it should be noted that not all of these musicians are human; indeed, most are not, and range from angels down to all kinds of beasts, undoubtedly affecting the manner in which they should be read.[14] Furthermore, the type of instrument which is played will also affect our reading, for whilst a harp, for example, has a delicate tone and may also carry positive associations with figures such as the romance hero Tristan, the biblical King David or

[13] Nicolas Bell, *Music in Medieval Manuscripts* (London: British Library, 2001), p. 5. On the variety of musicians to be found on English misericords, see Elaine C. Block with Frédéric Billiet, 'Musical Comedy in the Medieval Choir: England', in *Medieval English Comedy*, ed. Sandra M. Hordis and Paul Hardwick (Turnhout: Brepols, 2007), pp. 209–30.

[14] We shall consider the symbolic significance of animals in chapter 5.

even angels,[15] a set of bagpipes on the other hand is generally associated with low culture – we may think of Chaucer's raucous Miller here – even to the extent of carrying suggestions of coarse phallic imagery.[16]

To these players and entertainers so far considered may be added many others, including the lively company of fools who appear depicted throughout the country, performing in either outdoor or indoor settings. Instances of foolish behaviour may for convenience be divided most simply into two categories: those acts which are deliberate and those which are unwitting. The former may be seen in numerous carvings of the intentional performance of folly,[17] for example, the buttock-baring acrobats and contortionists, images of whom may be found with surprising frequency throughout England and mainland Europe and to whom we will return in chapter 4. As far as low comedy goes, the bared backside has never gone out of fashion, as evinced by the 'mooning' of drunken college sports teams the world over. Indeed, such actions fulfil the basic necessities of comedy, providing a frisson of surprise which elicits laughter, in this case heightened by the transgressive element of bodily exposure. As teachers from all levels of education will be aware, whether it is nudes in marginalia,[18] Chaucer's 'hende [courteous] Nicholas' at the denouement of his *Miller's Tale*, or Edward II, the introduction of the subject of buttocks is guaranteed to raise a giggle in any classroom. This response is surely not solely the result of the surprise elicited by the subject itself, but also to the context in which it occurs: it is not – at least initially – the sort of subject a pupil or student may expect to be broached by a teacher or tutor. This contextually compounded shock is undoubtedly heightened still further, particularly for modern viewers unacquainted with medieval art, when the location of the unexpected transgression is the choir of a church.[19]

[15] See, for example, the harpist in the trio of musical angels in St Mary, Enville. Whilst the harp is generally shown as having positive connotations, in Hereford Cathedral that arch deceiver, the fox, jovially plays the instrument as he dances with an ape upon the prone form of a trapped goose.

[16] See Kathleen L. Scott, 'Sow and Bagpipe Imagery in the Miller's Portrait', *Review of English Studies* 18 (1967), 287–90. As with the harp, however, the associations are not unequivocal: although the grossly comic piping pig, which will be discussed at length in chapter 5, may be found in Beverley Minster, Bishop Tunstall's Chapel, Durham Castle, Manchester Cathedral, St Mary, Richmond and Ripon Cathedral, we may also find a very elegant angel playing bagpipes in the Royal Foundation of St Katharine, London. Block, 'Musical Comedy in the Medieval Choir', p. 218, suggests that this latter image should be considered as a fallen angel although, as we shall see in chapter 5, not all bagpipers were necessarily considered to be of coarse, low status.

[17] To the dozen or so jesters depicted on misericords, identified by their caps and *marottes*, may be added grimacers and a number of acrobatic performers whose antics appear to be designed to provoke laughter in addition to (or even instead of) admiration of their athletic skill.

[18] Such as that in *The Rutland Psalter*, British Library MS 62925 fols 66v–67r, reproduced and discussed in Michael Camille, *Image on the Edge: The Margins of Medieval Art* (London: Reaktion Books, 1992), pp. 43–7 and Pls 21 and 22.

[19] A useful synopsis of modern interpretations of transgressive humour in the medieval margins is offered in Laurel Broughton, 'Joan's Drolleries: Humour in the Margins of Fitzwilliam MS 242', in *Medieval English Comedy*, ed. Hordis and Hardwick, pp. 127–30.

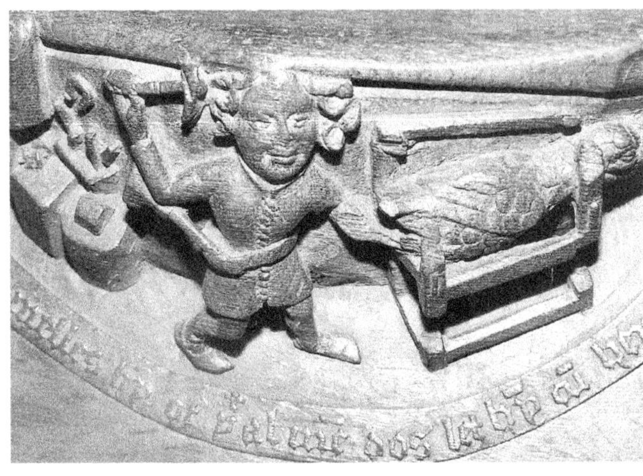

FIG. 4. ST MARY, WHALLEY MISERICORD

The second category of foolishness is perhaps best represented in scenes of proverbial folly – those Homer Simpson 'd'oh!' moments – such as 'putting the cart before the horse', seen in Beverley Minster, or the 'shoeing the goose' motif found in Beverley Minster and St Mary, Whalley (fig. 4). Depicted elsewhere in media as diverse as inexpensive popular prints and stone carvings in churches, this latter scene shows a foolish impossibility performed by one who knows no better, and we smile at the ridiculousness of the incongruity. In the Whalley carving, the sheer senselessness of the activity is made still more explicit by the addition of an accompanying inscription: 'Who so melles hy[m] of þ[at] al me[n] dos let hy[m] cu[m] heir & shog þe ghos' [Whoever concerns himself with the business of other men, let him come here and shoe the goose]. In other words, meddling in other people's business is a fruitless and foolish activity which the wise man will avoid. Both of these categories of folly to be found amongst the choir stalls share important elements in common, however. First, the humour of the image raises a smile or a giggle, rather than full-throated laughter. Secondly, as Janetta Rebold Benton notes of mischievous imagery in late medieval art in general, visual humour:

> is equally accessible to everyone, no matter what the viewer's origin, language, or level of education may be. One needs only to look, for no former familiarity or prior knowledge is required to *get the joke*.[20]

This, as is readily apparent, is the case with all of the above examples, which continue to raise a smile even amongst viewers separated from the culture in which they were commissioned and carved by five centuries or more.

Glancing briefly at these examples as representatives of our two broad categories, then, we could perhaps make a further distinction, in that – at least on the surface – the former type of deliberate performance appears to offer simple entertainment, whilst the latter folly of native stupidity shows the perpetrators to be unwitting, thereby offering amusement to the viewer but at the same time making a moral point. This is, of course, a very

[20] Janetta Rebold Benton, *Medieval Mischief: Wit and Humour in the Art of the Middle Ages* (Stroud: Sutton Publishing, 2004), p. 1.

imprecise – though I believe useful – generalisation, and there are certainly overlaps to be found at the borders. And it is these border areas to which we shall now turn, addressing the class of characters who, more than most, embody the very idea of borders and the transgression thereof: the fools. As Sebastian Brant would note in his *Ship of Fools* at the close of the fifteenth century, 'In jest and earnest evermore / You will encounter fools galore'.[21] Examples of both unwitting and intentional folly are to be found everywhere and, as Elaine Block has illustrated in her ongoing corpus of medieval misericords, the iconic fool may be found across the full geographical spread of surviving misericords throughout Europe.[22] Grinning and leering, gesturing and cavorting, singly or in the company of his fellows, the fool proudly declares his foolishness through his ass-eared cap and his bladder or *marotte*, as is so strikingly depicted in a figure on a misericord in Christchurch Priory (fig. 5).[23]

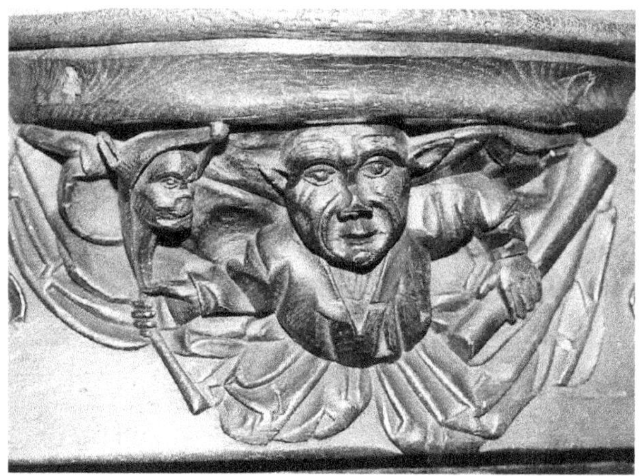

FIG. 5. CHRISTCHURCH PRIORY MISERICORD

The fool has been a significant element in western European culture since its earliest recorded manifestations, perhaps nowhere more so than in England, where his appeal is reflected in the lively profusion of visual representations of such entertainers in all media, including those upon misericords. And what place, we may ask, does the fool hold within the hustle and bustle of the scenes which are spread across misericords in the church choir? To begin to answer this, it is instructive to turn once more to Langland's *Piers Plowman*. In delineating the rich variety of inhabitants he sees going about their worldly business upon the 'fair feeld ful of folk',[24] it is not long before the narrator turns his critical attention upon entertainers, noting that:

[21] Sebastian Brant, *The Ship of Fools*, ed. and trans. Edwin H. Zeydel (New York: Dover Publications, 1962), p. 59.

[22] At the time of writing, Block's *Corpus of Medieval Misericords* volumes for France and Iberia have been published (Turnhout: Brepols, 2003 and 2004 respectively), with further volumes covering the rest of Europe being completed by colleagues following her death in 2008.

[23] Other fools may be found on the misericords of: Beverley Minster; St Botolph's, Boston; Chichester Cathedral; St Mary of Charity, Faversham; Henry VII's Chapel, Westminster Abbey; Winchester Cathedral; St George's Chapel, Windsor.

[24] Langland, *Piers Plowman*, B Prologue 17.

> ... somme murthes to make as mynstralles konne,
> And geten gold with hire glee – giltlees, I leeve.
> Ac japers and janglers, Judas children,
> Feynen hem fantasies, and fooles hem maketh –
> And han wit at wille to werken if they wolde.[25]

[some make entertainment as minstrels know how, and acquire gold with their singing, guiltless, I believe. But jesters and chatterers, children of Judas, create fantasies, and make fools of themselves – though they have ready intelligence to work if they so desired.]

The occupation of professional musician is seen as acceptable – after all, we find no shortage of angelic musicians on misericords and elsewhere in medieval ecclesiastical decoration – the verb *konne* here emphasising the learned skill required to thus earn a living.[26] It is perhaps worth noting, however, that this approval is far from being unconditional. Rather than offering commendation of musical entertainers, a limited approval is here framed in terms of negatives; for Will – and it is reasonable to surmise, by extension, for Langland himself – the performers are not actually praiseworthy, merely 'giltlees'. Furthermore, all judgement is couched within the uncertainty indicated by the fallible subjectivity of 'I leeve' – effectively, the opinion expressed seems to be a rather guarded 'I think they are harmless enough, but I may be wrong.' If the work of singers and musicians is thus viewed as being a little suspect, that of 'japers and janglers' is unequivocally censured. Indeed, it is explicitly defined as the *opposite* of the work in which they could, and by implication should, engage, 'if they wolde'. So, whilst all around them 'alle manere of men' are '[w]erchynge and wandrynge as the world asketh',[27] the fools make the choice not to work, earning themselves the epithet, 'Judas children', and placing themselves outside the natural order of God's world, towards which each man and woman should properly contribute to the utmost of their abilities.

Yet in spite of this censure within Langland's influential polemical work, deliberate foolishness was at times welcome in the church, such as in the topsy-turvy misrule of the Feast of Fools,[28] and in the proliferation of fools carved across the choir stalls. The particularly fine array of fools on the misericords in Beverley Minster, some of whom we shall meet again in chapter 3, has plausibly been attributed to Beverley's carnival culture, which was more vigorous than in most other towns and cities in England.[29] One misericord in particular shows an array of entertainments, with three fools dancing across the bulk of the console, whilst a further fool in the left

[25] Ibid., B Prologue 33–7.
[26] For an overview of angelic musicians see Jeremy and Gwen Montagu, *Minstrels and Angels: Carvings of Musicians in Medieval English Churches* (Berkeley: Fallen Leaf Press, 1998).
[27] Langland, *Piers Plowman*, B Prologue 18–19.
[28] On the limits of toleration of misrule during the Feast of Fools, and the consequent difficulties facing the modern interpreter, see Chris Humphrey, *The Politics of Carnival: Festive Misrule in Medieval England* (Manchester: Manchester University Press, 2001), pp. 48–9.
[29] Grössinger, *The World Upside-Down*, pp. 105–6.

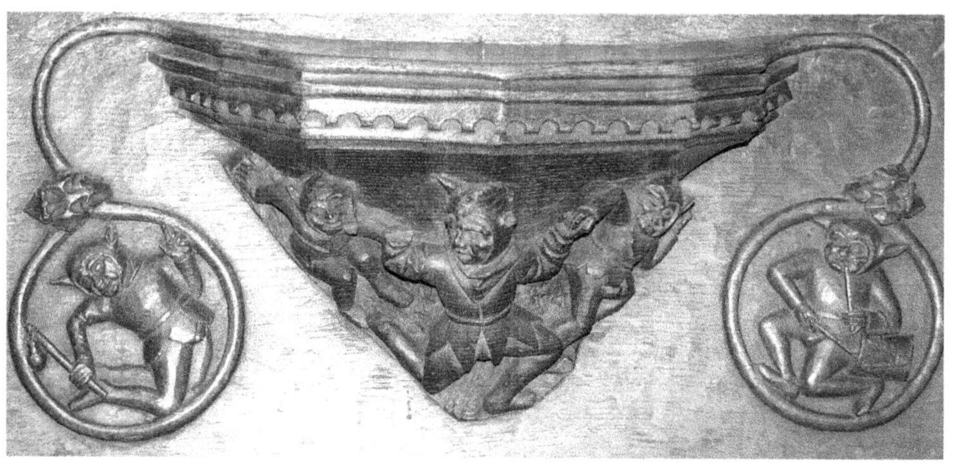

FIG. 6. BEVERLEY MINSTER MISERICORD.

supporter contorts himself whilst raising his finger – perhaps in a gesture of mock-seriousness – and, all the while, a fifth fool accompanies his fellows on pipe and tabor, that most common instrumental combination for the accompaniment of dancing (fig. 6).[30] Whilst this carving perhaps offers a documentary representation of activities which occurred during the Feast of Fools, it is nonetheless worth stating the obvious point that it is not an expression of misrule neatly constrained and controlled by a set time period, after which order is restored. Rather, it is a continuous disruption of decorum, carved and immobile, perhaps, but no more lifeless than the church's sculptural representations of the sacred which perpetually bear the weight of devotional and doctrinal truth for the viewer.

As John Southworth has shown in his comprehensive study of fools in the English court, the fool occupied a place which was set apart from the normally strict delineations of the social hierarchy – a position of exclusion which we saw earlier formulated in Langland's harsh dismissal of the 'japers and janglers'.[31] Southworth notes that,

> [b]eing neither lord nor cleric, freeman nor serf, [the fool] existed in a social limbo … In this, his situation was more extreme than that of the minstrels. Though obliged to sit at a separate table (when not performing), they at least had the companionship of their fellows: he was alone in his separation. In fifteenth-century scenes of court life he occupies otherwise empty spaces or is shown flitting from one group of courtiers to another, a barely corporeal presence.[32]

[30] Montagu, *Minstrels and Angels*, p. 63.

[31] Langland, *Piers Plowman*, B Prologue 35.

[32] John Southworth, *Fools and Jesters at the English Court* (Stroud: Sutton Publishing, 1998), p. 1.

We are reminded here of Langland's guarded acceptance of the role of the professional musician. Of particular note, however, is the fool's paradoxical state of drawing attention to himself, whilst at the same time existing outside acknowledged frames of reference, a position that seems to me in some ways to mirror the position of misericords. They too are marginal yet, by virtue of their location, readily accessible to satisfy the curiosity they arouse. And what is it that we discover upon looking closer? We are drawn into a world which, like Langland's field of folk, encompasses all aspects of life on earth, from the divine to the damned, the winners and wasters, the wise and the foolish. And within this chaotic world, the fool holds a unique place, at a remove from, yet commenting upon, the bustle of activity that surrounds him. We will look more closely at the implications of particular fools in chapter 3, but for now it is sufficient to bear in mind that the depiction of the most apparently frivolous – reprehensible even – of entertainers may hold a serious moral intent, both revealing and commenting upon the truth of that which he sees without fear of censure or reproach, as in the case of Langland's socially unconstrained 'lunatik' who is free to speak familiarly and openly to the King.[33]

As we look at the range of play, games and other entertainments of the common people depicted on misericords, we discover that not all scenes of pastimes are as good-natured as the Gloucester ball game to which we referred earlier. In a carving in Manchester Cathedral, for example, we find two men intent upon a game of dice or tables, a precursor of backgammon (fig. 7). Whilst this scene appears harmless enough, a misericord in St George's Chapel, Windsor, depicts a similar game but in this case it provokes an argument between the players which is on the verge of escalating into violence, as one of the protagonists reaches for a dagger hanging ready at his belt. Both of these scenes appear to be taking place in taverns,[34] a not uncommon interior to find beneath choir stalls, as may be seen at St Peter and St Paul, Hemington, for example, where a cellarer is depicted going busily about his business.

Although they are firmly rooted in the day-to-day activities of the world which surrounded the carvers and their patrons, these images may well also hold a significance beyond mere reportage of contemporary village – or, indeed, urban – life. The tavern, after all, was widely condemned by contemporary commentators for presenting a serious temptation away from righteous living. As Robert Mannyng of Brunne makes clear in his Prologue to *Handlyng Synne* (dated 'a þousynd and þre hundryd & þre'),

[33] Langland, *Piers Plowman*, B Prologue 123. This role for the fool as truth-teller, of course, is most familiar to modern audiences through the plays of Shakespeare and his post-medieval contemporaries.

[34] Although the figures which flank the game players in the Manchester carving are severely damaged, an ale cask is still clearly visible on the right-hand side.

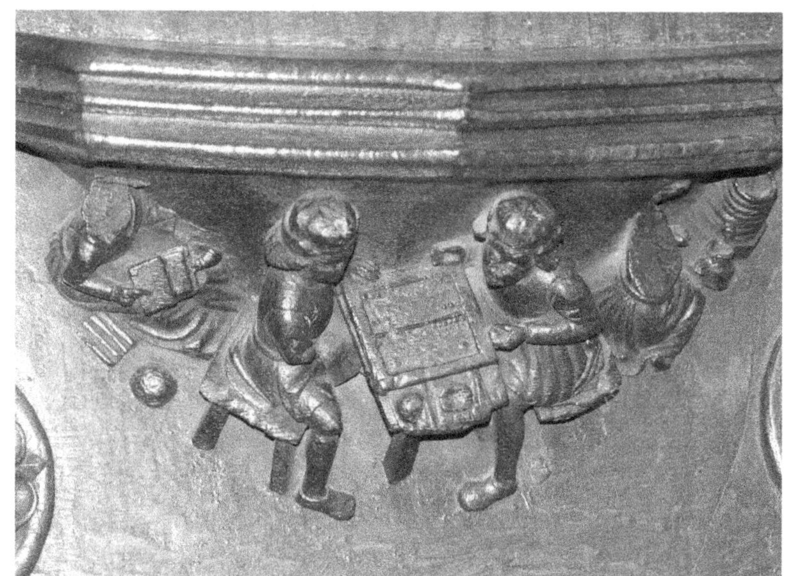

FIG. 7. MANCHESTER CATHEDRAL MISERICORD.

> … many beyn of swyche manere
> Þat talys & rymys wyle bleþly here
> Yn gamys, yn festys, & at þe ale,
> Loue men to lestene trotouale,
> Þat may falle ofte to velanye
> To dedly synne or outher folye.[35]

[… many are of such a disposition that they will gladly hear tales and rhymes. In games, at feasts, and at their drink, men love to listen to tittle-tattle that may often descend to villainy, to deadly sin or other folly.]

In considering the immoral allure of the tavern, we may also recall characters such as Chaucer's Friar who, rather than carrying out the apostolic duties of his calling amongst the poor and sick, 'knew the tavernes wel in every toun / And everich hostiler and tappestere',[36] as well as Langland's allegorical figure of Glutton, who is so easily distracted on his way to hear mass by the promise of 'good ale':

> There was laughynge and lourynge and 'Lat go the cuppe!'
> Bargaynes and beverages bigonne to arise;
> And seten so til evensong, and songen umwhile,

[35] Robert Mannyng of Brunne, *Handlyng Synne*, ed. Idelle Sullens (Binghamton, NY: Medieval and Renaissance Texts and Studies, 1983), ll. 76 and 45–50.
[36] Geoffrey Chaucer, *The Canterbury Tales*, in *The Riverside Chaucer*, ed. Larry D. Benson (Oxford: Oxford University Press, 1988), I (A) 240–1.

Til Gloton hadde yglubbed a galon and a gille.
His guttes bigonne to gothelen as two gredy sowes;
He pissed a potel in a Paternoster-while,
And blew his rounde ruwet at his ruggebones ende,
That alle that herde that horn helde hir nose after
And wisshed it hadde ben wexed with a wispe of firses![37]

[There was laughing and scowling and cries of 'Let go the cup!' Deals and drinking commenced; and they sat there until Evensong, singing occasionally, until Glutton had gulped a gallon and a gill. His guts began to grumble like two greedy sows; he pissed half a pint in the time it takes to say the Paternoster, and blew his round trumpet at the end of his spine, so everyone who heard that horn held their nose afterwards and wished it had been polished with wisp of furze.]

Putting aside for now the matter of base bodily functions in the latter example, to which we will have cause to return briefly in chapter 4, we may see a common line of polemic which focuses upon the stark opposition between devotion and the activities of the tavern, both in drinking and in the other moral misdemeanours to which this leads. Thus, it is not unrealistic to assume that this is how we should read tavern images upon misericords: as a warning against the excesses embraced by Chaucer's Pardoner's 'yonge folk that haunteden folye, / As riot, hasard, stywes, and tavernes',[38] which, with grim inevitability, will lead ultimately – as on the Windsor carving – to violence. One should rather, as Langland's figure of Repentance admonishes:

'... drynk nat over delicatly, ne to depe neither,
That thi wille by cause therof to wrathe myghte turne.
*Esto sobrius!*' he seide, and assoiled me after,
And bad me wilne to wepe my wikkednesse to amende.[39]

['... drink neither too daintily nor too deeply, that it may cause your will to turn to anger. Be sober!' he said, and afterwards absolved me, and commanded me to desire to weep to amend my wickedness.]

As he occupies the place thus carved, the cleric may both reflect that he has managed to resist such temptations as are offered by the tavern and remind himself to continue to do so. Nonetheless, we should perhaps also pause to consider the dishonest ale-wife (fig. 8) who is unceremoniously bundled naked across the shoulder of a devil and tipped into the gaping mouth of Hell – a scene which may be found in St Lawrence, Ludlow, and which calls to mind the woman in the Coventry Websters' Play of the Harrowing of Hell, who confesses that:

[37] Langland, *Piers Plowman*, B V 303 and 337–45.
[38] Chaucer, *Canterbury Tales*, VI (C) 464–5.
[39] Langland, *Piers Plowman*, B V 182–5.

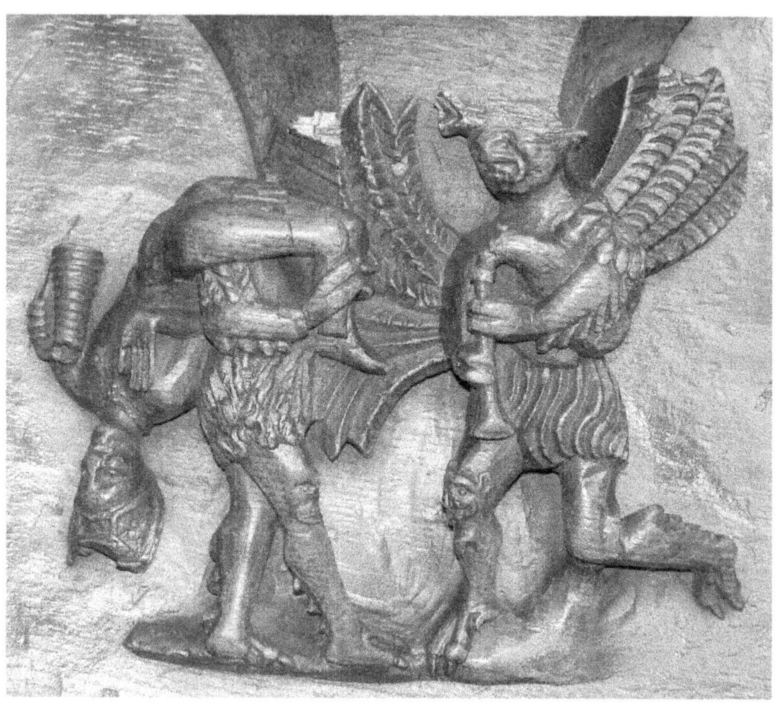

FIG. 8. ST LAWRENCE, LUDLOW MISERICORD.

> Sometyme I was a taverner,
> a gentle gossippe and a tapster,
> of wyne and ale a trustie bruer,
> which woe hath me wrought.
> Of kannes I kept no trewe measure.
> My cuppes I sould at my pleasure,
> deceavinge manye a creature.[40]

[For a time I was an innkeeper, a noble gossip and a barmaid, a trusty brewer of wine and ale, which has brought me suffering. I kept no true measure of my mugs. I sold my cups at my liking, deceiving many people.]

This dishonest ale-wife is consequently excluded from the mercy of Christ's rescue. As Satan informs her:

> Though Jesus be gonne with our meanye,
> yett shalt thou abyde here with mee
> in payne without ende.[41]

[Although Jesus has departed with our company, you shall nonetheless remain here with me in endless pain.]

[40] R. M. Lumiansky and David Mills (eds), *The Chester Mystery Cycle*, EETS s.s. 3 (London: Oxford University Press, 1994), p. 337.
[41] Ibid., p. 338.

Even those who provide the temptation should be minded to watch their step closely.

Reflecting upon the images thus far considered, then, it may be suggested that the depictions of leisure pursuits which proliferate on choir stalls fulfil a function akin to that of sermon *exempla* – so much a feature of the 'preaching revival' which gathered pace throughout the thirteenth and fourteenth centuries, following the Fourth Lateran Council of 1215 – and offer an illustrated catalogue of practices which lead to sin and are thus open to condemnation.[42] Again in Gloucester Cathedral, for example, we find barefoot, semi-clad wrestlers grasping each others' scarves as they each grapple for mastery. As Compton Reeves notes, the sport of wrestling was popular with both participants and observers, yet it was also one of many recreations of the body – indeed, few sports are so intensely physical, both in the demands placed upon the individual and in his physical connection with his opponent – which was frequently condemned by the Church as a distraction from devotion.[43] In considering these images, therefore, we should bear in mind Paulette E. Barton's cautionary observation that within the subjects depicted on misericords '[t]here are nuances and conventions that remain hidden or partially understood because the viewer is not of the culture that produced the image',[44] and we must endeavour, as much as we can, to bridge this cultural gap. Discussing the culture which gave rise to Langland's *Piers Plowman*, with particular reference to the wall paintings that filled medieval churches, C. David Benson makes an important point which is equally applicable to other forms of late medieval church decoration, including misericords:

> Long experience with the public art of their local churches must have acclimated contemporaries to forms of organization that may seem peculiar to modern audiences. Parish wall paintings would have trained parishioners to make sense of stylistic and narrative variety within a single structure.[45]

This conceptual unification of apparently diverse elements within – and, indeed, between – image and text would surely be even more acute amongst

[42] On preaching throughout the period, see Helen Leith Spencer, *English Preaching in the Late Middle Ages* (Oxford: Oxford University Press, 1993). The tenth Lateran decree had particularly stressed the importance of the appointment of suitable men to preach and hear confession: see Harry Rothwell (ed.), *English Historical Documents: 1189–1327* (London: Eyre and Spottiswoode, 1975), pp. 650–1.

[43] Compton Reeves, *Pleasures and Pastimes in Medieval England* (Stroud: Alan Sutton Publishing, 1995), pp. 95–6. See also G. R. Owst, *Literature and Pulpit in Medieval England: a Neglected Chapter in the History of English Letters and of the English People*, 2nd edn (Oxford: Blackwell, 1961), p. 33. For a brief history of English wrestling – and its changing position regarding the Church – see Roy Lomas, *Grasmere Sports: The First 150 Years* (Kendal: MTP, 2002), pp. 6–7.

[44] Paulette E. Barton, *Mercy and the Misericord in Late Medieval England: Cathedral Theology and Architecture* (Lewiston: Edwin Mellen Press, 2009), pp. 7–8.

[45] C. David Benson, *Public Piers Plowman: Modern Scholarship and Late Medieval English Culture* (University Park, PA: Pennsylvania State University Press, 2003), p. 200.

the clerical audience of the misericords, whose primary focus would be upon devotion in the world. Consequently, we should perhaps see these images not as mere representations of 'the daily life of humble folk',[46] lacking any Christian moralising intent, but rather as discrete yet interrelated reminders to question one's daily concerns and activities, thereby admonishing the viewer to good behaviour.

Alongside the scurrilous and downright sinful activities to be eschewed, a wide range of 'worthy' trades may also be found on carvings throughout the country. It is no surprise to find the workmen who were responsible for carving the misericords depicted on stalls more frequently than any other craft, with a particularly fine example originally from East Anglia now displayed in the Victoria & Albert Museum, London.[47] Elsewhere throughout Britain, a broad range of occupations from cloth maker to cook and from scribe to shipwright may be found.[48] By far the greatest number of scenes of labour, however, relate to agriculture. This proliferation of scenes from throughout the agricultural year – the 'labours of the months' which we considered earlier – takes in the cycle of crops from ploughing to harvest, as well as animal husbandry from feeding to slaughter, reflecting both late medieval Britain's dependence upon farming and the necessity of doing all things in their proper season. In addition, drawing together both sport and sustenance, we can see many scenes of hunting, mainly of indigenous animals such as deer and hare, and mainly by the upper classes although, as Richard Almond notes, '[o]wing to the various and disparate needs of medieval society, the functions of hunting ensured that it was widely engaged in throughout every community'.[49] As with the negative exemplars discussed above, we may read these carvings which depict honest work as illustrative approbation of assiduously fulfilling one's responsibilities to society in accordance with the estate to which one has been ordained by God, for 'labour of the hands', in the words of the homilist Master Ralph of Acton, 'confers four benefits. It destroys vices, it nourishes virtues, it provides necessaries, it gives alms.'[50] Regarding hunting, for example, whilst essential for both the acquisition of meat, skins and other animal products, and for

[46] Bond, *Wood Carvings in English Churches 1*, p. 87.

[47] Others may be found at: Beverley Minster; St Mary Magdalene, Brampton; Christchurch Priory; St Nicholas, Great Doddington; All Saints, Wellingborough. Carvers and their workshops will be discussed in chapter 3.

[48] Cloth makers are depicted at St Mary Magdalene, Brampton and St Andrew, Norton; cooks at All Saints, Maidstone and St Mary, Minster-in-Thanet; a scribe on a supporter at St Mary Magdalene, Brampton; and a shipwright at St David's Cathedral. Whilst the St David's carving appears to be simply a representation of the shipwright's craft, it could be related to the scene elsewhere on the cathedral stalls which has been identified as the voyage of St Govan: see Remnant, *Catalogue of Misericords*, p. 197 for full descriptions.

[49] Richard Almond, *Medieval Hunting* (Stroud: Sutton Publishing, 2003), p. 13. In the sequence from Ripple discussed earlier, for example, the month of June is signified by a young man riding out hawking. A rare example of hunting a more exotic beast can be found in St Botolph's, Boston, where a lion is caught with a rope.

[50] Cited in Owst, *Literature and Pulpit*, p. 569.

pest control, it was nonetheless frequently described further in terms of occupying a moral function:

> [T]he life of no man that useth gentle game and disport [is] less displeasable unto God than the life of a perfect and skilful hunter ... When a man is idle and reckless without work, and be not occupied in doing some thing, he abides in his bed or in his chamber, a thing which draweth men to imaginations of fleshy lust and pleasure. For such men have no wish but always to abide in one place, and think in pride, or in avarice, or in wrath, or in sloth, or in gluttony, or in lechery, or in envy. For the imagination of men rather turns to evil than to good, for the three enemies which mankind hath, are the devil, the world and the flesh, and this is proved enough.[51]

Although such arguments may not sound wholly persuasive to a modern reader, such passages provide ample illustration of the way in which all pastimes could be – and frequently were – framed as expressions of the good Christian life.[52]

In looking at these apparently secular activities – both those which are condemned and those which are encouraged – it is important to recognise that the distinction between sacred and profane in the Middle Ages was far from clear-cut. As Peggy Knapp puts it so succinctly, 'the fourteenth-century "Church" is not one entity so much as a number of contending hierarchies and orders',[53] and these 'hierarchies and orders' do not consist merely of those ordained into the institutional framework of the Church, for all Christians – both clerical and lay – were considered members of God's Church on earth. In his *Canterbury Tales*, for example, Chaucer may present to us the most celebrated diversity of fictional medieval characters, both exemplary and corrupt, whose relationship to organised religion ranges from the pious to the parasitic, but he is nonetheless clear in pointing out that 'pilgrimes were they alle';[54] whether devout or otherwise, the life of every Christian man and woman may be figured as a pilgrimage through life.[55] In delineating the characters in his motley band, Chaucer offers the reader few unequivocally exemplary pilgrims, but one in whom even the most ingenious critic has yet to find a trace of Chaucer's celebrated satirical irony

[51] Edward of Norwich, *The Master of Game*, ed. William A. Baillie-Grohman and F. N. Baillie-Grohman (Philadelphia: University of Pennsylvania Press, 2005), pp. 4–5.

[52] Some possible moral interpretations of specific hunting scenes are discussed in Barton, *Mercy and the Misericord*, pp. 188–90. Many sleeping or reclining figures may be read as symbols of Sloth, whilst Christa Grössinger has persuasively suggested that a carving in the chapel of New College, Oxford, depicting a naked woman reclining on a cushion, makes explicit the connection between sins of Sloth and Lust which we find in the quotation above: Grössinger, *The World Upside-Down*, p. 132.

[53] Peggy Knapp, *Chaucer and the Social Contest* (London: Routledge, 1990), p. 13.

[54] Chaucer, *Canterbury Tales*, I (A) 26.

[55] On the idea of pilgrimage – both actual and allegorical – throughout the medieval period, see Dee Dyas, *Pilgrimage in Medieval English Literature: 700–1500* (Cambridge: D. S. Brewer, 2001).

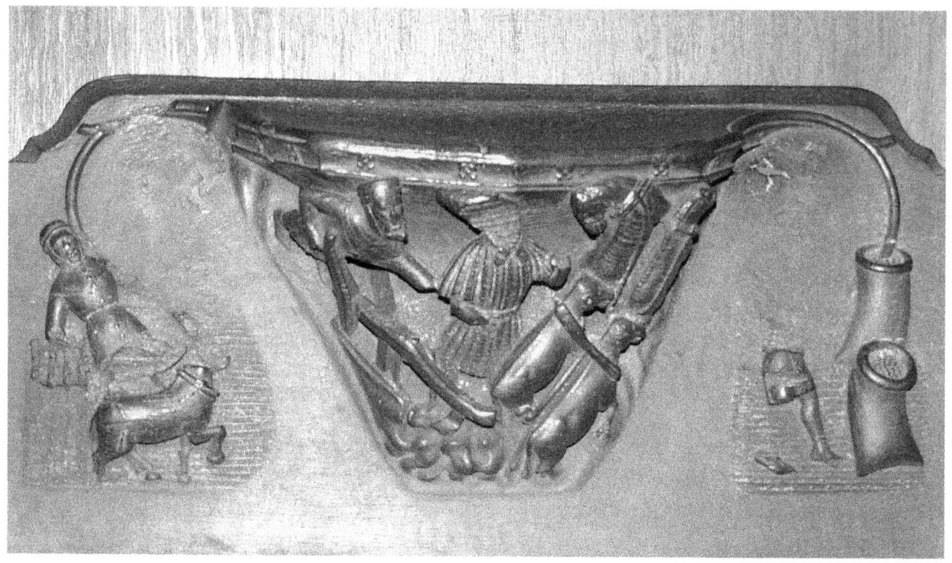

FIG. 9. LINCOLN CATHEDRAL MISERICORD.

is the most lowly: the humble, hard-working Plowman. And it is to the humble ploughman that we shall turn for the remainder of this chapter, as he provides a striking and particularly English illustration of the way in which even the most apparently secular of images could in the later Middle Ages resonate with allegorical depth.

In the late fourteenth-century stalls of Lincoln Cathedral may be found the only surviving English misericord carving showing the hard winter labour of ploughing (fig. 9), although drawings in the British Museum show that such a figure was also once depicted on the stalls of the long since demolished Carmelite Friary in Coventry.[56] The main scene of the Lincoln carving curves around the central console, with the ploughman positioned to the left and his team of four horses – disproportionately small by comparison, most likely on account of the spatial constraints of the medium – sweeping up the right-hand side. This tableau is completed by a central figure, now mutilated, who goads the animals, although the switch or other implement with which he is doing so is now missing. The supporters, which have fared even worse than this latter figure, show, on the left, what appears to be a scene of harrowing, again with a disproportionately small horse, and, on the right, two grain sacks. These sacks are presumably being either filled or, most probably, emptied for sowing, although only the lower abdomen,

[56] The drawings, from BL Lansdowne MS 209, ff. 254–5b, record the misericords which were relocated from the friary to King Henry VIII's Grammar School, Coventry. Many of these, including the ploughman, had been damaged or destroyed by the time Mary Dormer Harris made the first study of the Coventry stalls, in which both the surviving misericords and the drawings are reproduced: Mary Dormer Harris, 'The Misericords of Coventry', *Transactions and Proceedings of the Birmingham Archaeological Society* 52 (1927), 246–66.

left leg and right foot of the accompanying figure undertaking this task remain. Taking the three elements of the carving together, then, the misericord appears to depict the vital sequence of rural occupations which together provide the foundation of food production, with the ploughman placed – figuratively as well as literally – right in the centre of these activities.

The narrator of an early fourteenth-century alliterative poem which is generally referred to as the 'Song of the Husbandman' speaks eloquently of the hardships faced by a contemporary ploughman, as a result not only of the physically demanding labour itself but also of his lowly social position:

> Nou we mote worche, nis þer non oþer won,
> Mai ich no lengore lyue wiþ mi lesinge.[57]

> [Now we must work, there is no other course of action, I may no longer live with my lack.]

The poem is unusual in its narrative perspective, being composed in the voice of – if almost certainly not actually by – the ploughman himself. Written at a time during which labourers were held in strict obligation to their social superiors, it articulates the pressures and constraints under which these workers found themselves. Yet, in spite of his inferior social position, advances in ploughing technology throughout the Middle Ages, which consequently required a greater level of skill from agricultural workers, had resulted in a situation in which the ploughman was perhaps the most important member of the village labouring community and, indeed, of vital importance to society as a whole.[58] As Langland puts it:

> The Commune contrived of Kynde Wit craftes,
> And for profit of the peple plowmen ordained
> To tilie and to travaille as trewe lif asketh.[59]

> [The Common People made plans using the skills of Natural Understanding, and for the good of all people ordained ploughmen to till and work as honest life demands.]

[57] 'Song of the Husbandman', in *Historical Poems of the XIVth and XVth Centuries*, ed. Rossell Hope Robbins (New York: Columbia University Press, 1959), ll. 5–6.

[58] On the evolution of the plough during this period, see Lynn White, Jr, *Medieval Technology and Social Change* (Oxford: Oxford University Press, 1962), pp. 41–57. An anonymous treatise of the late thirteenth century enumerates the qualities necessary for ploughmen thus: 'The ploughmen ought to be men of intelligence, and ought to know how to sow, and how to repair and mend broken ploughs and harrows, and to till the land well, and crop it rightly.' See *Seneschaucie*, in Elizabeth Lamond (ed. and trans.), *Walter of Henley's Husbandry, together with an Anonymous Husbandry, Seneschaucie and Robert Grosseteste's Rules* (London: Longmans, Green and Co., 1890), p. 111. Georges Duby notes that by the mid-twelfth century the economic status of the ploughman had become such that the 'plough' (a term embracing the implement itself, the beasts which pulled it and the man who drove them) was the unit to reckon labour services in the Cluniac inventory – a practice which was adopted shortly afterwards by English landlords: Georges Duby, *Rural Economy and Country Life in the Medieval West*, trans. Cynthia Postan (London: Arnold, 1968), pp. 115–16.

[59] Langland, *Piers Plowman*, B Prologue 118–20.

It is only common sense, says Langland, to acknowledge that the very foundation of society's well-being depends upon those who:

> ... putten hem to the plough, pleiden ful selde,
> In settynge and sowynge swonken ful harde,
> And wonnen that thise wastours with glotonye destruyeth.[60]

> [... set themselves to the plough, very rarely played, worked very hard in setting and sowing, and obtained that which these wasters destroy through their gluttony.]

After all, without these hard-workers and providers, none may eat. In addition, it should be remembered that at the same time as the work had become more skilled as a result of the advances in and greater complexity of ploughing technology, by the latter part of the century the Black Death had made agricultural workers far less numerous than they had been when the 'Song of the Husbandman' was composed.

Addressing the frequent representation of ploughing in late medieval art, Michael Camille has described the scene as 'part of a traditional vocabulary of depicting agricultural life in manuscript illumination',[61] the harsh January toil notably introducing the oft-reproduced *bas-de-page* sequence of agricultural 'labours of the months' in the Luttrell Psalter. Elsewhere, the Limbourg brothers' remarkably landscaped calendar page for the *Très Riches Heures* of the Duc de Berry offers another famous example of this seasonal task which appears frequently in manuscript illustration.[62] These manuscript images are certainly not realistic representations of the impoverished agricultural labourers who had been given a voice in the 'Song of the Husbandman' and, although appearing far from happy in his lot, even the scowling ploughman of the Luttrell Psalter is in far richer array than that exaggerated example of his estate in the late fourteenth-century *Pierce the Ploughman's Crede*, of whom it is said that:

> His cote was of a cloute that cary was y-called,
> His hod was full of holes and his heer oute,
> With his knopped schon clouted full thykke;
> His ton toteden out as he the londe treddede,
> His hosen ouerhongen his hokschynes on eueriche a side,
> Al beslombred in fen as he the plow folwede ...[63]

> [His coat was of a poor cloth known as cary, his hood was full of holes and his hair stuck out, with his lumpy shoes wrapped thickly

[60] Langland, *Piers Plowman*, B Prologue 20–2. It is noteworthy that ploughing is the first occupation mentioned by name in the 'field of folk'.

[61] Michael Camille, *Mirror in Parchment: The Luttrell Psalter and the Making of Medieval England* (London: Reaktion, 1998), p. 186.

[62] In this case, the activity of ploughing is associated with the month of March. *Les Très Riches Heures du Duc de Berry*, with an introduction by Jean Longnon and Raymond Cazelles (London: Thames and Hudson, 1969), Pl. 4.

[63] *Pierce the Ploughman's Crede*, in *The Piers Plowman Tradition*, ed. Helen Barr (London: Everyman's Library, 1993), ll. 422–7.

> in rags; his toes poked out as he walked the land, his hose hanging behind his shins on each side, all sodden in mud as he followed the plough ...]

The labourers who are so often depicted at the plough in manuscripts are, in contrast, never shown in such rags, but instead have, as Camille notes, been 'dressed up' and 'cosmeticized' in order to appeal to the tastes of the aristocratic audience for which they were painted.[64] They are not, after all, images intended to offer a documentary record of the harsh conditions of agricultural labour but, rather, they provide decoration in keeping with the tastes of wealthy patrons.

Whilst it is clear and, indeed, perfectly understandable that these ploughmen are not depicted in order to provide a mirror of contemporary society, we may nonetheless wonder why such patrons would desire these agricultural images at all in the margins of their devotional manuscripts. It could, of course, be posited that the variety of labours to be found in these manuscripts may simply signify the lordship of the patron over the army of workers on his lands, thereby acting as a permanent record of his wealth, status and power.[65] Nonetheless, in view of the devotional nature of these texts, it is surely likely that an allegorical level of reading is also intended for these scenes, and there is a long and rich tradition to support this. Stephen Barney has demonstrated how, by the fourteenth century, there was an established tradition, firmly rooted in scriptural exegesis, in which the office of priesthood was described in agricultural metaphors, the act of preaching itself becoming seen as labour with 'the ploughshare of the tongue'.[66] This in turn contributed to a subsequent proliferation of agricultural metaphors which stretched to encompass devotional matters beyond the purely sacerdotal; after all, as Luke 9:62 reminds us, 'No man, having put his hand to the plough, and looking back, is fit for the kingdom of God.' In view of this, we may see the ploughmen who decorate manuscripts, and, indeed, the Lincoln misericord, as true Christians, diligently ploughing their furrows. In order to illuminate the way in which these images of ploughing and related activities were used to enumerate the requirements of Christian life, it will be fruitful to focus upon one specific, though widespread, instance of the employment of such agricultural metaphors: the fourteenth-century preachers' manual, *Fasciculus morum*.[67]

[64] Camille, *Mirror in Parchment*, p. 184.

[65] This is noted by Camille, *Mirror in Parchment*, pp. 180–2.

[66] Stephen A. Barney, 'The Plowshare of the Tongue: The Progress of a Symbol from the Bible to *Piers Plowman*', *Mediaeval Studies* 35 (1973), 261–93. Whilst Elizabeth D. Kirk, 'Langland's Plowman and the Recreation of Fourteenth-Century Religious Metaphor', *Yearbook of Langland Studies* 2 (1988), 1–21, seeks to qualify some of Barney's assertions by foregrounding the proliferation of ploughmen as negative *exempla*, it does not detract from Barney's observations upon the development of the metaphorical uses which had become commonplace by the late fourteenth century.

[67] All references taken from, *Fasciculus morum*, ed. and trans. Siegfried Wenzel (London: Pennsylvania State University Press, 1989).

It was originally compiled around 1300 by a Franciscan for use by other friars, but variations throughout the many fourteenth- and fifteenth-century manuscript survivals indicate that *Fasciculus morum* also became widely known and used by secular clergy.[68] In addition, there is evidence for extensive borrowing from the work in sermon collections well into the fifteenth century.[69] It is safe to assume, then, that the modes of expression employed within the collection would be common to the devotional culture within which it proved so popular. If we turn to chapter 5.25 of *Fasciculus morum*, we find the theme of 'those things which hinder almsgiving' (*que elemosinam impediunt*) explored through the analogy of a seed which is prevented from bearing fruit.[70] The hindrances which stand in the way of the free giving of alms are shown to be the seven deadly sins, the effects of which are described in terms relating to the original agricultural metaphor: pride is that which exposes the seed to 'the wind of human praise' (*vento humane laudis*) when it should rather be covered by 'the earth of humility' (*terra humilitatis*); avarice is the planting of the seed too deeply; and so on. Whilst the notion of almsgiving bearing fruit may relate to the rich history of tree imagery in Christian allegorical tradition,[71] what is interesting in this particular case is the manner in which the reader – or auditor – is exhorted to nurture the vulnerable seed. Each of the sins is an aspect of spiritual sloth, the remedy for which is appropriately described in terms of active good husbandry:

> First, before the seed is cast upon the soil, the latter must be carefully prepared; if sterile, it must first be burned with the fire of contrition and then be ploughed with the ploughshare of confession.
>
> [*Prima est quod antequam iaciatur in terram, necessaria est diligens preparacio terre, quia si sit infructuosa, debet primo comburi igne contricionis et postea arari vomere confessionis.*]

The team of oxen which draws the plough is composed of the five senses along with the faculty of memory; the servant who leads the plough is 'hope of future glory' (*spes future glorie*); and the oxen are goaded by 'fear of punishment' (*timor pene*).

As we can see, from at least the beginning of the fourteenth century, through to the sixteenth century, a popular preachers' manual – a document

[68] Frances A. Foster, 'A Note on the *Fasciculus morum*', *Franciscan Studies* 8 (1948), 202–4. Twenty eight known copies survive. On date and authorship, see Siegfried Wenzel, *Verses in Sermons: Fasciculus morum and its Middle English Poems* (Cambridge, MA: Medieval Society of America Publications, 1978), pp. 26–34.

[69] See Alan J. Fletcher and Susan Powell, 'The Origins of a Fifteenth-Century Sermon Collection: MSS Harley 2247 and Royal 18 B XXV', *Leeds Studies in English* n. s. 10 (1978), 74–96.

[70] *Fasciculus morum*, pp. 544–5. This elaborates an earlier comparison between alms and the seed, which provides the subject matter for chapters 5.23 and 5.24.

[71] For a discussion of this tradition, see, for example, A. Joan Bowers, 'The Tree of Charity in *Piers Plowman*', in *Literary Monographs* 6, ed. Eric Rothstein and Joseph Anthony Wittreich Jr (Madison: University of Wisconsin Press, 1975), pp. 1–34.

compiled with the specific intention of offering materials for the preacher to transmit widely to the laity – was employing a metaphorical *schema* which figured the hard work of living as a Christian in terms of agricultural labour. It is, then, no surprise to find such labour depicted in the margins of devotional texts, as well as in church decoration such as the Lincoln misericord. Indeed, given the allegorical significance of the ploughman during this period, it comes as something of a surprise that the Lincoln carving is the only representation to be found in the corpus of surviving English misericords. Yet, as we have seen, allegorical labourers – ploughmen in particular – not only appear in marginal decoration, but also occupy a prominent place in a number of devotional texts of the later Middle Ages, and it is here that we may find possible clues to explain the scarcity of ploughmen on misericords. Turning for now from *Fasciculus morum*, it is illuminating here to return to a vernacular work mentioned earlier in this chapter, *Pierce the Ploughman's Crede*, in order to illustrate how far the symbol of the ploughman could be taken in discussion of doctrinal matters by the early years of the fifteenth century.

Deriving from, and making explicit reference to, a reading of Langland's *Piers Plowman* – itself likely indebted in part to the agricultural imagery of *Fasciculus morum*[72] – the overtly Lollard *Pierce the Ploughman's Crede* nonetheless differs from its more widely circulated antecedent in almost all key respects. Most significant to the present discussion is the lack of apparent allegory in the later work. *Crede* has no dream framework and, rather than complex allegorical figures such as Lady Mede, Anima and the many others who guide, beguile and baffle Langland's Will, the narrator of the later poem is merely confronted by representatives of the four orders of corrupt, all too worldly friars as he seeks for one, either 'lered' or 'lewed' [lettered or unlettered],[73] who may teach him the Apostle's Creed, a fundamental expression of faith which all Christians were expected to commit to memory. Consequently when, at the mid point of the poem, the narrator comes across 'a sely man [who] on the plow hongen' [a simple/blessed man who hung onto the plough],[74] we may initially read the description – already quoted in part above – of the impoverished Piers and his pitiful family as, in the words of H. S. Bennett, 'an unforgettable vignette … from a side of life Chaucer does not choose to depict in detail'.[75] However, the vivid pictorial quality of the description should not blind us to the fact that this is no more an accurate representation of the lot of the late medieval agricultural

[72] The possible relationship between *Piers Plowman* and *Fasciculus morum* is touched upon, although not elaborated, by Alan J. Fletcher in his review of Wenzel's edition of *Fasciculus morum*, which appears in the *Yearbook of Langland Studies* 4 (1990), 184–7. If we are to believe the 'autobiographical' interpolation of the C-text of *Piers Plowman*, Langland is precisely the sort of minor cleric for whom *Fasciculus morum* would have been written.

[73] *Crede*, l. 25.

[74] Ibid., l. 421.

[75] H. S. Bennett, *Chaucer in the Fifteenth Century* (Oxford: Clarendon Press, 1947), p. 72.

labourer than is the brightly dressed ploughman of the Luttrell Psalter.[76] For all of the poem's apparent concern with realism in its evocation of tangible physical details, the *Crede* poet employs the character of Piers as a monumental symbolic figure of what he believes to be the true Christian, offering both narrator and reader hope of spiritual fecundity in contrast to the sterility of both the friars and the winter landscape, itself as psychologically resonant as that described in *Sir Gawain and the Green Knight* or, indeed, Langland's 'wildernesse'.[77] For, in the wake of *Piers Plowman*, the figure of the ploughman had become not simply a representative of the good Christian but, rather, the lay spiritual authority at the centre of Lollard ideology: witness the Wycliffite contention that,

> A simple Pater noster of a plouȝman þat his in charite is betre þan a þousand massis of coueitouse prelates & veyn religious ful of coueitise & pride & fals flaterynge & norischynge of synne.[78]
>
> [A simple 'Our Father' of a charitable ploughman is better than a thousand masses of covetous prelates and vain clergy full of covetousness, pride, false flattering and the nurture of sin.]

Consequently, as soon as the poor ploughman of *Crede* reveals himself to be 'Peres ... the pore man, the plowe-man',[79] the narrator, along with the assumed reader, eagerly anticipates the voice of truth and trenchant anticlericalism for which the figure had become known. This is a response which is echoed in the later, pseudo-Chaucerian *Plowman's Tale*, in which the ploughman, newly arrived upon the pilgrimage, is exhorted – and indeed expected – by the Host to 'tell us some holy thynge'.[80]

Throughout the late fourteenth century and early fifteenth century, then, the iconic, ideal ploughman as, in Chaucer's phrase, a 'trewe swynkere', working 'for Cristes sake, for every povre wight',[81] had become appropriated as a Lollard figurehead and spokesman. As a result of this, it is little surprise if by the fifteenth century the orthodox Church was prone to 'smelle a Lollere in the wynd' whenever the ploughman raised his head.[82] An example of a response to such perceptions may perhaps be discerned in Bodleian Library MS Greaves 54, a fifteenth-century miscellany which contains an item that Alan Fletcher has termed 'a unique, if fragmentary, Middle English

[76] On the Luttrell Psalter ploughman's clothing, see Camille, *Mirror in Parchment*, pp. 184–5.
[77] Langland, *Piers Plowman*, B Prologue I 12.
[78] F. D. Matthew (ed.), *The English Works of Wyclif, Hitherto Unprinted*, rev. edn, EETS o.s. 74 (London: Kegan Paul, 1902), p. 274.
[79] *Crede*, l. 473.
[80] *The Plowman's Tale: The c.1532 and 1606 Editions of a Spurious Canterbury Tale*, ed. Mary Rhinelander McCarl (New York: Garland, 1997), c.1533 edition, l. 46. Although the poet of *The Plowman's Tale* appears to claim authorship of the earlier *Crede* ('Of freres I have tolde before, / In a makynge of a Crede': ll. 1065–6), the somewhat inferior verse of the latter work renders this most unlikely. Nevertheless, that such a claim is made offers clear evidence of the currency of the figure of the ploughman in suppressed Lollard discourse.
[81] Chaucer, *Canterbury Tales*, I (A) 537.
[82] Ibid., II ($B^1$) 1173.

translation of the *Fasciculus* [*morum*].[83] Notably, the manuscript contains an extended metaphor of sin as earth which blocks the ears of the sinner to the good words of the gospel, referring to:

> A covetise Man . his eris buth stoppid with erth . ffor he coveitith nouȝt to her[e] his s[er]vyse / butt off the covetise of the world the whiche is butt erth.[84]
>
> [A covetous man's ears are blocked with earth, for he does not desire to hear his service, but covets the things of the earth which is merely earth.]

As we have seen, *Fasciculus morum* contains the metaphor of the 'ploughshare of confession', so it is surprising that the later writer, clearly sufficiently familiar with the work to borrow many useful *exempla*, chooses not to employ this apposite metaphor as a means of breaking up the 'earth of sin'. This is all the more striking as the 'water of penance' is prescribed in order to quench the fire of lust,[85] whilst the problem of 'earth' remains unresolved. This omission of the expected motif offers a glimpse of what we may think of as an 'anti-*Piers Plowman* tradition', in which the metaphor of ploughing is removed from orthodox discourse because of the accumulation of heterodox connotations which it had accrued by this time.

The very nature of such a programme, of course, renders it difficult to prove in retrospect that there was a concerted excision of the ploughman – particularly if it was successful – but a further example from a preaching aid of the fifteenth century may here be cited in support of the assumption. John Mirk's *Festial*, a sermon collection of the late fourteenth century,[86] records an interesting anecdote concerning the birth of Christ:

> That same tyme as men of þe countrey ȝeden at þe plogh, exen speken to the plogh-men and sayden: 'Þese sedys schull encrese and men schull wax few'.[87]
>
> [At the same time as men of the country worked at the plough,

[83] This comment occurs in his review of Wenzel's edition of *Fasciculus morum*, published in the *Yearbook of Langland Studies* 4 (1990), 185. In a later review of Helen Leith Spencer, *English Preaching in the Late Middle Ages*, published in the *Yearbook of Langland Studies* 9 (1995), 197–203, Wenzel maintains that Greaves 54 does not constitute a translation, 'not even a "fragmentary" one' (202). However, one may certainly detect *Fasciculus morum* as a prominent source for the later work.

[84] Greaves 54 f.120v. Similar examples occur at ff. 121v, 122r and 123v. The metaphorical possibilities of earth are possibly most fully explored in the short poem 'Erthe upon Erthe', the two versions of which survive in numerous manuscripts dating from the late fifteenth century and beyond: see *Erthe upon Erthe, Printed from Twenty-Four Manuscripts*, ed. Hilda M. R. Murray, EETS o.s. 141 (London: Oxford University Press, 1911).

[85] Greaves 54 f. 125v.

[86] On dating and distribution of Mirk's *Festial*, see Susan Powell, 'John Mirk's *Festial* and the Pastoral Programme', *Leeds Studies in English* n. s. 22 (1991), 85–102.

[87] John Mirk, *Festial*, ed. Theodore Erbe, EETS e.s. 96 (London: K. Paul, Trench, Trübner and Co., 1905), p. 23. This apocryphal tale may well derive from Isaiah 1:3: 'The ox knoweth his owner, and the ass his master's crib, but Israel doth not know, my people doth not consider.'

> oxen spoke to the ploughmen and said: 'These seeds shall increase and men shall wax few'.]

Later recensions of this sermon, however, whilst remaining largely faithful to Mirk's model, omit this incident.[88] Susan Powell accounts for this absence by suggesting that it is an example of the omission of 'dubious and unauthenticated facts asserted by Mirk',[89] yet it is surely equally likely that, in a period during which the suppression of Lollardy was a major concern of the Church, this was the result of uneasiness about an anecdote which could be interpreted as showing God to have singled out the potentially problematic ploughman as a privileged recipient of His word.

Given the prominence of the ploughman in late medieval Christian allegory, it is unlikely that the Lincoln misericord and the now lost Coventry carving accounted for the only representations of the subject to be found on English choir stalls in the later Middle Ages. In particular, for example, we may expect to find a carving of a ploughman amongst the misericords of Chester Cathedral, which are clearly and directly influenced by Lincoln, closely reproducing a dozen designs from the earlier scheme.[90] Of course we have, over the centuries, lost the great majority of medieval misericords in England, many through deliberate iconoclasm, others by accident, some by recent theft, and the remainder by any number of causes which may arise over half a millennium. However, in view of the textual excisions explored above in the light of Lollard appropriation of the figure of the ploughman, it appears likely that the loss of such carvings – whilst less contentious (though no doubt equally allegorical in intention) agricultural scenes survive[91] – may well be due to systematic targeting of such representations of the ploughman in the years immediately leading up to 1400 and beyond.

As we survey the 'fair feeld ful of folk' which spreads before us beneath the choirs of English medieval churches, then, we may at first glance see, as did Bond, 'a large and interesting class [of misericord carvings] in which there is no ulterior intent other than to portray faithfully the daily life of humble folk'.[92] However, when we begin to consider these folk, whether at work or at play, in the light of the concerns of their contemporary clerical

[88] Susan Powell (ed.), *The Advent and Nativity Sermons from a Fifteenth-Century Revision of John Mirk's Festial, edited from B. L. MSS Harley 2247, Royal 18 B XXV and Gloucester Cathedral Library 22* (Heidelberg: C. Winter, 1981), p. 82. On the nature and sources of subsequent revisions, see Susan Powell, 'A Critical Edition of the *Temporale* Sermons of MSS Harley 2247 and Royal B XXV' (unpublished D.Phil thesis, University of London, 1980), vol. 2, p. 48.

[89] Powell (ed.), *Advent and Nativity Sermons*, p. 29.

[90] See M. D. Anderson, *The Choir Stalls of Lincoln Minster* (Lincoln: Friends of Lincoln Minster, 1967), pp. 10–11 and 24–5.

[91] A misericord in Winchester College Chapel, for example, shows three scenes of shepherds, in which we may discern the words of Christ from John 10:11 – 'I am the good shepherd: the good shepherd giveth his life for the sheep.'

[92] Bond, *Wood Carvings in English Churches 1*, p. 87.

patrons and audience, an altogether richer reading emerges. For, just as for the medieval Christian all life on earth is part of God's creation, so all human activity is seen – and, in consequence, either approved or admonished – in terms of the ideals of Christian behaviour. It is, of course, inevitable that such a perspective should be intimately tied up with devotional and doctrinal concerns, some of which we have here addressed in passing, particularly in relation to the fool and the ploughman. The irony is that whilst scenes of the raucous activities which should be piously eschewed – such as gambling, drinking and brawling – have survived on misericords, one of the most vital Christian allegorical symbols of the period, the ploughman, has all but disappeared. We shall pursue the Church's teachings further in the following chapter, in which we will turn to carvings which deal more explicitly with piety and devotion and, indeed, the unrest which arose in England from the late fourteenth century concerning devotional practices.

# 2 DOCTRINE AND DEBATE

In the previous chapter, we explored the ways in which the scenes of everyday activities which abound on medieval misericords can be seen to have carried a spiritual message for a specifically clerical audience which was attuned to their iconographic significance and by whom, after all, they were commissioned. Without the barrier of such unacknowledged symbolism to distract us, we may expect images which address devotional and doctrinal matters more explicitly to communicate directly with the viewer and, in consequence, to be in some ways more readily understandable to a modern audience no longer steeped in the subtleties of the Christian visual culture of England in the later Middle Ages. Whilst this is often the case, we shall see in the present chapter that even symbols at the heart of Christianity may, depending on the contexts in which they appear, create perplexing puzzles for the viewer. Images, after all, have always had the potential to create disagreements. Writing around the middle of the fifteenth century, Bishop Reginald Pecock was moved to defend the use of images in churches from Lollard criticism in what are essentially commonplace terms:

> [T]he iye sight schewith and bringith into the ymaginacioun and into the mynde withynne in the heed of a man myche mater and long mater sooner, and with lasse labour and traueil and peine, than the heering of the eere dooth. And if this now seid is trewe of a man which can rede in bokis stories writun, that myche sooner and in schortir tyme and with lasse labour and pein in his brayn he schal come into remembraunce of a long storie bi sight, than bi the heering of othere mennys reding or bi heering of his owne reding; miche rather this is trewe of alle tho persoones whiche kunnen not rede in bokis, namelich sithen thei schulen not fynde men so redi for to rede a dosen leeuys of a book to hem, as thei schulen fynde redy the wallis of a chirche peintid or a clooth steyned or ymagis sprad abrood in dyuerse placis of the chirche.[1]

[1] Reginald Pecock, *The Repressor of Over Much Blaming of Clergy*, 2 vols, ed. Churchill Babington (London: Longman, Green, Longman and Roberts, 1860), I, 212–13. For a

> [Seeing with the eye shows and brings into the imagination and into the mind within a man's head much information, and a great deal of information sooner and with less labour, work and effort, than hearing with the ear does. And if this is true of a man who is able to read stories written in books – that he shall much more quickly and immediately and with less labour and effort in his brain come to remember a long story by sight than by hearing other men's reading or hearing his own reading – so much more is this true of those persons who are not able to read in books, namely since they shall not as easily find men to read a dozen pages of a book to them as they shall easily find the painted walls of a church, a dyed cloth, or images spread throughout various parts of the church.]

The greatest emphasis of Pecock's argument is, as we may see, placed upon the long-established classification of images as 'books of the unlearned', a view most famously propounded by Gregory the Great some eight centuries earlier, which promoted images as near-equivalent substitutes for words, their chief value being that they were legible to the illiterate. However, it is interesting to note that Pecock not only perceives images as being superior to books for the illiterate, but also extols their superior virtue for one who is able to read, as they entail less 'labour and pein in his brayn'. We shall return to Pecock later, but it is appropriate to invoke his comments now in order to foreground the problem – familiar to all with an interest in the 'ymagis sprad abrood in dyuerse placis of the chirche' – of what it is that we and our forebears are and were actually reading. We have seen in the previous chapter how, from the late fourteenth century, debates concerning Lollardy focused upon the allegorised figure of the ploughman, and later in this chapter we shall explore further the resonance of apparently profane subjects within the doctrinal climate of late medieval England. In order to place these sometimes enigmatic images more firmly in context, however, it will be useful to begin with a survey of the subjects to be found on misericords which relate most explicitly to matters of religious devotion.

In considering expressions of devotion, it is important not to overlook the scores of crests and heraldic devices which survive throughout the country. Whether representing families, individuals, guilds, towns or other social or ecclesiastical groupings, these signs denote the commitment – most commonly a specifically financial commitment – of the bearer to the church in which they appear. One example from the vast number which could be cited is found on the only remaining medieval misericord in All Saints, North Street, York, on which the motif of the pelican in her piety is flanked in the supporters by the initials and coat of arms of John Gilliot,

chronology of Pecock's works, see Charles W. Brockwell, Jr, *Bishop Reginald Pecock and the Lancastrian Church: Securing the Foundations of Cultural Authority* (Lewiston: Edwin Mellen Press, 1985), p. x–xii.

Master of the Corpus Christi Guild and Vicar of All Saints (1467–72).[2] That his arms – *ermine on a bend sable three lucies' heads couped argent* – also appear on a boss at the east end of the fine carved roof demonstrates both the generosity of Gilliot's gift and also that he did not wish that generosity to be forgotten. It is, of course, easy in our somewhat cynical age to suspect that motives of temporal self-aggrandisement were paramount in such conspicuous displays by patrons and, indeed, the religious foundations themselves, and such judgements likewise provided fuel for both satire and complaint in the Middle Ages. We have already come across the early fifteenth-century Lollard poem *Pierce the Ploughman's Crede*, the antifraternal satire of which is characteristically terse when it comes to the matter of lay patronage in ecclesiastical buildings. The poem's narrator, seeking spiritual sustenance, approaches a Franciscan friar, whose materialistic response sums up a strain of contemporary complaint in no uncertain terms:

> … we buldeth a burwgh – a brod and a large –
> A chirche and a chapaile with chambers a-lofte,
> With wide windowes y-wrought and walles well heye,
> That mote ben portreid and paynt and pulched ful clene,
> With gaie glittering glas glowing as the sonne.
> And myghtestou amenden vs with money of thyn owne,
> Thou chuldest cnely before Crist in compass of gold
> In the wide windowe westwarde wel nighe in the myddell,
> And seynt Fraunces himself schall folden the in his cope,
> And presente the to the trynitie and praie for thy synnes.[3]

> [… we build a convent – broad and long – a church and a chapel with high chambers, built with wide windows and high walls, that must be decorated and painted and polished very brightly, with gay, glittering glass glowing like the sun. And if you could help us with your own money, you could kneel before Christ encircled in gold in the wide west window, right near the middle, and Saint Francis himself shall wrap you in his cloak, and present you to the Trinity and pray for your sins.]

The caustic satire speaks of a mercenary clergy preying upon both the piety and the vanity – so close that they are almost indistinguishable – of the laity in order to fund sumptuous decorative schemes. In this case funds are sought for the glazing of a window, but we may just as easily substitute the carving of a set of choir stalls. Yet we should not be too hasty to reach such negative conclusions

[2] On Gilliot's identification and patronage, see Anonymous, *All Saints', North Street, York*, 2nd edn (York: York Civic Trust, 1989), pp. 11–12 and 14. Remnant identifies more than a hundred family heraldic devices, some of which occur in more than one location. To these may be added unidentified shields, along with crests and insignia, bringing the total number of misericords bearing the marks of patrons close to two hundred: G. L. Remnant, *A Catalogue of Misericords in Great Britain* (London: Oxford University Press, 1969), pp. 214–16.

[3] *Pierce the Ploughman's Crede*, in *The Piers Plowman Tradition*, ed. Helen Barr (London: Everyman's Library, 1993), ll. 118–27. In this there is more than an echo of *Piers Plowman* B III, in which Lady Mede offers to pay for a window in return for the friar's absolution.

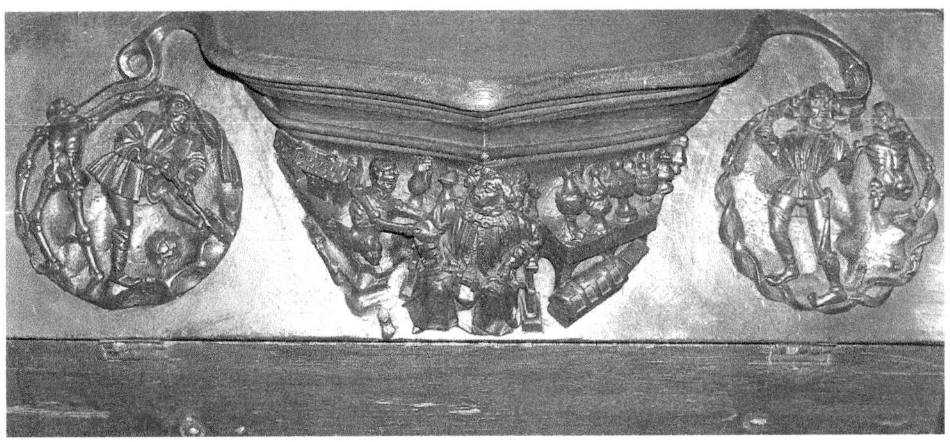

FIG. 10. ST GEORGE'S CHAPEL, WINDSOR MISERICORD.

about patronage of ecclesiastical art, and should keep in mind that even when varying degrees of earthly self-regard are indeed present, this nonetheless need not entirely preclude an essential piety. It has rightly been said that,

> Wherever one turns in the sources for the period one encounters the overwhelming preoccupation of clergy and laity alike, from peasant to prince and from parish clerk to pontiff, with the safe transition of their souls from this world to the next, above all with the shortening and easing of their stay in Purgatory.[4]

Putting aside considerations of expense and display, there is a sense that the life eternal is, after all, of more concern than earthly fame, and that the prayers offered by the choir stalls' occupants will continue to provide more lasting benefit for donors than any transitory worldly aggrandisement. This truth is strikingly brought home on the one surviving English misericord bearing scenes from the *Danse macabre*, located in St George's Chapel, Windsor, which, in its main carving, shows a haughty, richly dressed man seated in luxury and surrounded by opulent material goods and a treasure chest (fig. 10). In the supporters he is flanked by labourers digging and threshing: Death comes to each. It was a stark reminder, during a time of recent plague and frequent wars, that Death does not discriminate between rich and poor, nor does he necessarily defer to the apparent strength and vigour of his intended victim. As Hans Holbein the Younger would neatly summarise in his celebrated sixteenth-century *Les simulachres et historiees faces de la mort*:

> Malheureux qui uiuez au monde
> Tousiours remplis d'aduersitez,
> Pour quelque bien qui uous abonde,
> Serez tous de Mort uisitez.

[4] Eamon Duffy, *The Stripping of the Altars: Traditional Religion in England 1400–1580* (New Haven and London: Yale University Press, 1992), p. 301.

> [Woe! woe! inhabitants of Earth, / Where blighting cares so keenly strike, / And, spite of rank, or wealth, or worth, / Death—Death will visit all alike.][5]

A further example of the subject is known to have existed across three misericords in St Michael's Cathedral, Coventry, but this was destroyed when the cathedral was bombed during the night of 14 November 1940. On these misericords, the central carvings depicted scenes of the Corporal Acts of Mercy as described in Matthew 25:35–6 – clothing the naked, visiting the sick and burying the dead – flanked in the supporters by the skeletal figure of Death hand-in-hand with a range of characters, both lay and clerical, offering an unequivocal exhortation to guard one's immortal soul by undertaking charitable acts towards one's fellow men while one still has the opportunity.[6]

As we have seen in the case of the arms of John Gilliot, not all of the heraldic devices found on misericords are secular in signification. In All Saints, Leighton Buzzard, for example, there is a set of choir stalls which is believed to have been made originally for nearby St Albans Abbey. The heraldry on these stalls relates not only to nobility who were connected in some way with the abbey, but also includes the shield of Thomas Thornburgh, a late fourteenth-century abbey steward, and the emblem of the abbey itself. This is just one of several locations in which we can find such evidence of mixed lay and ecclesiastical patronage within the choirs of greater churches. The self-representation of the clergy, however, is not limited purely to the symbolic, and we may encounter many ecclesiastics throughout the country, though often in guises we may not initially expect.

The monks carved in Ely Cathedral, St Mary, Framsden or St Andrew, Norton, the priest at St Andrew, Isleham, the praying cleric at the Royal Foundation of St Katharine, London, or any of the number of mitred heads to be found throughout the country may be memorial portrait representations of figures who were involved with the construction or financing of the stalls.[7] Many other ecclesiastics, however, are depicted in a less flattering light. At St Nicholas, Castle Hedingham, a unique misericord depicts a

[5] Hans Holbein the Younger, *The Dance of Death: A Complete Facsimile of the Original 1538 Edition of Les simulachres et historiees faces de la mort* (New York: Dover Publications, 1971), p. 20; translation by Frederick H. Evans from ibid., p. 110.

[6] These misericords are described in Mary Dormer Harris, 'The Misericords of Coventry', *Transactions and Proceedings of the Birmingham Archaeological Society* 52 (1927), 262–3 and illustrated in Pl. V–VII. A similar telling juxtaposition may be observed in the stained glass of All Saints, North Street, York, which has windows depicting both the Acts of Mercy and the final fifteen days of the world (the so-called 'Prick of Conscience' window), the latter surmounted in the tracery by an image of the blessed entering Heaven and the damned consigned to Hell.

[7] Mitred heads may be found in: St Catherine, Beaumaris; St Mary the Virgin, Beddington; St Botolph, Boston; St Mary, East Lavant; The National Museum of Antiquities of Scotland, Edinburgh (provenance unknown: possibly English); St Peter and St Paul, Lingfield; St Lawrence, Ludlow; Norwich Cathedral; St Stephen, Norwich; All Souls College Chapel, Oxford; Wells Cathedral; St Peter and St Paul, West Wittering; and Winchester Cathedral.

monk slung by his ankles over the shoulder of a muscular fox, who stands erect on his hind legs in an attitude of proud self-satisfaction. The monk appears understandably nonplussed as his arms trail on the ground and his head drags in the fox's brush. Kenneth Varty sees this as a comment upon hypocrisy, the monk captured by the legendarily sly fox:[8] whatever the nature of the monk's fall, however, as his habit falls to his chin, we may certainly say that that which he would usually keep hidden has been revealed by the fox.

We will consider the fox at length within a broader discussion of animal symbolism in chapter 5, but such is the nature of the ubiquitous Reynard that he will not be constrained within such rigidly imposed limits, and in discussing carvings of ecclesiastics it is impossible not to refer to the considerable number of representations of foxes in ecclesiastical vestments. From his earliest appearance in Wells Cathedral around 1330, the ecclesiastical fox most frequently crops up in the role of a preacher, and it is surely no coincidence here that we may note a number of similarities between preaching practice and the images we find on misericords. Brief English inscriptions of the kind that we saw in the last chapter accompanying the shoeing of the goose at St Mary, Whalley, for example, are reminiscent of the frequently colloquial English tags which are often included as pithy aides-memoires in both Latin and French sermon collections produced in England in the later Middle Ages.[9] However, as Christa Grössinger has noted, the closest parallel is between misericord iconography and the growing currency of *exempla* in preaching from the thirteenth century onward, both of which often shared the characteristics of 'a humorous twist to a moral tale and the combination of sacred and profane'.[10] And one of the most popular humorous misericord images with undoubtedly serious moral connotations is the preaching fox. Whilst this disguise may be familiar from medieval Beast Epic, it is not clear why such a figure should be represented on misericords in more than a dozen English churches – not to mention in other media in many more locations – generally in the company of an oblivious congregation of geese, poultry or other birds.[11] Varty observes that in the earliest surviving literary adventures of Reynard the Fox, there is little ecclesiastical satire; however, 'with the arrival of the friar in the thirteenth century, sharp satire does appear, and the friar is often the object of it'.[12] We

[8] Kenneth Varty, *Reynard the Fox: A Study of the Fox in Medieval English Art* (Leicester: Leicester University Press, 1967), p. 56.

[9] For two examples from the early fourteenth century, see the Latin *Fasciculus morum*, ed. Siegfried Wenzel (London: Pennsylvania State University Press, 1989), and Nicole Bozon, *Les Contes Moralisés*, ed. Lucy Toulmin Smith and Paul Meyer (Paris: Librairie De Firmin Didot, 1889), for French.

[10] Christa Grössinger, *The World Upside-Down: English Misericords* (London: Harvey Miller Publishers, 1997), p. 115.

[11] These are listed and discussed in Elaine C. Block and Kenneth Varty, 'Choir-Stall Carvings of Reynard and Other Foxes', in *Reynard the Fox: Social Engagement in the Beast Epic from the Middle Ages to the Present*, ed. Kenneth Varty (New York and Oxford: Berghahn Books, 2000), pp. 140–8.

[12] Varty, *Reynard the Fox*, p. 58.

may, then, view the proliferation of preaching and other ecclesiastical foxes from the early fourteenth century onward as an extension of this, being a visual manifestation of 'the antagonism between parish priest and itinerant friar'.[13] Perhaps a more likely reading, though, is that depictions of the inveterate trickster in such garments were designed to act as a warning against false words in righteous array, a possibility which will be explored at more length in chapter 5. Indeed, as the fourteenth century drew to a close with the growing threat and attempted suppression of Lollardy, we may even see such images – for example the fox preacher and his congregation of hens at St Botolph, Boston, dated to c.1390, one supporter of which shows another fox engaged in the decidedly suspicious activity of reading a book – as pointed anti-Lollard statements, drawing attention to the inevitable dire outcome when the role of preacher is usurped by one who is plainly unsuitable.

Writing of the physical location of misericords, Christa Grössinger has noted that,

> In spite of the overall sacredness of the church choir, lower spaces were exempt from spiritual subject-matter, and the lower parts of walls surrounding the altar were often decorated with ornamental borders, curtains or secular scenes.[14]

Whilst this may indeed apply as a general rule, misericords – as in so many other ways – do not appear to be bound by such conventions, for a wide array of unequivocally religious subjects may still be seen on English choir stalls. These include episodes from both the Old and New Testaments, scenes from the lives of saints, and many non-canonical images with overt devotional or doctrinal content. From the Old Testament, Adam and Eve are the most frequently depicted figures and may be found in St Mary's, Blackburn, Bristol Cathedral, Ely Cathedral, Winchester Cathedral and Worcester Cathedral (fig. 11).[15] The Blackburn misericord is unique in combining more than one scene in order to convey an unfolding narrative: the serpent coils around the Tree in the centre of the carving, with the left supporter showing Adam and Eve naked, presumably prior to temptation, and the right showing them partially clothed in shame, in flight from the angel with the flaming sword. Worcester Cathedral contains more Old Testament scenes than anywhere else in the country. Here, the Temptation and Expulsion of Adam and Eve extend across two misericords, the first showing the two figures holding the fruit to either side of the Tree, around which a long-eared, dragon-like serpent coils, the second showing them covering themselves with leaves as, once again, they cower before a sword-

[13] Block and Varty, 'Choir-Stall Carvings', p. 145.

[14] Grössinger, *The World Upside-Down*, p. 73.

[15] Remnant describes the Winchester figures as 'boy with foliage', but on account of the apple held by the right-hand figure I am more persuaded by Barton's identification of these characters as Adam and Eve: Remnant, *Catalogue of Misericords*, p. 59; Paulette E. Barton, *Mercy and the Misericord in Late Medieval England* (Lewiston: Edwin Mellen Press, 2009), p. 190.

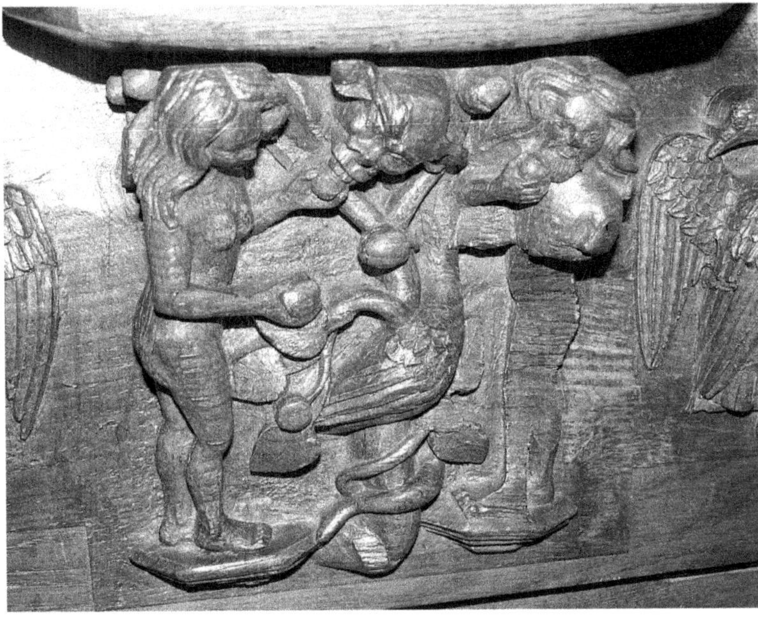

FIG. 11. ST MARY'S, BLACKBURN MISERICORD.

bearing angel. Elsewhere, Abraham and Isaac with an angel staying the point of Abraham's sword, Moses with the Tables of the Law, the Judgment of Solomon with supporters showing the mother delivering her child to the swordsman and subsequently carrying the dead infant, and Samson grasping the jaws of the lion are all to be found throughout the choir.

Far more numerous than Old Testament scenes are depictions of figures and narratives from the New Testament. Gloucester Cathedral's depiction of three shepherds, for example, is distinguished from other the instances of agricultural labour which we looked at in the last chapter by virtue of the inclusion of the Star of Bethlehem. From the opposite end of the story of Christ, Lincoln Cathedral, as well as boasting a lavish image of the Resurrection, complete with angels and sleeping soldiers, and flanked by Mary Magdalene with a jar of spices and Christ as gardener, also has a unique Ascension scene. Although it is far from clear at first glance what the two kneeling figures of this rather awkward latter composition are doing, closer inspection reveals them to be gazing with rapt attention at the feet of Christ and the hem of His garment as he ascends into clouds.[16] Discounting episodes from the life of Christ, the most frequently depicted New Testament image is that of the Last Judgement, that constant reminder of the end result of one's acts on earth, which can be found at St Mary, Gayton, St Nicholas, Montgomery, and Sherborne Abbey. However, by far the most common figures depicted are Christ and the Virgin Mary.

[16] Another Resurrection scene may be found, though in rather poorer condition, at St Mary Magdalene, Leintwardine.

As Richard Marks has shown, a growing cult of the Virgin Mary across Europe in the fourteenth century led to a proliferation of Marian images in all media,[17] and scenes from the life of the Virgin occur on a number of English misericords. St Mary with St Bartholomew, Tong, for example, has a particularly interesting Annunciation which depicts Christ crucified on the stem of the lily,[18] whilst a Nativity scene may be found in Lincoln Cathedral. Again in Lincoln is a richly canopied Coronation of the Virgin, an apocryphal image proving popular elsewhere too.[19] As these few instances of the representation of the Virgin will suggest, most images of Mary show her in combination with Christ and, as one would expect, we find a number of further scenes taken from the life of Christ, with the main preference being for images relating to the Nativity and the Passion and Resurrection, a particularly fine example of the latter being the Lincoln Cathedral misericord mentioned above. Yet, taken overall, biblical subjects account for a very small proportion of surviving images and in the instances of the Virgin and Christ it is questionable whether we should consider them first and foremost as examples of Bible illustrations at all. As C. M. Kauffmann has noted in his wide-ranging study of medieval biblical imagery,

> [a] great deal of religious imagery was to be found in late medieval churches but it must be admitted that much of it was not biblical. Images of the Virgin and Child and of saints – the principal intercessors – predominated in wall-paintings, stained glass and three-dimensional artefacts alike.[20]

It is in this active, intercessory role that we should, perhaps, view at least most of the depictions of the Virgin and Christ on misericords, rather than as visual representations of specific biblical narratives. Other carvings may indeed be intended to represent biblical figures or episodes, but lack any distinctive features by which to differentiate them from more generic scenes. Paulette E. Barton, for example, has identified two seated figures in Chester Cathedral as Noah and his wife,[21] yet there are no distinctive attributes which denote anything other than a seated domestic couple who are possibly, on account of their postures – side by side yet facing slightly away from each other – in a state of disharmony, a subject which we shall address in chapter 4.

[17] See Richard Marks, *Image and Devotion in Late Medieval England* (Stroud: Sutton Publishing, 2004), pp. 121–56.
[18] The lily crucifix may also once have been part of a damaged misericord at All Saints, Gresford which possibly shows an Annunciation scene. See Remnant, *Catalogue of Misericords*, p. 194.
[19] The Coronation of the Virgin occurs at: Carlisle Cathedral; Chester Cathedral; Lincoln Cathedral; and Norwich Cathedral.
[20] C. M. Kauffmann, *Biblical Imagery in Medieval England 700–1550* (London: Harvey Miller Publishers, 2003), p. 255.
[21] Barton, *Mercy and the Misericord*, p. 158.

Allowing for such problems of identification – not all carvings are as unmistakably recognisable as that of John the Baptist, whose head is presented to Herodias beneath a stall at Ely Cathedral – there are perhaps twenty or so saints to be found on English misericords.[22] As Ronald C. Finucane notes, '[b]efore the Reformation … the great age of saint-making was the thirteenth century',[23] and the veneration of saints as intercessors was at its height between the late thirteenth and early sixteenth centuries. The number of people from all walks of life undertaking pilgrimages to saints' shrines at which relics were displayed in elaborate reliquaries may appear the most remarkable expression of this devotion, but it is also reflected in all media of church decoration; for whilst countless palmers may have wended their way to Canterbury, 'The hooly blisful martir for to seke, / That hem hath holpen whan that they were seeke',[24] he could also be found beneath the choir stalls at St Martin's, Fornham in Suffolk. If, indeed, 'intention rather than distance' was the key element of pilgrimage for many,[25] we may deduce that contemplation of a saint's image in some ways fulfilled the same function for the devout – particularly for ordained clergy who would perhaps be unable to take time away from their duties in order to make a lengthy journey – and St Thomas Becket of Canterbury is but one of the many saints of whom only one misericord carving survives. Occasionally the saint thus depicted may reflect the dedication of the church in which it is found, such as the martyrdom of St Andrew which is carved in St Andrew's, Norton, but this is far from being a general rule: the St Andrew's stalls, for example, also boast a carving of the martyrdom of St Edmund. By far the most common saint depicted on misericords is St George – invariably shown battling the dragon – with perhaps ten surviving images,[26] reflecting the growing cult around him and his becoming established, probably from around the middle of the fourteenth century, as

[22] As well as in scenes from lives or of martyrdoms, such as the boiling in oil of St John the Evangelist in Lincoln Cathedral, saints may also be recognised by the metonymic use of their attributes alone, as in the striking wheel of St Catherine on a misericord in St Lawrence, Canon Pyon.

[23] Ronald C. Finucane, *Miracles and Pilgrims: Popular Beliefs in Medieval England* (London: J. M. Dent and Sons, 1977), p. 130.

[24] Geoffrey Chaucer, *The Canterbury Tales*, in *The Riverside Chaucer*, ed. Larry D. Benson (Oxford: Oxford University Press, 1988), I (A) 17–18.

[25] Dee Dyas, referring specifically to Margery Kempe, in *Pilgrimage in Medieval English Literature: 700–1500* (Cambridge: D. S. Brewer, 2001), p. 130.

[26] Whilst often the figure of St George may be identified by his arms, in their absence there is always the possibility that it is another dragon-slaying narrative which is being illustrated. The knight battling the wyvern on the stalls of St Mary, Beverley, for example, may represent St George but, as Remnant acknowledges (*Catalogue of Misericords*, p. 177), this is by no means definite. Elsewhere, it has been suggested that the knight fighting the dragon at St Botolph, Boston, may depict a scene from Chrétien de Troyes's *Yvain* or the Middle English *Ywain and Gawain*: see Jennifer Fellows, 'Romance among the Choir Stalls: Middle English Romance Motifs on English Misericords', in *Profane Images in Marginal Arts of the Middle Ages*, ed. Elaine C. Block with Frédéric Billiet, Sylvie Bethmont-Gallerand and Paul Hardwick (Turnhout: Brepols, 2008), p. 136.

the patron saint of England.[27] Elsewhere, saints with more limited regional significance may be depicted, such as St Govan in the cathedral dedicated to his nephew, St David, or St Werburga of Chester in Chester Cathedral.[28] Even St Margaret of Antioch, so common in other forms of ecclesiastical decoration, only appears on one surviving misericord, possibly on account of her patronage of women in childbirth being of little relevance to the male occupants of the choir.[29]

In addition to saints, a great many angels – the winged messengers between man and God – may be found on misericords, attesting to their importance in late medieval thought. *The Golden Legend* discusses man's relationship with angels, stressing their importance both in this life and beyond, for which they should be honoured. The most pertinent points to note in relation to the present discussion are that 'we owe them honor because they are our guardians' and also 'because it is they who present our prayers before God',[30] two very important matters when considering the efficacy of the devotional work taking place within the choir. As well as angels, the four evangelists –those more tangible intercessors and carriers of God's word – are also present in the form of their symbols,[31] each surviving in six or seven locations.

Not all of the images relating to the Christian life are so positive, however. We have already seen how the clerically garbed fox could be interpreted as an admonitory analogue to eschew the 'wolf in sheep's clothing' or, indeed, to avoid becoming the wolf – or, at least, the fox – oneself. For those needing a still more direct lesson, a score of devils may still be seen going eagerly about their business of temptation and torment across misericords throughout the country. Whether depicted individually, leading the unwary astray or, as in a wonderfully vivid scene in Bristol Cathedral in which a devil welcomes a naked woman who leads a quartet of bound apes into the mouth of Hell – itself a proverbial fate awaiting the spinster – meting out punishment to sinners, these figures unequivocally remind the choir's occupants of the

[27] The continued popularity of St George in the post-Reformation period doubtless accounts for the greater number of survivals than for images of other saints. On the development and survival of the cult of St George, see Samantha Riches, *St George: Hero, Martyr and Myth* (Stroud: Sutton Publishing, 2005), pp. 1–35. Riches notes that the earliest explicit reference to St George as patron saint of England is from the calendar of patent rolls and can be dated to 1351. Whilst in the present book I have tended to downplay the borders between England and the rest of Britain, it is perhaps nonetheless worth remarking in passing that no images of England's patron saint may be found on misericords in Scotland, Wales or Ireland.

[28] The curious legend which is depicted, of St Werberga and her restoration to life of a goose after it had been eaten, may be found in William of Malmesbury, *Gesta Pontificum*, and is translated in Helen Waddell, *Beasts and Saints*, new edn (London: Darton, Longman and Todd, 1995), pp. 63–4.

[29] St Margaret was one of the most popular saints of the later Middle Ages. Her association with childbirth stems from the legend that she burst from the belly of Satan, who swallowed her in the form of a dragon. The surviving misericord is in Sherborne Abbey.

[30] Jacobus de Voragine, *The Golden Legend: Readings on the Saints*, trans. William Granger Ryan, 2 vols (Princeton: Princeton University Press, 1993), II, 207–11.

[31] See p. 56.

necessity of spiritual rectitude at all times, particularly when occupied in the core devotional work of the Church.[32] In all, then, a broad range of lively images relating explicitly to devotional activities pertinent to the life and work of the Church may be found throughout the country. Nonetheless, taken as a group they represent a relatively small proportion of surviving misericord carvings, and it is worth pausing to consider why this may be the case. Francis Bond suggests that patrons 'did not wish a delineation of sacred things to be placed where it would normally be in contact with the least honourable portion of the human person'.[33] As we will see towards the end of this chapter, the functional location of misericords in such a lowly position may well affect the manner in which we interpret images in some cases, yet the religious subjects that we have briefly surveyed above would tend to undermine any claims to universality of Bond's view. After all, the number of representations of Christ and the Virgin alone, whilst not great, is far from insignificant and is certainly sufficient to demonstrate that such positioning was not considered in any way inappropriate for images of the most holy of Christian figures. Although impossible to prove, it is surely more likely that explicitly religious material was once much more common, but that such subjects would have drawn the especial ire of iconoclasts from the Reformation and beyond.[34] Whatever the reason may be for this relative paucity of biblical and other overtly religious material, it is surely more surprising to the modern viewer to observe the breadth and scope of the apparently profane subjects which do survive. However, as we have already seen with the examples of the fools and the Lincoln ploughman in the last chapter, that which initially appears to be a profane subject may upon closer consideration be revealed to possess a devotional or doctrinal aspect which is frequently lost to the modern observer.

William Granger Ryan, in discussing that great medieval 'best-seller' and invaluable iconographic resource, *The Golden Legend*, notes that, in substantiating the points he makes by citing scriptural authority, Jacobus de Voragine frequently gives only the first few words of the biblical texts quoted, trusting in the ability of his (presumably clerical) audience to recognise and expand the references themselves.[35] It is also useful to apply this idea of a

[32] On the motif of the spinster leading apes in Hell, first attested in written sources some forty years after the carving of the Bristol misericord, see Malcolm Jones, *The Secret Middle Ages: Discovering the Real Medieval World* (Stroud: Sutton Publishing, 2002), pp. 93–4. Chained apes frequently represent worldly, specifically bodily, concerns. Whilst it is tempting to view the woman's nakedness as a comment upon the sins of the flesh, it should be remembered that souls in medieval art – whether damned or saved – are generally represented without clothes. The most commonly depicted devil on misericords is Tutivillus, the scourge of gossips, who will be discussed in chapter 4.

[33] Francis Bond, *Wood Carvings in English Churches 1: Misericords* (London: Oxford University Press, 1910), p. 129.

[34] On the process of Reformation iconoclasm, see Margaret Aston, 'Iconoclasm in England: Official and Clandestine', in *Iconoclasm vs. Art and Drama*, ed. Clifford Davidson and Ann Eljenholm Nichols (Kalamazoo: Medieval Institute Publications, 1989), pp. 47–91.

[35] Introduction to Jacobus de Voragine, *The Golden Legend*, I, xvi.

process of expansion upon allusion by an audience imbued with the same cultural referents when approaching the visual arts, for, as Eamon Duffy has observed, the religious culture of the Middle Ages was 'rooted in a repertoire of inherited and shared beliefs and symbols, while remaining capable of enormous flexibility and variety'.[36] Regarding the symbols of the evangelists mentioned above, for example, the inexpert modern viewer may only see a carving of a winged lion but one steeped in this shared culture of medieval Christianity is led by this to ponder upon St Mark and the reasons for his being thus represented.[37] We will look in more detail at the significance of representations of animals in chapter 5, but should nonetheless note here that the rich medieval tradition of beast allegory makes it unlikely that a carving of any creature – particularly when it is located in the devotional heart of the church building – would not carry with it a complex range of associations for its patrons and audience. Few images are more common, for example, than the pelican vulning or wounding itself as a representation of Christ's self-sacrificial love.[38] Alongside the pelican, a vast menagerie of domestic, exotic and fanciful beasts is depicted in apparently playful or satirical situations, and it is to one such example that we will now turn in order to begin to explore the layers of meaning which may be found therein.

The image in question is located amongst the choir stalls of St Mary, Beverley (fig. 12), which date from c.1445, about the same time as Pecock was writing his *Repressor of Over Much Blaming of Clergy*, with which we began this chapter. Before we can begin to explore what it means, however, we must first negotiate the primary issue of what exactly is depicted – an issue which is, in itself, rather more difficult than one may suspect. Like the fox we met earlier, the ape is seemingly omnipresent in medieval art, and the central figure in the St Mary carving is generally recognised as an ape physician, identified by the common iconographic device of the urine flask which he appears to be inspecting. The scene has been interpreted as one in which the ape is offering his services to a wealthy man – probably a cleric – who holds a large coin, whilst at the same time pointedly shunning the other figure. It has been

FIG. 12. ST MARY'S, BEVERLEY MISERICORD.

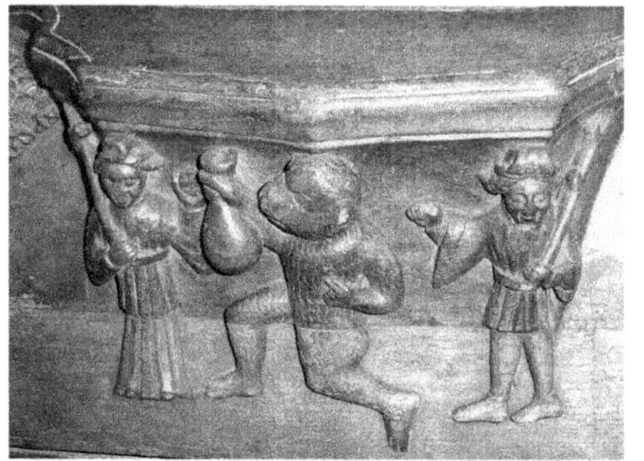

[36] Duffy, *The Stripping of the Altars*, p. 3.

[37] The four evangelists are associated in Christian tradition with the four beasts which surround God's throne in Revelation 4:6–10. Whilst there is some disagreement between early Christian authors, by the later Middle Ages the correspondences were generally considered to be: Matthew = man/angel; Mark = lion; Luke = ox; John = eagle.

[38] The pelican is by far the most frequently occurring bird to be found on misericords, with around thirty-five surviving carvings throughout England, although none remain elsewhere in Britain. The iconography of the pelican will be discussed in the next chapter.

suggested that this latter figure may perhaps be a poor labourer, whom Remnant describes as 'holding up what appears to be bread'.[39] It is possible that an element of the carving may have been lost subsequent to Remnant's description, but even a close inspection of the figure affords no clear indication of what the now damaged right hand may originally have been holding. However, this somewhat enigmatic scene, which we may at first sight relate to a contemporary satirical tradition against the medical profession,[40] becomes more enigmatic still if we follow Christa Grössinger's persuasive suggestion that the item raised by the figure on the left is not a coin but, rather, the Eucharistic Host.[41]

As Eamon Duffy reminds us, 'the liturgy lay at the heart of medieval religion, and the Mass lay at the heart of the liturgy'.[42] For most people in England in the later Middle Ages, receiving communion, as with confession, was an event which only took place once a year, generally at Easter.[43] Yet throughout the year the elevation of the Host was a regular customary element of the Church's liturgical ritual which, taking place in the choir, was visible to, yet out of reach of, the laity. Consequently, for the laity, who saw the Host far more frequently than they actually consumed it, the elevation itself became a moment of particular devotional significance.[44] Indeed, Michael Camille has gone so far as to suggest that the Host was the single most important image to medieval Christians from the middle of the thirteenth century onward, perhaps even overtaking veneration of the cross.[45]

Evidence of this reverence in England in particular may be found in a number of places. First, as attested by surviving documents such as bequests, there is the significant number of individuals and guilds who made specific provision for wax lights to illuminate the elevation. Secondly, there is the considerable number of depictions of the elevation to be found in contemporary representations of the seven sacraments. As Ann Eljenholm Nichols has observed,

39 Remnant, *Catalogue of Misericords*, p. 177; Ben Chapman, *Yorkshire Misericords* (Beverley: Highgate Publications, 1996), p. 16; Marshall Laird, *English Misericords* (London: John Murray, 1986), p. 59.

40 See David A. Sprunger, 'Parodic Animal Physicians from the Margins of Medieval Manuscripts', in *Animals in the Middle Ages*, ed. Nona C. Flores (New York and London: Routledge, 1996), pp. 67–81. The ape physician will be discussed at length in chapter 5.

41 Grössinger, *The World Upside-Down*, p. 101.

42 Duffy, *The Stripping of the Altars*, p. 91.

43 The obligation of the laity to confess annually to their parish priests was imposed following the Fourth Lateran Council of 1215. Misericords in Ely Cathedral and New College Chapel, Oxford, have been identified as showing scenes of confession: Remnant, *Catalogue of Misericords*, p. 210.

44 Ibid., pp. 95–102. See also Rossell Hope Robbins, 'Levation Prayers in Middle English Verse', *Modern Philology* 40 (1942), 131–46, which notes the prominence of vernacular verse prayers on the elevation in the late fourteenth and early fifteenth centuries.

45 Michael Camille, *The Gothic Idol: Ideology and Image-Making in Medieval Art* (Cambridge: Cambridge University Press, 1989), p. 215. On the place of the Eucharist in the later Middle Ages, see Miri Rubin, *Corpus Christi: The Eucharist in Late Medieval Culture* (Cambridge: Cambridge University Press, 1991).

> [i]n contrast to the range of eucharistic subjects found in continental seven-sacrament series, English iconography overwhelmingly preferred the elevation of the mass. It is the only subject preserved in glass and predominates in … font reliefs.[46]

In order to draw the attention of those engaged in private prayer within the church building to the consecration and elevation of the Host, this significant act was signalled by the ringing of a bell.[47] As noted above, there is no clear evidence of what may once have been held by the figure on the right of the St Mary's misericord, but in view of these contemporary practices surrounding the elevation of the Host, one possibility is surely that the damaged hand originally clasped a bell. Lastly, the importance of the sacrament is attested by the prominence it is accorded not only in the visual arts, but in a variety of textual sources. John Mirk's fifteenth-century manual of *Instructions for Parish Priests*, for example, unequivocally states the importance of the instruction of the laity on this matter, as he enjoins his diligent reader to:

> Teche hem þenne wyth gode entent,
> To be-leue on that sacrament;
> That þey receyue in forme of bred
> Ys goddes body þat soffered ded
> Vp-on the holy rode tre,
> To bye owre synnes & make vs fre.[48]

> [Teach them, therefore, with good intent to believe in that sacrament; that which they receive in the form of bread is God's body that suffered death on the holy cross in order to purchase our sins and make us free.]

As well as stressing the doctrinal importance of the Eucharist, Mirk's verse may perhaps aid our understanding – or at least clarify the iconography – of the Beverley misericord. For not only is the Host the body of Christ; the body of Christ is also described as that with which our entry into heaven is purchased. The object to which our ape physician addresses himself, then, could be both Host and, as the poem 'Salve lux mundi' puts it, 'journey-money for our pilgrimage' through this life and into the next.[49] Consequently, to the initiated 'reader' of the image, the elevated disc may simultaneously signify both actual Eucharistic Host and metaphorical coin.

[46] Ann Eljenholm Nichols, *Seeable Signs: The Iconography of the Seven Sacraments 1350–1544* (Woodbridge: Boydell Press, 1994), p. 251. Nichols offers a number of illustrations of the elevation in Pls 58–68.

[47] This may be clearly seen on the font at Badingham in Suffolk, which is illustrated in Duffy, *The Stripping of the Altars*, Pl. 42.

[48] John Mirk, *Instructions for Parish Priests*, ed. Gillis Kristensson (Lund: CWK Gleerup, 1974), ll. 244–9. A representative example of fifteenth-century poems on the Eucharist may be found in Carleton Brown (ed.), *Religious Lyrics of the Fifteenth Century* (Oxford: Oxford University Press, 1939), pp. 180–3.

[49] 'Salve lux mundi' is quoted in Duffy, *The Stripping of the Altars*, p. 91.

We must remember, however, that by the mid-fifteenth century the significance of the Eucharist within Christian belief and practice had caused it to become one of the most controversial elements of doctrine in the English Church. From the late 1370s, Wyclif had rejected the orthodox doctrine of transubstantiation, instead arguing that although the spiritual being of Christ also became present, the bread and wine remained materially unchanged by consecration. Whilst Wyclif's followers frequently simplified his complex theology, by the late fourteenth century, as Miri Rubin has noted, 'views on the Eucharist were … the very central area of [Lollard] criticism, and the one which the Church could least allow to pass uncorrected'.[50] Unfortunately, no copy of Pecock's *The Book of Eukarist* survives, but he notes in his *Reule of Crysten Religioun* that 'manye of þe lay partye bileeven amys in mater of þe eukarist' [many of the laity believe inaccurately in the matter of the Eucharist], a state of affairs for which he places the blame firmly upon 'summe clerkis, namelich Johan Wiccliffe and hise disciplis, which token, bi occasioun of holy writt not wele vndirstondyn, þe seid errour to þe comoun peple' [some clerks, namely John Wyclif and his followers, who, because of imperfect understanding of holy writ, took the said error to the common people].[51] Given that, perhaps surprisingly, the fifteenth-century Lollard poem known as *Pierce the Ploughman's Crede* places the blame for confusion on the matter of transubstantiation firmly at the door of 'flaterynge freres',[52] we may see that Mirk's insistence upon the clear teaching of orthodox belief regarding the sacrament is of particular significance – to both Church orthodoxy and Lollard dissenters – during this period.

Whilst anything from wilful non-attendance at Mass to, at the most extreme, profanation of the Host could be interpreted as an indication of heretical beliefs,[53] a simple reticence on the part of an individual to commit to the doctrine of transubstantiation was, in itself, a Lollard commonplace.[54] This is well illustrated by reference to a Lollard debate poem of c.1400, subsequently expanded and printed in the second quarter of the sixteenth century as *The Plowman's Tale*, in which the Pelican – who, in his pure piety, represents the Lollard viewpoint against the unnatural Griffon of the established ecclesiastical order – claims that:

[50] Rubin, *Corpus Christi*, p. 327. On Wyclif's Eucharistic theology, and Lollard adoption thereof, see Rubin, *Corpus Christi*, p. 319–34 and Anne Hudson, *The Premature Reformation: Wycliffite Texts and Lollard History* (Oxford: Oxford University Press, 1988), pp. 281–90. See also Anne Hudson, *Lollards and their Books* (London: Hambledon Press, 1985), pp. 111–23, in which she addresses the difficulty in deciding whether recorded Lollard views are accurately represented in examination records.

[51] Reginald Pecock, *The Reule of Crysten Religioun*, ed. William Cabell Greet, EETS o.s. 171 (London, 1927), pp. 95 and 34. *The Book of Eukarist* is mentioned in Pecock, *Repressor*, II, p. 564.

[52] *Crede*, l. 819.

[53] This point is made by Duffy, *The Stripping of the Altars*, pp. 99–100 and 126.

[54] See Hudson, *Premature Reformation*, p. 282–3.

I say sothe thorowe trewe rede
His fleshe and blode, through his mastry
Is there/ in the forme of brede
Howe it is there/ it nedeth not stryue
Whether it be subgette or accydent
But as Christ was/ when he was on-lyue
So is he there uerament.[55]

[I say the truth through true understanding: His flesh and blood, through his subtle works, is there in the form of bread. In what manner it is present need not be debated, whether as subject or accident, but as Christ was when he was alive, so He is truly there.]

Although not going so far as to argue against the orthodox doctrine of transubstantiation, the Pelican remains resolutely non-committal, itself a position sufficient to identify the poet's heterodox stance. For this Lollard writer, it is the Real Presence that is the significant matter, whilst theological subtleties are at best unimportant and, he strongly suggests, may indeed provoke unnecessary confusion.[56]

The matter of the Host/coin thus addressed, we should turn our attention once more to the dominant central figure of the ape. As David A. Sprunger notes, '[w]ith their physical resemblance to humans and their capacity to mimic but not understand human behavior, apes have long been used for human parody'.[57] Certainly, the thirteenth-century bestiary MS Bodley 764 states that 'Apes are so called because they ape the behaviour of rational human beings',[58] a view which perhaps lends weight to the suggestion that the Beverley image may be a criticism of irrational doubt concerning the orthodox doctrine of the sacrament. Are we, then, to interpret the ape as representing a debased mockery of the human form, merely 'aping' man's devotion to the elevated Host whilst being unable to see its true nature? If this is the case, we may perhaps conclude that the St Mary's misericord is to be read as an anti-Lollard statement of some description.

By the time this misericord was produced in the middle of the fifteenth century, the rationality of lay belief had indeed become a matter which could not be ignored by ecclesiastical authorities and, consequently, had to be addressed directly. Throughout the fourteenth century, in response to

[55] *The Plowman's Tale: The c.1532 and 1606 Editions of a Spurious Canterbury Tale*, ed. Mary Rhinelander McCarl (New York: Garland, 1997), c.1533 edition, ll. 1218–24. On the dating of *The Plowman's Tale*, see Andrew N. Wawn, 'The Genesis of *The Plowman's Tale*', *Yearbook of English Studies* 2 (1972), 21–40.

[56] It is important to recognise, however, that the term 'Lollardy' does not itself denote a single agreed doctrinal perspective and that, as Anne Hudson notes, there was some Lollard denial of the Real Presence following consecration. See Hudson, *Premature Reformation*, pp. 282–3.

[57] Sprunger, 'Parodic Animal Physicians', p. 72.

[58] Richard Barber (ed. and trans.), *Bestiary, Being an English Version of the Bodleian Library, Oxford MS Bodley 764* (Woodbridge: Boydell Press, 1993), p. 48.

growing demand, vernacular texts had proliferated in order to aid lay understanding of orthodox Christian doctrine, including the Mass.[59] In addition, however, there was an increasing number of vernacular theological texts of questionable orthodoxy, alongside which, of course, the Bible itself had been translated into English. Janet Coleman effectively summarises the situation, noting that,

> the ability to read was coupled with a desire to become increasingly involved, not only in understanding injunctions to the simple Christian life as set out in the gospels, but in understanding certain current theological issues, popular in the schools, which reached the theologically unsophisticated laity in various literary forms.[60]

A sermon of around 1400 pointedly addresses this lay tendency to engage with topics traditionally deemed to be outside their province, with a particularly pointed reference to the debates concerning the nature of the Host:

> Crist with oo loffe þis day, þat is ys owen precious body in þe forme of brede, fediþ many hundreþ þousandes of men. But I prey þe, what is þe releue of þis brede? For-sothe þei be þe argvmentes and þe skill þat may be of þe Sacramente, and þat longeþ not to þe, shewynge well Crist, þat he wold lat no man geþur þe releue but is disciples, shewynge to þe þat arte a lewd man þat it is inowȝþ to þe to beleven as holychurche techeþ þe and lat þe clerkes alone with þe argumentes. For þe more þat þou disputes þer-of, þe farþur þou shall be þer-fro.[61]
>
> [Christ with one loaf today – that is his own precious body in the form of bread – feeds many hundreds of thousands of men. But I ask you, what is the remainder of this bread? Truly they are the arguments and the reasoning that concern the sacrament, and which do not belong to you, Christ bids clearly, that he would let no man gather the remainder but his disciples, instructing you who are an unlettered man that it is enough for you to believe as Holy Church teaches you and leave the clerks to themselves with the debates. For the more you dispute the matter the further you shall be from its significance.]

This kind of exhortation to the laity, to 'lete auctoritees, on Goddes name, / To prechyng and to scoles of clergye',[62] is often repeated throughout a wide range of vernacular texts of the period. Coleman, for example, singles out

[59] See, for example, *The Lay Folks Mass Book*, ed. Thomas Frederick Simmons, EETS o.s. 71 (London: Oxford University Press, 1879).
[60] Janet Coleman, *English Literature in History 1350–1400: Medieval Readers and Writers* (London: Hutchinson, 1981), p. 207.
[61] Woodburn O. Ross, *Middle English Sermons edited from British Museum MS. Royal 18 b. xxiii*, EETS o.s. 209 (London: Oxford University Press, 1940), p. 128.
[62] Chaucer, *Canterbury Tales*, III (D) 1276–7.

Langland's *Piers Plowman* as one of many texts that reprove laymen for involving themselves in theological debate. Yet ironically, as we saw in the previous chapter, this is a work which by the fifteenth century found itself appropriated and interpreted in a heterodox manner, a situation which offers a forceful example of the unforeseen problems posed by the combination of increasingly active lay piety and growing vernacular literacy.[63]

Following Arundel's *Constitutions*, which Nicholas Watson has succinctly characterised as 'the linchpin of a broader attempt to limit religious discussion and writing in the vernacular',[64] it became increasingly difficult to combat Lollardy by means of reasoned argument, however desirable this may have been. One notable figure who did attempt this, however, was Pecock, who claimed that,

> I have spoke oft tyme, and bi long leisir, with the wittiest and kunnyngist men of thilk seid sort, contrarie to the chirche [i.e. Lollards], and which han be holde as dukis amonge hem, and which han loved me for that y wolde pacientli heere her evydencis, and her motyves, without exprobacioun. And verrili noon of hem couthe make eny motyve for her parti so stronge as y my silf couthe have made therto.[65]
>
> [I have frequently spoken, and at great length, with the most intelligent and knowledgeable men of that sort who are against the Church, and who are regarded as dukes amongst them, and who have loved me because I would patiently listen to their evidence and ideas without censure. And truly none of them could put forward any ideas for their party as strongly as I could have done myself.]

Whilst we may detect some of Pecock's customary arrogance in these claims concerning his persuasive powers against Lollard leaders, it is nonetheless evidence of a belief that error and heresy were the fault of imperfect reason which could, through patient and persuasive logical explanation, be corrected. The St Mary's ape, then – physically resembling a human but lacking human understanding – would appear to be an ideal symbol of the Lollard's irrational nature.

However, in turning to one last – though arguably the most significant – point, this reading becomes problematised. Why, we may ask, is the ape

[63] On the literature of dissent influenced by *Piers Plowman*, see David Lawton, 'Lollardy and the *Piers Plowman* Tradition', *Modern Language Review* 76 (1981), 780–93; Anne Hudson, 'Epilogue: The Legacy of *Piers Plowman*', in *A Companion to Piers Plowman*, ed. John A. Alford (Berkeley: University of California Press, 1988), pp. 251–66; Barr (ed.), *Piers Plowman Tradition*.

[64] Nicholas Watson, 'Censorship and Cultural Change in Late-Medieval England: Vernacular Theology, the Oxford Translation Debate, and Arundel's Constitutions of 1409', *Speculum* 70 (1995), 824.

[65] Reginald Pecock, *Reginald Pecock's Book of Faith*, ed. J. L. Morison (Glasgow: J. Maclehose and Sons, 1909), p. 202.

depicted as a physician? As mentioned earlier, animal physicians frequently relate to the rich vein of satire of the medical profession, of which Chaucer's gold-fixated Doctour of Phisik, with his 'urynals and … jurdones', is only the most famous human example in the literature of the period.[66] Notwithstanding this, in a theme which we shall explore in more detail in chapter 5, a considerable number of late medieval texts refer to Christ as a spiritual doctor, a metaphor which is further extended to the clergy as His representatives on earth. St Jerome, for example, a much quoted authority throughout the Middle Ages, notes specifically that, 'indeed, an apostle is a spiritual physician'.[67] In this context, we could perhaps view the ape physician on the St Mary's misericord not as unreasonable or in any way degraded, but rather simply as a shorthand representation of 'the physical'. What, indeed, could be more explicitly concerned with bodily matters than a doctor? Yet, as we can see, within the overall design, the carving shows this animal representation of the physical turning towards matters of the spirit, as represented by the elevated Host. Indeed, if we look once more at the ape's gesture, we will notice that he appears to be pointing through the raised flask, by which physical health was gauged,[68] towards this most potent symbol of union with the divine. Far from conveying a satirical message, then, the carving may be offering a commentary on the nature of transformation, both of and through the sacrament, from the physical to the spiritual.

As Grössinger has stressed, the audience for medieval misericords was the clergy and 'even the scatological carvings were didactic rather than comical'.[69] This acknowledgement of a didactic intent, whilst persuading us that there is a serious meaning to be found within what at first may strike us as a comical scene, is nevertheless unlikely to help us when trying to interpret the St Mary's carving, as both anti-Lollard sentiment and the mystery of transubstantiation may be considered appropriate subjects for this audience at this time. Of course, as Michael Camille has noted, we should not neglect to consider the physical position of misericord carvings. Camille concentrates upon the manner in which these carvings 'were literally debased and made subservient to those "above" them [i.e. the clergy]'.[70] Whilst, as we saw earlier in this chapter in our consideration of biblical and related subjects, it is unwise to make such a claim in all cases, it is nonetheless something we may wish to take into consideration. If we do bear this in mind, it will perhaps sway the viewer towards a satirical

[66] Chaucer, *Canterbury Tales*, VI (C) 305. The pilgrim's portrait may be found in I (A) 411–44.
[67] St Jerome, 'Letter to Eustochium', in *Gender and Sexuality in the Middle Ages*, ed. Martha A. Brozyna (Jefferson: McFarland, 2005), p. 27.
[68] On the practice of uroscopy, by which a patient's health was assessed through the examination of urine, see Carole Rawcliffe, *Medicine and Society in Later Medieval Europe* (Stroud: Sutton Publishing, 1995), pp. 46–52.
[69] Grössinger, *The World Upside-Down*, pp. 73–83.
[70] Michael Camille, *Image on the Edge: The Margins of Medieval Art* (London: Reaktion, 1992) p. 94.

interpretation of the scene. Yet, by the same token, in the post-*Constitutions* world of fifteenth-century England, it is perhaps the discussion of the nature of transubstantiation itself that is being suppressed and, quite literally, 'sat upon' in this position.

In 1457, in a cruelly ironic turn of events, the passionately anti-heretical Reginald Pecock, who has provided something of a commentary throughout our consideration of the St Mary carving and other doctrinal matters in this chapter, was condemned for his writings and imprisoned in Thorney Abbey.[71] Amongst the several charges levelled against him, one of the most prominent was his rationalism, his over-reliance upon the faculty of reason with which he hoped to combat error in others. Although not explicitly stated in criticism of Pecock, it is nonetheless clear that his gravest error was to engage in these debates in the vernacular at all, thereby, as Wendy Scase puts it, 'borrow[ing] from the modes of discourse current among the anticlericals and heretics' and, in consequence, implicitly validating the viewpoints he sought to oppose.[72] Following Pecock's condemnation and the subsequent order for the destruction of his books, little of his writing survives, with his aforementioned *Boke of Eukarist* being one of the many works consigned to the flames. The fate of Pecock and his works provides a vivid illustration of the fact that, in the fifteenth century, open discussion of doctrinal matters, even by the avowedly orthodox, was considered to be dangerous indeed.

As Pecock noted in the passage from *The Repressor of Over Much Blaming of Clergy* which we considered at the start of this chapter, images depicted throughout 'dyuerse placis of the chirche' are there to be read by the lettered and unlettered alike. They are there to convey 'stories' to the viewer. But what 'storie' concerning an ape physician and the elevation of the Host are we to read beneath the stalls of St Mary, Beverley? *Pierce the Ploughman's Crede*, the Lollard descendant of *Piers Plowman* to which we referred earlier, in addressing theological discussions concerning transubstantiation makes the astute point that '[t]he more the matere is moved the masedere hy worthen' [the more the subject is debated, the more baffled they become].[73] This is certainly true also of the Beverley carving, the contemplation of which seems to multiply rather than clarify possible interpretations. But the larger 'storie' of the devotional climate we may perhaps read is one of doctrinal controversy in which all discussion may only take place in the most veiled of terms, in a prescribed area of the church which is accessible only to the few.

[71] On Pecock, see Brockwell, *Bishop Pecock and the Lancastrian Church*, and Wendy Scase, 'Reginald Pecock', in *Authors of the Middle Ages* 3, ed. M. C. Seymour (Aldershot: Variorum, 1996), pp. 75–146.

[72] Scase, 'Reginald Pecock', p. 117. On the centrality of Pecock's use of the vernacular to his condemnation, see Paul Hardwick, 'Breaking the Rules that "ben not written": Reginald Pecock and the Vernacular', *Parergon* n.s. 19.2 (2002), 101–18.

[73] *Crede*, l. 821.

In surveying the range of images on misericords which relate specifically to matters of devotional practice, then, we can see evidence of a number of approaches. Biblical figures, saints and angels represent the core focus of the medieval Church, whilst the wily fox in preacher's array and the company of devils illustrate the consequences which arise from the corruption of Christian truth. This latter concern mounted throughout the medieval period in England and came to a head in the late fourteenth and fifteenth centuries in the wake of Wyclif. Acknowledgement of the consequent culture of suppressed debate and re-statement of the authority of the Church may in turn illuminate our reading of enigmatic images such as the curious Eucharistic symbolism in Beverley or even, as we saw in chapter 1, apparently secular images, highlighting the contemporary significance of that which, taken out of context, may otherwise appear mundane or comic. It may be seen, then, that for those responsible for these carvings, the world of the flesh and the world of the spirit could not in any way be separated: all is, quite literally, at the heart of the Church, and the Church had dominion over all. We shall explore this further in later chapters, but now that we have broadly surveyed the interweaving worlds of substance and spirit beneath the choir stalls, it is time for us to pause and address the question of how these images came to be there.

# 3 INFLUENCE AND INVENTION

In discussing the standard of workmanship found on English choir stalls, M. D. Anderson laments the absence of detailed records, both of the process by which such work was commissioned and of the craftsmen who were responsible for undertaking the work, before reflecting that,

> [o]n the whole, the level of workmanship is high, even in small churches, which suggests that their misericords may have been obtained from workshops in some larger centre. This was certainly done in the case of monumental effigies, but if the principle of shop-work was adopted for misericords the almost inexhaustible versatility of their designs shows little evidence of it.[1]

This discrepancy between the high quality of workmanship displayed in surviving sets of stalls and the level of craftsmanship a modern viewer may perhaps expect in a small village church is, however, resolved when we consider the nature of crafts needs in the medieval period. 'Local labour resources were not sufficient for a large project such as an abbey or cathedral,' notes Patricia Basing,

> and workers had to be gathered from other areas. In particular, masons were itinerant workers, because of the relatively small amount of stone building that took place, while carpenters found plenty of employment in their local towns, where most houses were of wooden construction and naturally contained wooden fitments.[2]

There is, as we shall see, much evidence to suggest a fruitful exchange of ideas across different areas of the country and beyond – sometimes apparently even involving some movement of craftsmen – but it is important to remember that craftsmanship in wood was necessary for all communities,

[1] M. D. Anderson, *Misericords: Medieval Life in English Woodcarving* (Harmondsworth: Penguin Books, 1954), pp. 8–9.
[2] Patricia Basing, *Trades and Crafts in Medieval Manuscripts* (London: The British Library, 1990), p. 67.

however small, in an era in which it was the primary material for construction. It is no surprise, then, that within the relatively small number of tradesmen and craftsmen who are depicted on misericords, carvers are amongst those who appear most frequently, with half a dozen images surviving, including one in Beverley Minster which we shall look at more closely later in this chapter.[3] Certainly, all the surviving material evidence suggests that those who commissioned the stalls wanted the best possible work from the anonymous local carvers who they paid by the day, for, as we saw in the introduction, when stalls were being planned considerations of decoration and display appear to have figured prominently alongside considerations relating to comfort and the primary liturgical function of the furniture.[4] But what of the subjects which were chosen for display? Where did this dizzying panorama of life, devotion and imagination originate?

Unfortunately, no documents survive which give details of subjects to be carved on English choir stalls, but the view that misericords offered 'a rare opportunity for self-expression to carvers employed', whilst attractive, appears on closer inspection to be highly unlikely.[5] In a world in which details of both stone sculpture and stained glass, high in the shadows of the loftiest, darkest ecclesiastical buildings, were treated with the same care as details at eye level – to an omnipresent God, after all, nothing is hidden – there is every reason to assume that the design of misericords was as carefully considered. Whilst Malcolm Jones points to contracts for misericords in Amiens Cathedral, the abbey of St Clare in Gent-brugge and the abbey of St Nicholas in Veurne that grant a considerable degree of artistic freedom,[6] the specific context of post-Wyclif unease in the English Church which was considered in the previous chapter would surely makes such licence rather less likely in England. Paulette E. Barton suggests a process by which a decorative scheme would have been decided upon:

> In leading this discussion [on themes to be depicted] the abbot would consider the composition of the community. He would also consider the levels of ability in reading and writing within the community as well as the varying intellectual abilities. Members of the community would have a favorite image from a Psalm, an illustrated manuscript, a childhood story, an event in their lives before profession and all of these images could fit into an

[3] The others are to be found in: St Mary Magdalene, Brampton; Christchurch Priory; St Nicholas, Great Doddington; All Saints, Wellingborough; and the Victoria & Albert Museum, London (identified by Remnant as being of unknown East Anglian origin: G. L. Remnant, *A Catalogue of Misericords in Great Britain* (London: Oxford University Press, 1969), p. 94).

[4] Charles Tracy, *English Gothic Choir-Stalls 1200–1400* (Woodbridge: Boydell Press, 1987), p. xix.

[5] Anderson, *Misericords*, p. 5.

[6] Malcolm Jones, 'The Misericords of Beverley Minster: a Corpus of Folkloric Imagery and its Cultural Milieu, with special reference to the influence of Northern European Iconography on Late-medieval and Early Modern English Woodwork', unpublished PhD thesis (Polytechnic of the South West, 1991), pp. 344–5 and n. 24.

> illustrative microcosm of God's universe. The examples of misericords found in other quires would be a tested resource for images that could be used without fear of controversy in the new quire. Suggestions were respectfully made, discussed and argued in Chapter before the abbot who, in counsel with his senior administrative staff, would make the final decision.[7]

This account is, of course, speculative, but whilst the implied openness to all subject matter and the impression of the democratic ideal in action within the community may perhaps be overstated, there is certainly no doubt that a lot of thought would have gone into a commission entailing such expense – not to mention disruption within the choir – for furnishings with such a degree of permanence. In consideration of the time spent by the holder of a particular position within the choir each day, Charles Tracy has suggested that '[i]t is most likely that in English secular cathedrals at least the prospective stallholders were given the opportunity to specify the design of their own misericord',[8] which could account for the lack of clear iconographic schemes linking all the carvings in almost every surviving set.[9] Nonetheless, whether or not this is the case in terms of each individual stall, it is hard to imagine such work being produced without close supervision from planning to completion. To take an example which is rarely remarked upon, the more than a hundred heraldic shields which still survive on misericords offer clear evidence of specific patrons' requirements, as we saw in the case of John Gilliot in All Saints, North Street, York, in chapter 2. Indeed, as we shall see shortly, the carvings on a number of the early sixteenth-century misericords in Beverley Minster explicitly identify their original occupants. Whilst such personal identification was no doubt intended to serve a commemorative function, there is no reason to suspect that other motifs on misericords – whether selected by an individual or a community – were chosen with any less care and deliberation, for there is no shortage of evidence to suggest that for those who built and decorated churches throughout the period posterity was a real concern.

During the course of the last two chapters we have seen how representations of both the apparently secular and the explicitly doctrinal may be read as elements of a single worldview which is bounded by the

[7] Paulette E. Barton, *Mercy and the Misericord in Late Medieval England: Cathedral Theology and Architecture* (Lewiston: Edwin Mellen Press), pp. 148–9.

[8] Tracy, *English Gothic Choir-Stalls 1200–1400*, p. xx.

[9] The only surviving clearly coherent set of carvings is the 'Labours of the Months' sequence in St Mary, Ripple, which was discussed in chapter 1. Several short sequences of thematically linked misericords, of course, survive within larger groupings of unrelated carvings throughout the country. As we saw in chapter 2, the now-lost choir stalls of Coventry Cathedral contained three misericords which combined Dance of Death motifs with scenes from the Corporal Acts of Mercy, offering at least the possibility that they once, along with four further Acts of Mercy, formed a coherent iconographic group alongside the other carvings which up to the destruction of the stalls in 1940 included explicitly devotional images such as the Tree of Jesse, the Last Judgement and the binding of Satan.

Church. The key to this reading is the location – both architecturally and ideologically – of these images within the late medieval English Church. Before we turn to further images which may initially be yet more surprising to a modern viewer – including the apparently playful, the obscene or the simply bizarre – it will be illuminating to consider the sources of the motifs which we find, for, whilst variety is indeed the most striking characteristic of this rich corpus of carvings, we may nevertheless note the occurrence of many repeated subjects and, indeed, similar designs. The question, therefore, is: once the subject for the misericord carving had been selected, how was the form this subject would take decided upon? In considering this question, we shall have cause to look particularly closely at the ways in which motifs were both understood and, indeed, misunderstood.

M. D. Anderson suggests that '[m]ost scenes of agricultural labour shown on misericords were probably copied from calendar illustrations in books of devotion',[10] and whilst this is certainly a likely hypothesis, actual manuscript sources for specific carvings have so far remained elusive. The ploughman in Lincoln Cathedral which was discussed in chapter 1, for example, whilst having many manuscript analogues, has no known clearly identifiable model. Indeed, as we saw, its curiously cramped design is profoundly affected by the constraints of the three-dimensional space available on the misericord console, constraints which pose very different challenges to the craftsman than those which are encountered on the flat plane of manuscript illumination. Likewise, in discussing the proliferation of animals to be found in church decoration in all media, Beryl Rowland observes that '[t]he similarity apparent between the animals of manuscript miniatures and those of other ecclesiastical ornamentation suggests that the carver simply used the copy-book models or the manuscripts themselves'.[11] From this she concludes that 'their creator was not much concerned with zoological accuracy. But the medieval craftsman may not have been greatly interested in symbolic truth either.'[12] Inherent in this reasoning is the assumption that the craftsman himself was responsible for the selection of decorative motifs, the unlikelihood of which has already been addressed. Nonetheless, we may easily imagine that once a patron had settled on a subject – with, as we shall see in the case of animals in chapter 5, both an awareness of and an interest in its symbolic truth – the carpenter would turn to nature or, more likely, to a pattern book or possibly a picture supplied by the patron, in order to fulfil the commission. Alternatively, he may have looked to the carvings made by his predecessors.

In an early study, J. S. Purvis noted that 'certain subjects were used over and over again by successive generations of artists':

[10] M. D. Anderson, 'The Iconography of British Misericords', in Remnant, *Catalogue of Misericords*, p. xxviii.
[11] Beryl Rowland, *Blind Beasts: Chaucer's Animal World* (Kent, OH: Kent State University Press, 1971), p. 9.
[12] Ibid.

> Subjects which are familiar to us from the decorations of illuminated manuscripts reappear translated into wood, and it is clear that many such were widely accepted as stock designs traditionally popular.[13]

Whilst exact models in manuscripts prove elusive, printed material offers us evidence of a number of instances in which designs were clearly used as a basis for subsequent carvings. Purvis was the first to address in depth the use of the increasingly popular prints which were imported from the Continent and sometimes employed as direct models for later English misericords, a study which has been further explored in the work of Christa Grössinger and Malcolm Jones.[14] With the advent of printing in the fifteenth century, relatively cheap images could be reproduced in large numbers, and it is here that we begin to see designs which were copied closely onto the three-dimensional medium of misericord consoles. We should note, however, that the mass reproduction of images created a much greater chance for at least one copy of a given motif to survive the depredations of time, thereby making comparison today possible: it is very likely that a number of manuscripts which in their time fulfilled the function of exemplars – whether in the manner of the unique English Pepysian model-book, in which 'many of the drawings seem to be models for use in a workshop',[15] or simply by virtue of containing one or two appealing individual illuminations – have been lost over the centuries. Of the few biblical scenes to be found on English misericords, Purvis identifies four designs found in Ripon Minster as being copies of prints from the *Biblia Pauperum*, one of the most widely circulated wood-block books of the period.[16] Another image with an identifiable source in Continental prints is derived from a popular engraving of c.1475–80 by the Master bxg which was widely disseminated throughout Europe in the last quarter of the fifteenth century, showing an old woman, presumably under the influence of the contents of the flask to which she

[13] Rev. J. S. Purvis, 'The Use of Continental Woodcuts and Prints by the "Ripon School" of Woodcarvers in the Early Sixteenth Century', *Archaeologia* 85 (1935), 116.

[14] Ibid., pp. 107–28. See also, Christa Grössinger, *The World Upside-Down: English Misericords* (London: Harvey Miller, 1997), especially pp. 65–71; Christa Grössinger, *Humour and Folly in Secular and Profane Prints of Northern Europe, 1430–1540* (London: Harvey Miller, 2002), especially pp. 13–53; Malcolm Jones, 'German and Flemish Prints as Design-Sources for the Misericords in St George's Chapel, Windsor (1477×84)', in *Windsor: Medieval Archaeology, Art and Architecture of the Thames Valley*, ed. Laurence Keen and Eileen Scarff, *The British Archaeological Association Conference Transactions* 25 (2002), 155–65; Malcolm Jones, 'Metal-Cut Border Ornaments in Parisian Printed Books of Hours as Design Sources for Sixteenth-Century Works of Art', in *Publishing the Fine and Applied Arts, 1500–2000*, ed. Giles Mandelbrote (forthcoming).

[15] Jonathan Alexander and Paul Binski (eds), *Age of Chivalry: Art in Plantagenet England 1200–1400* (London: Weidenfeld and Nicholson, 1987), p. 402. Grössinger draws attention to the similarities between designs found therein and images carved on misericords: *The World Upside-Down*, p. 64.

[16] Purvis, 'The Use of Continental Woodcuts and Prints', pp. 120–1. These scenes are: Samson carrying off the Gates of Gaza; Jonah cast overboard; Jonah coming out of the whale; and Joshua and Caleb with the grapes from the brook of Eshcol.

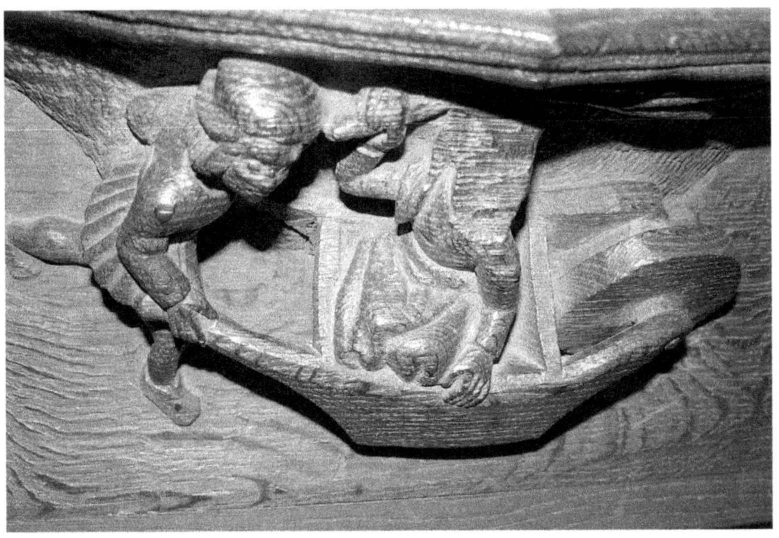

FIG. 13. BISHOP TUNSTALL'S CHAPEL, DURHAM CASTLE MISERICORD.

clutches, being wheeled on a barrow by a raggedly attired man (fig. 13). This provides the model for a misericord now located in Bishop Tunstall's Chapel in Durham Castle which we shall consider shortly.[17] Other misericords based on printed models include the 'Rabbits' revenge' in Manchester Cathedral which closely follows a print by Israhel van Meckenem from the closing years of the fifteenth century, and a scene in Henry VII's Chapel, Westminster Abbey, of a cowering man with a distaff being birched on his naked behind by a woman which, as Grössinger has suggested, is close enough to a playing card design of c.1528 by Erhard Schön to suggest a shared model.[18] Indeed, several of the Westminster Abbey carvings make use of prints as patterns, including a number by Albrecht Dürer.[19] In studying the stalls in St George's Chapel, Windsor, Malcolm Jones has demonstrated that, as we may expect of such a prestigious royal commission, the carvers had access to 'the latest imported sources',[20] in the form of prints by the Master of the Berlin Passion, the Master E.S. and, possibly, Israhel van Meckenem, attesting to an enthusiasm to embrace this new medium of design transmission.

Whatever manuscript or print exemplars may now be lost, then, it may be confidently asserted that printed sources provided the models for a

[17] The motif is repeated with slight variation in Beverley and Ripon Minsters. On the print's popularity, see Christa Grössinger, *Picturing Women in Late Medieval and Renaissance Art* (Manchester: Manchester University Press, 1997), p. 126.
[18] Grössinger, *The World Upside Down*, p. 67. We shall return to this latter image in the next chapter.
[19] Ibid. Those images which have been identified as deriving from Dürer are: unequal couple; Samson and the lion; man and woman facing each other; man in foliage.
[20] Jones, 'German and Flemish Prints as Design-Sources for the Misericords in St George's Chapel', 155.

number of later English misericords, and there is the very real possibility that, as the corpus of Continental prints becomes more widely known, further examples will be identified. In the case of multiple carvings deriving from a known source, however, it is interesting to speculate upon whether each carving was made with reference to the print or if, returning to a point made by Barton above, a patron would perhaps ask for a copy of a carving that had taken his fancy elsewhere. Certainly, we may detect instances in which earlier carvings have influenced later work. It is likely that substantially the same group of craftsmen worked on the stalls of Lincoln Cathedral and Chester Abbey around the last quarter of the fourteenth century, explaining not only similarities of style but also the repetition of a dozen subjects.[21] Further north, whilst Charles Tracy's meticulous stylistic analyses have discredited early assertions of a 'Ludlow School' of carvers working in the north-west of England and North Wales,[22] the 'many affinities' between the stall work and misericords in groups of churches such as St Mary with St Bartholomew, Tong, All Saints, Gresford, and St Cuthbert, Halsall, suggest that when it came to the design and construction of new sets of choir stalls, the emulation of popular styles was far from unknown.[23]

The problematic nature for the modern viewer of unravelling the strands of influence and inspiration which led to the carving of a misericord may be most effectively explored by focusing at length upon what seems to be an almost deliberately mocking challenge that faces us in the choir of Beverley Minster: the head of a gurning, gesticulating fool who is flanked in the supporters by two rather startled-looking geese (fig. 14). In order to begin to understand this image, it is first necessary to place it in its immediate cultural context amongst the choir stalls in the town of Beverley in the early sixteenth century. This will allow us to speculate upon possible iconographic interpretations which will, in turn, suggest that the image itself may be the result of a misunderstanding on the part of the Beverley carver. In consequence, whilst casting some light on the manner in which designs came to be reused in different churches, we may at the same time be able to posit a lost model for this particular carving.

The choir stalls at Beverley Minster belong to the very last years of late medieval English church furnishing, having been installed – in a building which in its present form has otherwise remained largely unchanged since the close of the fourteenth century – in c.1520.[24] This date may be attributed with

[21] M. D. Anderson, *The Choir Stalls of Lincoln Minster* (Lincoln: Friends of Lincoln Minster, 1967), pp. 10–11 and 24–5. For a broader discussion of the place of Lincoln and Chester in the stylistic development of English choir stalls in the second half of the fourteenth century, see Tracy, *English Gothic Choir-Stalls 1200–1400*, pp. 49–55.

[22] Charles Tracy, *English Gothic Choir-Stalls 1400–1540* (Woodbridge: Boydell Press, 1990), pp. 9–15 and 41–6.

[23] Ibid., p. 45.

[24] On the chronology of the building work, see Paul Barnwell and Rosemary Horrox's Introduction to *Beverley Minster: An Illustrated History*, ed. Rosemary Horrox (Beverley: Friends of Beverley Minster, 2000), pp. 3–11.

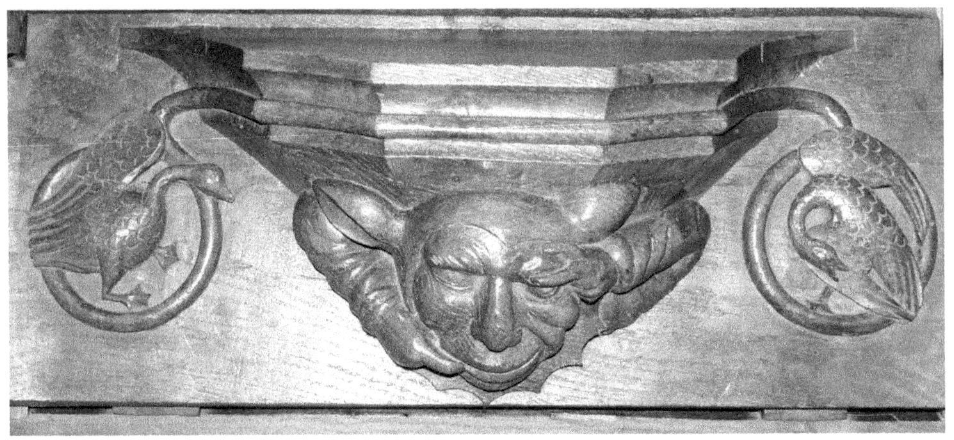

FIG. 14. BEVERLEY MINSTER MISERICORD.

uncharacteristic precision because it appears in the design on the stall of the sacrist, William Tait, one of four church officials to be specifically identified by name in the carvings.[25] Sixty-eight stalls survive *in situ* and, whilst Charles Tracy has plausibly suggested a possible loss of two return stalls in the eighteenth century to accommodate the installation of a new choir screen, it is entirely possible that the original overall plan remains intact, albeit with the distinct possibility of some re-ordering of individual misericord seats.[26] As such, then, the Beverley scheme represents a particularly valuable corpus of motifs from the very eve of the English Reformation.

In addition to the carvings which refer directly to the stalls' original occupants, there is an extensive and apparently unrelated range of subjects depicted. As we may now have come to expect, few of these subjects are explicitly religious in content. The ubiquitous pelican in her piety appears twice, significantly prominent on the stalls of the highest-ranking minster dignitaries – the precentor and the Archbishop of York – suggesting that, at least on these stalls, specific instructions were given concerning the iconographic emblems of selfless piety appropriate to elevated clerical rank which were to be carved.[27] Elsewhere, we may find Joshua and Caleb, returning from the expedition into the land of Canaan upon which they were sent by Moses:

> And they came to the brook of Eschol, and cut down from thence a branch with one cluster of grapes, and they bare it between two upon a staff . . . And they returned from searching of the land after forty days.[28]

[25] The other three are: William Wight, Chancellor; ? Donyngton, Precentor; John Sperke, Clerk of Works.

[26] Tracy, *English Gothic Choir-Stalls 1400–1540*, p. 23. The possibility of re-ordering is addressed below.

[27] This point is noted in Malcolm Jones, 'The Misericords', in *Beverley Minster*, ed. Horrox, pp. 159–60.

[28] Numbers 13:23.

The scene, which shows the 'spies', as they are often called, bearing a staff supporting a bunch of outsized grapes – presumably signifying the abundance to be found in the 'land of milk and honey' – is, like four misericords in Ripon Minster, derived from an image in the block-book *Biblia Pauperum*.[29]

Amongst the apparently less pious scenes depicted on the Beverley Minster misericords is another example of the ubiquitous fox preacher we met in the last chapter, here addressing his attentive congregation of proverbially foolish geese. Nearby, although not adjacent – a fact which perhaps suggests some re-ordering of the misericords subsequent to their initial installation – the geese may be seen to exact their revenge upon the fox at the gallows, a common companion piece which may be found, for example, on a misericord in Bristol Cathedral and on a bench end in the church of St Michael, Brent Knoll. Whilst specific models cannot be identified, it is quite possible that these scenes may owe their designs to lost manuscript illustrations of this popular figure.[30] A second, again interrupted, narrative sequence depicts four scenes relating to the capture, transportation and baiting of a bear (fig. 15); these have been plausibly related to the exhibition of dancing bears which is recorded as having taken place in the marketplace at Beverley in 1520, a date contemporary with the construction of the stalls.[31] We will meet both the fox and the bear again in chapter 5.

FIG. 15. BEVERLEY MINSTER MISERICORD.

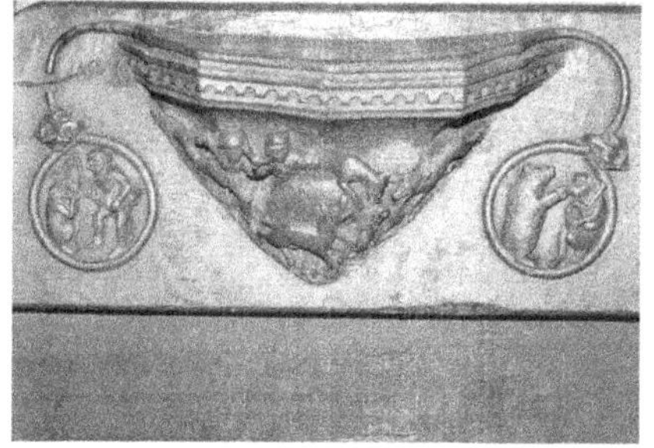

Alongside these natural, observable and anthropomorphised animals, beasts of a more fabulous nature may be found, including a unicorn, a dragon and more than one griffin – fantastic beasts of a type which we shall consider more closely in chapter 6. Like these often allegorised mythical and legendary creatures, the realistic yet exotic elephant and castle may send us searching within the bestiary for an explanation,[32] although Malcolm Jones plays

[29] This is the only one of the scenes derived from the *Biblia Pauperum* which is repeated outside Ripon. It may also be found in Manchester Cathedral.

[30] See Kenneth Varty, *Reynard the Fox: A Study of the Fox in Medieval English Art* (Leicester: Leicester University Press, 1967), pp. 81–3. On medieval illustrations in all media of the death and subsequent resurrection of the fox, see Kenneth Varty, *Reynard, Renart, Reinaert and Other Foxes in Medieval England: The Iconographic Evidence* (Amsterdam: Amsterdam University Press, 1999), pp. 131–62. For an overview of misericord carvings of the fox, see Elaine C. Block and Kenneth Varty, 'Choir-Stall Carvings of Reynard and Other Foxes', in *Reynard the Fox: Social Engagement and Cultural Metamorphoses in the Beast Epic from the Middle Ages to the Present*, ed. Kenneth Varty (New York and Oxford: Berghahn Books, 2000), pp. 125–62.

[31] Jones, 'The Misericords', p. 160.

[32] The elephant and castle motif is fairly common, with a further local example in St Mary's, Beverley, with others further afield in Cartmel Priory; St Helen's, Garstang; Gloucester Cathedral; St Katharine's Foundation, London; Manchester Cathedral; and two in St George's Chapel, Windsor. The curiously shaped ears of the Beverley elephant, described by Remnant as 'webbed like a bat's', suggest that it was not modelled from life. The symbolism of the elephant will be considered in chapter 5.

down the metaphorical possibilities which are suggested by bestiary symbolism.[33] However, other subjects undoubtedly ask to be read in a specific manner as they clearly refer to proverbial sayings. We have already come across depictions of 'shoeing the goose' at St Mary, Whalley, in chapter 1, a motif which appears here as a supporter to the preaching fox. This proverbial trope denoting futility may also be found closer to Beverley on a capital in the north choir aisle of York Minster, and in both cases it is presented without the accompanying text we saw in Whalley, thereby suggesting a sufficiently common currency for the image and its signification which thus required no additional explanation. Elsewhere in the Beverley stalls, there is a further example of proverbial folly in a scene of the cart being placed before the horse.[34] The foolishness of this act is further compounded in the right-hand supporter, in which a maid milks a bull. And it is in this category of vernacular proverbial sayings that the misericord of the gurning fool and his flanking geese is usually considered to belong.

The Beverley Minster choir stalls contain no shortage of fools: fools who grin from beneath their ass-eared hoods; others who cavort with their baton and bauble; and others who dance wildly and play on the pipe and drum. As Christa Grössinger acknowledges, '[i]t may be that the Feast of Fools, celebrated in Beverley every Christmas, when the clergy and others dressed up as fools and held mock services, was responsible for this predilection for the fool'.[35] Nonetheless, whilst surviving records indeed attest to a vital dramatic culture in Beverley in the later Middle Ages, these images seem to me to suggest more than a simple desire to record contemporary festivities. After all, as we saw in chapter 1, the fool appears to hold a particular significance in this period as a disinterested, stringently truthful commentator upon society. Grössinger has noted a similarity of posture between the Beverley misericord depicting fools dancing the wild moresca and an engraving of c.1490 by Israhel van Meckenem, in which men cavort around the central figure of a woman who is proffering an apple – symbolic of carnal desire – whilst a fool stands open-armed in rapt

[33] Jones, 'The Misericords', pp. 160–1. On the place of bestiaries in medieval thought, see Ron Baxter, *Bestiaries and their Users in the Middle Ages* (Stroud: Sutton Publishing, 1998).

[34] It is interesting to note that *The Oxford Dictionary of Proverbs*, ed. Jennifer Speake, 4th edn (Oxford: Oxford University Press, 2003), cites R. Whittington's *Vulgaria* of c.1520 – that is, roughly contemporary with the Beverley carvings – as the first recorded use of the proverb 'That teacher setteth the carte before the horse that preferreth imitacyon before preceptes.'

[35] Christa Grössinger, 'Humour and Folly in English Misericords of the First Quarter of the Sixteenth Century', in *Early Tudor England: Proceedings of the 1987 Harlaxton Symposium*, ed. Daniel Williams (Woodbridge: Boydell Press, 1989), pp. 82–3, citing Francis Bond, *Wood Carvings in English Churches 1: Misericords* (London: Oxford University Press, 1910), p. 110. For evidence of other forms of drama in Beverley during this period, see Alan H. Nelson, *The Medieval English Stage: Corpus Christi Pageants and Plays* (Chicago and London: Chicago University Press, 1974), pp. 88–99.

adoration at her feet.[36] In this further example of a Continental print that provides the model for an English misericord, albeit with adaptation on account of its new location and medium, desire leads the men in a foolish dance as they relinquish their power to the self-possessed temptress – a trap much abhorred and feared in the misogynist culture of the late Middle Ages, particularly within the Church, as we shall see in the next chapter. In the light of this comparison, Grössinger suggests that the group of contorted, dancing fools in Beverley may be playing out their foolish carnal desires.[37] Referring to another misericord, Jones identifies the two birds pecking at a fool's hood as coots and points to the roughly contemporary *Philip Sparrow* (c.1508), in which Skelton gives us our first recorded usage of the phrase 'the mad coot'.[38] In the light of this, it is certainly possible that both Skelton and the Beverley carver are making reference to the same contemporary proverbial attribute of the bird.

This latter figure of the mobbed fool is flanked by supporters depicting geese, which are also interpreted by Jones with reference to one of Skelton's ornithological insults, 'as witless as a wild goose', thereby suggesting that they compound the folly of the main carving in the way that we saw earlier in the example of the bull-milking scene on the supporter of the depiction of the cart being driven before the horse. As this symbolic system, whereby the supporters add a further layer of emphasis to the meaning of the main carving, is clearly employed on more than one of the Beverley misericords, it is reasonable to attribute the same function to the geese in the supporters of our misericord of the gurning fool. Jones considers there to be a unity between the three elements of the carving, interpreting them thus:

> As for the meaning of the fool's face, it might, of course, be purely whimsical, a piece of *grotesquerie* merely, yet both gestures [made with his hands] considered separately can be assigned conventional meanings. The iconography of historical gesture is still in its infancy but, in an admittedly modern survey, the gesture termed 'the eyelid pull' signifies, 'I'm alert, I'm no fool'. Could this fool, paradoxically, be trying to tell us he is no fool? Both supporters depict geese. However unjustly, the goose is considered a proverbially foolish bird in English.

In addition, he goes on to cite a homiletic phrase, 'Shall I stand still, like a goose or a fool, with my finger in my mouth?', the first surviving written occurrence of which can be dated to 1547, a short enough time after the

[36] Grössinger, *Humour and Folly*, 115–17. On the dance represented in van Meckenem's engraving, see John Forrest, *The History of Morris Dancing: 1458–1750* (Toronto: University of Toronto Press, 1999), pp. 56–91. Although considering the influence of the engraving upon the famous Betley Hall window of c.1621 (pp. 153–6), in his discussion of Morris dancing and the Church, Forrest does not discuss the Beverley misericord.
[37] Grössinger, *The World Upside-Down*, pp. 106–7.
[38] Jones, 'The Misericords', p. 162.

construction of the Beverley stalls to assume that it may well have been in common circulation at the time of the carvings, noting that,

> [t]his quotation significantly combines three of the elements which go to make up this misericord carving – the fool, the goose, and the finger in the mouth – and constitutes valuable proof that the goose supporters are not merely whimsical, decorative additions.[39]

Jones is surely right to attribute a single, coherent meaning to the combination of the main carving and the supporters for – as we have already begun to see, and shall observe further in future chapters – this is a feature common to the minster misericords. Nevertheless, to explain the symbolism of the arrangement in terms of the phrase 'shall I stand still, like a goose or a fool, with my finger in my mouth' still falls short of encompassing all elements of the design, as it omits the gesture towards the eye which Jones, as he himself acknowledges, addresses rather tentatively. In view of this, it seems that we need to seek further for an alternative reading which incorporates all of the carved elements.

We have already encountered a number of carvings of fools in chapter 1, of whom we have observed that, as Clifford Davidson reminds us, '[i]n the Middle Ages and subsequently, the fool is a paradoxical figure of the greatest complexity who deserves to be examined from different perspectives'.[40] In seeking to unravel the meanings of this paradoxical figure, the location of the misericord carvings with which we are currently concerned, right in the devotional heart of the church, may logically lead us to look to the Bible for examples of fools, and it is here that the greatest paradox may indeed be found. For whilst Psalm 52 (*AV*: 53) says of those who deny God, 'The fool has said in his heart, There is no God', St Paul's letter to the Corinthians (I Corinthians 4:10) states that 'We are fools for Christ's sake'. Depending on where we look, then, the fool may be viewed as either apostate sinner or holy innocent, rendering a scriptural reading tantalisingly inviting yet elusive. However, if we consider these scriptural allusions in the light of Beverley's aforementioned lively dramatic culture, it may perhaps suggest a resolution to this puzzle.

Whilst records of Beverley's Feast of Fools suggest one possible dramatic context for our image of the fool and geese, further light may be cast by a very different type of dramatic performance which was then current. Although no text has survived, Beverley is known to have had its own cycle of mystery plays; but if we turn to those mystery cycles from the north of

[39] Ibid., p.162. The importance of gesture cannot be overstated for, as Jody Enders notes, even in spoken or dramatic performance, gesture could be considered to 'speak' even before words: Jody Enders, 'Of Miming and Signing: The Dramatic Rhetoric of Gesture', in *Gesture in Medieval Drama and Art*, ed. Clifford Davidson (Kalamazoo: Medieval Institute Publications, 2001), pp. 10–11.

[40] Clifford Davidson, Introduction to *Fools and Folly*, ed. Clifford Davidson (Kalamazoo: Medieval Institute Publications, 1996), p. 5.

England that have survived – those of Wakefield and of York – we see that in both of them Christ himself is mocked as a Christmas fool.[41] And it is in the York plays that we may find a clue to interpretation of the Beverley carving. When Christ is brought before Herod in the Litsters' Play, he is mockingly introduced as an entertaining fool, the First Soldier characterising their intent in presenting Christ thus: 'My lord, we fare fools to flay / That to you would forfeit.'[42] [My lord, we come to punish fools who would cause you offence.] Herod, in turn, can barely contain his enthusiastic anticipation:

> Oh, my heart hops for joy
> To see now this prophet appear.
> We shall have good game with this boy—
> Take heed, for in haste ye shall hear.
>
> I leve we shall laugh and have liking
> To see how this lidderon here he ledges our laws.[43]

> [Oh, my heart jumps for joy to see now this prophet appear. We shall have good sport with this boy – listen, for you shall soon hear. I believe we shall laugh and have fun to see how this rascal here expounds our laws.]

When, however, in spite of pleas and increasing threats, Christ fails to provide the expected entertainment, refusing to speak or even move, it is Herod himself who adopts the role of fool, exclaiming unintelligible nonsense – 'Kyte oute yugilment. Uta! Oy! Oy!' – in hope of encouraging the silent and immobile Christ to participate in his 'gauds full good and games'[44] [excellent sport and games], but to no avail. As Sandra Billington points out,

> [h]ad Christ said a single word, he would have contributed to the Fool-game that he was placed in and so would have betrayed the Christian aspect of the Fool. The audience would have been fully aware of the two sides to the name [of fool] and would have been waiting for any possible slip. One can imagine the humour combined with tension when Herod pulls faces and makes gurgling noises to encourage Christ.[45]

This complex response, equal parts humour and tension, is precisely what is engendered by the carving of the gurning fool beneath the Beverley Minster choir stall; as it surprises us with its grimace, we are amused by the foolish expression, yet at the same time we are made acutely aware of

[41] See A. C. Cawley (ed.), *The Wakefield Pageants in the Towneley Cycle* (Manchester: Manchester University Press, 1958), p. 87 and Richard Beadle and Pamela King (eds), *York Mystery Plays: a Selection in Modern Spelling* (Oxford: Oxford University Press, 1995), pp. 176–91.
[42] Beadle and King (eds), *York Mystery Plays*, p. 179.
[43] Ibid., p. 182.
[44] Ibid., p. 185.
[45] Sandra Billington, *A Social History of the Fool* (Brighton: Harvester Press, 1984), p. 19.

its inappropriateness within the sacred space. In effect, it presents a challenge to the viewer not to laugh, and to refrain from participation in sinful foolishness.

But what of the fool's hand gestures to eye and mouth? Whilst one finger could possibly, as Jones suggests, be in the fool's mouth, it appears to me that, rather, the fool is actually making a gesture *towards* his mouth. Likewise, rather than pulling at his eyelid, his other hand appears to be pointing *towards* his eye. Taken thus, the gestures may be read as drawing attention to the faculties of speech and sight, in which case the foolish geese to either side may contribute to a reading of the whole as an exhortation to avoid foolish interpretation or speech. At risk of appearing foolish myself, I would, however, like to take this reading one step further, for which it will be necessary to turn to the construction of the Beverley Minster choir stalls and the influence of earlier stalls in northern England upon their design, particularly in relation to the subjects depicted on the misericords.

Whilst the notion of the 'Ripon School' of carvers proposed by J. S. Purvis in 1929 has subsequently been shown to be an overly specific epithet,[46] the Beverley Minster stalls show a marked stylistic similarity – characterised by Tracy as a 'regional period style' – to earlier northern examples, including Ripon but with a particular closeness to those found in Manchester Cathedral (c.1506) and some of those which are now located in the Tunstall Chapel in Durham Castle (1508–22).[47] Although the Beverley Minster carvings display rather less skilled craftsmanship in their overall execution than is evident in earlier work elsewhere, a number of stylistic details on the misericords betray the influence of earlier northern motifs, most notably in the manner in which at both Manchester and Beverley the line of the seat is extended into a descending arc which loops around the supporter and is 'tied' with a foliate motif.[48] Furthermore, a number of scenes which occur on earlier misericords are repeated in the later work. For example, a lively

[46] J. S. Purvis, 'The Ripon Carvers and the Lost Choir-Stalls of Bridlington Priory', *Yorkshire Archaeological Journal* 29 (1929), 157–201. A persuasive qualification of Purvis's view is offered in Tracy, *English Gothic Choir-Stalls 1400–1540*, pp. 16–17.

[47] Records refer to the transfer of 'Stalls in the Highe Chapell' of Auckland Castle being transferred to the chapel of Durham Castle in the time of Bishop Tunstall. Striking stylistic differences between the misericords now in the Tunstall Chapel, however, show that they are clearly not a unified set, suggesting a rather more complex history than the documentary evidence reveals. Perhaps the stalls came to Durham from more than one location or, equally likely, the misericords transferred from Auckland Castle themselves have a chequered provenance. See Emma Phipson, *Choir Stalls and their Carvings: Examples of Misericords from English Cathedrals and Churches* (London: B. T. Batsford, 1896), p. 91; Remnant, *Catalogue of Misericords*, p. 42. On the dating of the Manchester stalls, see H. A. Hudson, *The Medieval Woodwork in Manchester Cathedral* (Manchester: Sherratt and Hughes, 1924), pp. 13–14.

[48] As Tracy notes, this is one of the ways in which Manchester shows a possible influence from St George's Chapel, Windsor. At Windsor, however, the supporters are 'tied' further up the stem towards the seat, creating a more pointed effect than at either Manchester or Beverley. This, then, suggests a rather general influence exerted by a prestige royal commission, rather than the closer affinity between Manchester and Beverley. The relationship between Windsor and Manchester is discussed in Tracy, *English Gothic Choir-Stalls 1400–1540*, pp. 27–8.

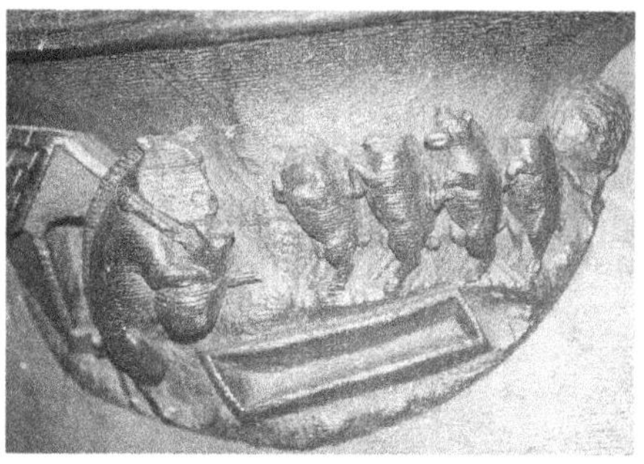

FIG. 16. MANCHESTER CATHEDRAL MISERICORD.

image of a piping sow playing for her dancing piglets occurs in both Manchester (fig. 16) and Beverley, although in the latter location the scene is reversed and has some minor variation of detail. Elsewhere, other images found in Manchester which are reproduced more or less exactly by the Beverley carver include a fox making off with a goose, a gang of apes rifling the pack of a sleeping pedlar, an ape holding a swaddled baby, and an ape physician examining a uroscopy flask. We shall be considering several of these animal motifs more closely in chapter 5, but for now it is sufficient to note this extensive repetition of motifs from Manchester in the choir at Beverley Minster.[49] In addition to those already mentioned, a scene showing a Wild Man attacking a dragon with a club is found on a misericord in Durham Castle, as well as beneath the stalls at Manchester and Beverley.[50] It should nonetheless be stressed that, whilst the Beverley carvings are close to their models, none is an exact copy, suggesting that the later carvers may have worked from sketches, or even memory, rather than from shared patterns. Jones, for example, notes that details of the Beverley carving showing a man pushing a woman in a wheelbarrow – a motif also found in Ripon – suggest that the carver may have misunderstood the possibly damaged version of the scene derived from the print by the Master bxg which we encountered above in Durham:

> The Durham Castle scene ... shows the woman holding onto the side of the wheelbarrow with one hand while she raises her branch with the other, on the point of thrashing her hapless husband with it – the central portion of the branch is now broken such that, at first glance she appears to be pulling the man's hair, so that it is curious that the Beverley crone, one hand similarly on the barrow's side, is indeed pulling her man's hair – is it possible that the Beverley carver, a generation later, based his design on the Durham Castle misericord and misunderstood the *already broken* branch, just as a modern viewer might?[51]

In a general discussion of misericord design, M. D. Anderson refers to the

[49] I have discussed a number of these images in the following articles: 'Through a Glass, Darkly: Interpreting Animal Physicians', *Reinardus* 15 (2002), 63–70; 'Foxing Daun Russell: Moral Lessons of Poultry on Misericords and in Literature', *Reinardus* 17 (2004), 85–94; 'The Merchant, the Monkeys and the Lure of Money', *Reinardus* 19 (2006), 83–90.
[50] These correspondences are discussed in Jones, 'The Misericords of Beverley Minster', pp. 46–51. See also, Jones, 'The Misericords', p. 158 and Grössinger, *The World Upside-Down*, pp. 54–6. We shall consider Wild Men in chapter 6.
[51] Jones, 'The Misericords of Beverley Minster', p. 47. Jones notes the apparent derivation of this motif from an engraving by the late fifteenth-century German artist known as 'Master bxg'.

possibility that the carver sometimes 'worked from his inaccurate memory of a picture he had seen but not fully understood',[52] and it is very probable that with the carving of the Beverley barrow we are witnessing just such an occasion. Clearly not derived directly from the popular print itself, it seems almost certain that the craftsman was here relying either on memory or – more likely, considering the closeness to the damaged Durham carving – upon a sketch, possibly made in haste, either by himself or even by another, in what T. Tindall Wildridge long ago described evocatively as the 'minster gloom' beneath the stalls.[53] In consequence, this has led the carver to misunderstand the action of the scene when reproducing it in Beverley. And it is to the matter of the very real possibility of misunderstanding when copying images that we shall now turn.

Discussing medieval European representations of non-native animals, E. H. Gombrich comments upon the tendency of artists to adapt that which they observe into familiar schemata. What they see is, in effect, transformed by what they know,[54] a process that may well have occurred in the case of the Beverley misericord of the fool and the geese, on which the carver may have been working – again probably via memory or a sketch – from a now lost exemplar where the supporters were rather different. For whilst, in the town in which 'the popular medieval Feast of Fools seems to have survived longest in England',[55] the foolish geese may have seemed logical companions to the grimacing fool, the gestures of the central figure and the postures of the geese suggest otherwise. The right-hand supporter shows the goose with its neck curved backwards, tucking its beak into its breast. Such a gesture is common in all media of medieval art, including around three dozen English misericords, but in these cases it is not a goose that is depicted; rather, such a pose is more characteristic of the pelican (fig. 17). Enumerating the qualities of the pelican and, characteristically, using

FIG. 17. ALL SAINTS, NORTH STREET MISERICORD.

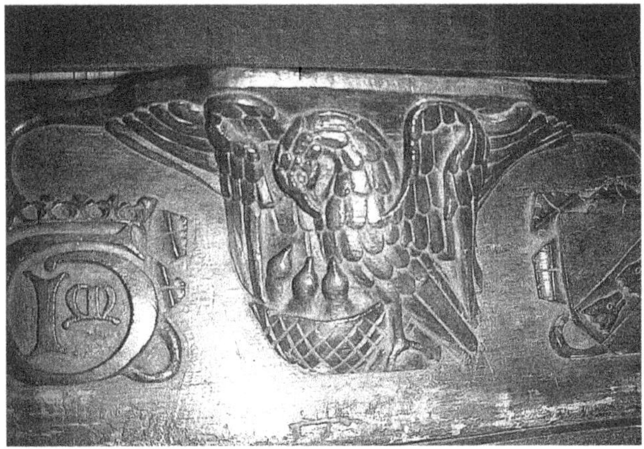

[52] Anderson, 'The Iconography of British Misericords', p. xxiv.
[53] T. Tindall Wildridge, *The Misereres of Beverley Minster: A Complete Series of Drawings of the Seat Carvings in the Choir of St John's, Beverley, Yorkshire; with Notes on the Plates and Subject* (Hull: J. Plaxton, 1879), p. 2.
[54] E. H. Gombrich, *Art and Illusion: a Study in the Psychology of Pictorial Representation*, 5th edn (Oxford: Phaidon Press, 1977), pp. 67–73.
[55] Jones, 'The Misericords', p. 162.

these observations as a basis to draw out an allegorical interpretation, the bestiary tells us that:

> [i]t shows exceeding love towards its young. If it has brought offspring into the world, when these grow up they strike their parents in the face. The parents strike back and kill them. After three days, their mother opens her own breast and side, and lies on her young, pouring all her blood over the dead bodies, and thus her love brings them back to life. So our Lord Jesus Christ, who is the author and originator of all creatures, begot us, and, when we did not exist, He made us. But we struck Him in the face; as Isaiah said: 'I have begotten sons and raised them up, but they have despised me'. Christ ascended the Cross and was struck in the side: blood and water came forth for our salvation, to give us eternal life.[56]

If the original model for the carving had indeed been a pelican, our fool's gesture towards his eye could, therefore, indicate that he looks upon this traditional symbol of Christ's love which was so widespread throughout the Middle Ages. If so, we may perhaps read the other hand pointing towards his mouth as a gesture denoting speech. But of what, we may ask, does the fool speak?

As the form of the right-hand goose suggests a pelican, so the left-hand goose, with its rather awkward rendering of its hindmost feathers, suggests another often-depicted creature: the griffin (fig. 18). Of the griffin, the *Bestiary* tells us little, other than that '[t]he hinder part of its body is like a lion; its wings and face are like an eagle ... and if it comes face to face with a man, it will attack him'.[57] Nonetheless, this deadly hybrid occurs frequently in late medieval art, and may be found on a number of misericords, including many elsewhere in Yorkshire: at St Mary, Beverley; St Mary, Old Malton; Ripon Minster; St Mary, Swine, and, indeed, on another misericord in Beverley Minster itself.[58] Significantly, when we turn to examples from contemporary literature, a griffin also appears in a Lollard debate poem – first printed in 1532, around a decade after the construction of the Beverley Minster choir stalls, though undoubtedly composed earlier – where it is engaged in a *flyting* with none other than a pelican.[59] In *The Plowman's Tale*, as this poem has become known since its spurious attribution to Chaucer in the sixteenth century, the pious Pelican is employed as a mouthpiece in order to articulate the views of those of whom the poet considers the true

[56] Richard Barber (ed. and trans.), *Bestiary, Being an English Version of the Bodleian Library, Oxford MS Bodley 764* (Woodbridge: Boydell Press, 1993), p. 147.

[57] Ibid., p. 39.

[58] More than two dozen griffins appear on misericords throughout the country.

[59] *The Plowman's Tale: the c. 1532 and 1606 Editions of a Spurious Canterbury Tale*, ed. Mary Rhinelander McCarl (New York and London: Garland, 1997). On the dating of elements of the poem, see Andrew N. Wawn, 'The Genesis of *The Plowman's Tale*', *Yearbook of English Studies* 2 (1972), 21–40.

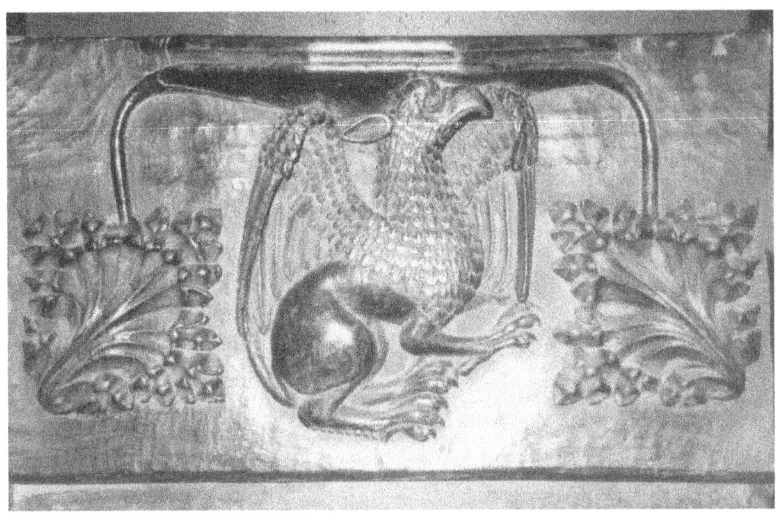

FIG. 18. LIMERICK CATHEDRAL MISERICORD.

Church to be composed – namely the 'poore and pale' Lollards[60] – whilst the unnatural and deadly Griffin stands for the perceived corruption and hypocrisy of the institutionalised Church. Whilst it would be unwise to go so far as to suggest a Lollard interpretation of the Beverley misericord, if the identification of the lost models for the geese as a pelican and a griffin is correct, the fool's gestures may denote him as one who looks upon Christ's truth, yet nonetheless speaks corruptly, falsely and even dangerously. And, like Herod in the York play, he challenges the viewer – who, we must remember, would originally have been a cleric – to remain aloof from the folly of such behaviour which, as we have seen in chapter 2, was of particular concern during the post-Wyclif, pre-Reformation period.

Of necessity, failing a distinctly unlikely discovery, my hypothetical source for the Beverley carving must remain unproven. Nevertheless, as we have seen, there is certainly evidence for the Beverley carvers freely adapting motifs from elsewhere in the north of England. Furthermore, in the case of the man pushing the woman in the barrow, there is evidence to suggest that when designs were copied they could, for whatever reason, be misunderstood. Finally, roughly contemporary textual evidence shows that the pelican and the griffin were used as symbolic protagonists in the debates concerning doctrinal interpretation that resonated at the heart of the pre-Reformation Church. As proverbial readings of the Beverley misericord suggested by Jones do not quite address all of its design elements – and one of the distinctive features of many Beverley Minster misericords is the thematic unity of main carving and supporters – it may be conjectured that

[60] *Plowman's Tale*, 1533 version, l. 69. The descriptive phrase employed here suggests connotations of the Lollard 'poor priests': see Anne Hudson, 'A Lollard Sect Vocabulary?', in *Lollards and their Books*, ed. Anne Hudson (London: Hambledon Press, 1985), pp. 170–1.

one of the now-lost carvings from one of the fragmentary series of misericords now located in the choir stalls of Bishop Tunstall's Chapel in Durham Castle may well have shown a fool flanked to his left by a pelican and to his right by a griffin. Failing to understand the didactic implications, a carver from Beverley, steeped in a culture of festive misrule, misread a sketch of the winged creatures on the supporters – itself perhaps inaccurate because of a damaged original and, indeed, the poor lighting beneath choir stalls – as proverbially foolish geese.

That a certain degree of playfulness is at work in the designs of the Beverley Minster choir stalls is undeniable. In addition to the scenes of folly to which we have already referred, a delightful misericord, with supporters showing what appear to be two apprentices thumbing their noses at the main central scene of two craftsmen who are engaged in a mock battle, perhaps expresses a degree of joy in the skill and invention of the stalls. As John Dickinson notes, the exclusively clerical prime audience of medieval misericords meant that, in comparison to images in the nave,

> the decoration contained therein could be more sophisticated in nature and more subtle in didacticism; rather than a single message, it would create multiple meanings, each overlaying the next in a manner designed to be accessible only to the more learned monk.[61]

It is unlikely that the craftsmen themselves would recognise the symbolic didacticism of many of the images which they were required to reproduce, hence the misunderstanding of my suggested model for the gurning fool and his iconographically complex supporters. Consequently, the apparent playfulness in this carving of the craftsmen is itself suggestive of the play of meaning, the battle for both articulation and comprehension, and the potential for foolishness in making such an engagement.

However, when attempting to unravel such puzzles on misericords, one sometimes suspects that it is the patrons of the stalls, along with their anonymous craftsmen, who have the last laugh at the expense of those of us who, in spite of being so temporally distant from the iconographic vocabulary which informed their work, take up their silent challenge. They are, as it were, playfully thumbing their noses at us as we attempt to interpret that which we see whilst studiously endeavouring to avoid falling into folly ourselves. And it is to one of the treacherous temptations towards folly – or worse – most feared by the medieval Church that we shall now turn.

[61] John Dickinson, *Misericords of North West England: Their Nature and Significance* (Lancaster: Centre for North-West Regional Studies, 2008), p. 5.

# 4 MASCULINITY AND POWER

The importance of the choir stalls at Ripon Minster – dated to the closing years of the fifteenth century – has long been acknowledged, in terms of the arrangement of elements, the vigour and variety of misericord carving and, as we saw in the last chapter, their influence upon subsequent work in a number of significant churches in the north of England: Beverley Minster, Manchester Cathedral, All Saints, Wensley, and the stalls now located in Bishop Tunstall's Chapel in Durham Castle.[1] However, when faced with such a bewildering iconographic richness as the Ripon stalls display, it is not uncommon for both the scholar and the more casual visitor to be unsure of where to start to explore the symbolic significance of the carvings. In order to avoid the many tempting distractions offered beneath the choir stalls, then, it is perhaps advisable to begin this chapter by focusing in the first instance upon just one small detail of the Ripon carving which is frequently overlooked by both guides and academics, but which nonetheless provides a useful stimulus to initiate a discussion of the visual demonstration of masculinity and power in the late medieval English Church, a topic which, as we shall see, was of particular concern in the pre-Reformation period. A curious visitor, captivated by the misericords and, indeed, by the fine carving throughout the choir as a whole, is very likely to miss this particular image unless it is pointed out to them by someone 'in the know'. In my case, this was done by a group of giggling choristers, a circumstance which I suspect may have been repeated on countless occasions throughout the past five centuries. For, partially obscured in one of the spandrels of the elaborate north return stall canopies – very likely one of the earliest sections of the choir woodwork to be carved – the keen eye may spot a relief carving depicting the figure of a standing cleric who gleefully raises his garments in order

[1] See J. S. Purvis, 'The Ripon Carvers and the Lost Choir-Stalls of Bridlington Priory', *Yorkshire Archaeological Journal* 29 (1929), 157–201. A more subtle reading of the stylistic evidence is explored in Charles Tracy, *English Gothic Choir-Stalls 1400–1540* (Woodbridge: Boydell Press, 1990), pp. 23–31.

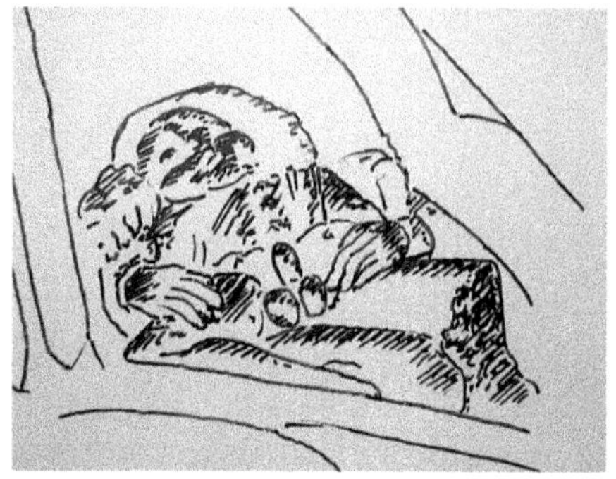

FIG. 19. RIPON MINSTER CANOPY DETAIL. ILLUSTRATION BY SIBYLLE ZIPPERER.

to expose his private parts to those who sit below (fig. 19).[2] Although he is not the only human figure to be depicted in the canopies, he is nonetheless the only one who confronts the viewer in such a forthright manner. By looking at this little figure in the context of other ecclesiastical images likely to provoke similar responses of amusement – perhaps even mixed with shock – from the modern viewer, along with some contemporary literary and non-literary texts, this chapter aims to unravel the mystery of what such an apparently scurrilous, or even scandalous, character may be doing in so lofty a position in the cathedral choir.

Although he is isolated in the canopy of the stalls of Ripon Minster, this figure is certainly not alone in the sphere of late medieval art. The male sexual organ is flagrantly displayed – occasionally even in a curiously disembodied form – in a variety of media ranging from stone sculpture to manuscript painting, by way of the numerous frankly bizarre lead badges which have been discovered throughout Europe, particularly in the Schelde estuary in the Netherlands. These latter apparently carnivalesque representations of animated genitalia, a number of which are even depicted in what seem to be coarse parodies of sacred observances, present a fascinating enigma to which we shall return later in the present chapter.[3] European choir stalls, being the site of some of the most lively decoration in late medieval art, unsurprisingly carry their own fair share of phallic images, and this is as true for England as it is elsewhere. At All Saints, Gresford, for example, an acrobat swings on a pole which is carried by three of his companions and brazenly confronts the viewer with raised and splayed legs as he draws his feet level with his ears. A sole crowned figure in St Mary, Swine, adopts a similar pose, although without even offering any evidence of an explanatory context of acrobatic performance to justify

[2] On the sequence of construction, see Charles Tracy, 'Misericords as an Interpretative Tool in the Study of Choir Stalls', in *Profane Images in Marginal Arts of the Middle Ages*, ed. Elaine C. Block with Frédéric Billiet, Sylvie Bethmont-Gallerand and Paul Hardwick (Turnhout: Brepols, 2008), pp. 6–7.

[3] Whilst mainly found in mainland Europe, a few examples have been found in England, in London and Salisbury: see A. M. Koldeweij, 'A Barefaced *Roman de la Rose* (Paris, B.N., ms. fr. 25526) and some Late Medieval Mass-Produced Badges of a Sexual Nature', in *Flanders in a European Perspective: Manuscript Illumination around 1400 in Flanders and Abroad*, eds. Maurits Smeyers and Bert Cardon (Leuven: Uitgeverij Peeters, 1995), p. 500. A broad introduction to the array of such images may be found in Malcolm Jones, *The Secret Middle Ages: Discovering the Real Medieval World* (Stroud: Sutton Publishing, 2002), pp. 248–73. See also: Malcolm Jones, 'The Secular Badges', in *Heilig en Profaan*, Rotterdam Papers 8, ed. H. J. E. van Beuningen and A. M. Koldeweij (Cothen: Stichting Middeleeuwse Religieuze en Profane Insignes, 1993), pp. 99–109; Malcolm Jones, 'The Sexual and the Secular Badges', in *Heilig en Profaan* 2, Rotterdam Papers 12, ed. H. J. E. van Beuningen, A. M. Koldeweij and D. Kicken (Cothen: Stichting Middeleeuwse Religieuze en Profane Insignes, 2001), pp. 196–206.

his genital display (see front cover). Christa Grössinger places these carvings in the context of the scatological imagery which was popular throughout Europe in the late fifteenth century and which, she suggests, was intended to stun the viewer, the juxtaposition of the face and the 'lower face' serving to provide a graphic reminder of the constant proximity of 'the deadliest of vices, the vilest of passions'.[4] Just such a juxtaposition of man's higher ideals against his lower bodily functions may be found in the English morality play *Mankind*, which can be dated to somewhere between 1464 and 1471 – that is, predating the Ripon carvings by between fifteen and thirty years – in which the disruptive devil Titivillus distracts the protagonist from his prayers by diverting his mind to altogether more physical thoughts concerning his bowels:

> Of thy preyer blin.
> Thou art holier then ever was any of thy kin.
> Arise and avent thee! Nature compels.[5]
>
> [Leave off your prayer. You are more pious than ever was any of your family. Arise and relieve yourself! Nature demands.]

Readily heeding the insinuating voice, and thus becoming satisfied with his limited show of devotion, Mankind duly abandons his beads in order to answer the call of base nature and 'do that needs must be done'.[6] Following the demands of the body is here explicitly equated with sin: his devotion forgotten, Mankind is off, as Titivillus tells us, 'to shit leasings' [lies].[7]

In the light of the view of bodily functions expressed in *Mankind*, then, Grössinger's reading of bared bottoms on misericords as acting as correctives to straying thoughts by confronting and repelling the mind with such a shocking incursion of transgressive physicality is certainly persuasive. This is perhaps even more so in cases in which the perpetrator of such an act is either an animal or a monster, thereby drawing the viewer's attention to the bestial nature of bodily functions and, as with the episode from *Mankind* cited above, creating a pointed contrast to the elevated status of spiritual works. One of the most clear representations of this can be found on a misericord in Great Malvern Priory, on which a monk is shown inserting a pair of bellows into the behind of an ape-like creature (fig. 20) – a very literal depiction of the righteous countering the unholy blasts issuing from a base

[4] Christa Grössinger, *The World Upside-Down: English Misericords* (London: Harvey Miller Publishers, 1997), pp. 73 and 109–11. For a discussion of scatology in relation to the rise – and consequent threat – of vernacular language, see Paul Hardwick, 'Talking Dirty: Vernacular Language and the Lower Body', in *The Playful Middle Ages: Meanings of Play and Plays of Meaning. Essays in Memory of Elaine C. Block*, ed. Paul Hardwick (Turnhout: Brepols, forthcoming).

[5] *Mankind*, in *Three Late Medieval Morality Plays*, ed. G. A. Lester (London: A. C. Black, 1990), ll. 558–10. On the date of the play, see pp. xiii–xiv. The relationship between intellect, spirituality and bodily evacuations in medieval thought is explored in Valerie Allen, *On Farting: Language and Laughter in the Middle Ages* (New York: Palgrave Macmillan, 2007).

[6] *Mankind*, l. 563.

[7] Ibid., l. 568.

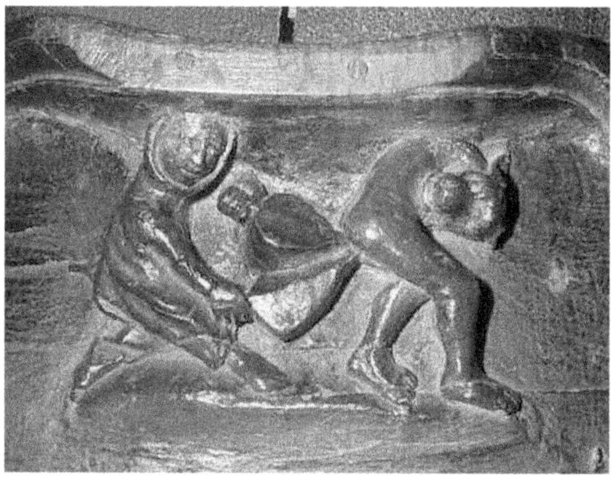

FIG. 20. GREAT MALVERN PRIORY MISERICORD.

being.[8] Nonetheless, in the case of other carvings such as, for example, those which we have already encountered in All Saints, Gresford, and St Mary, Swine, such an explanation does not account for that which they share with our figure in the Ripon canopy – the overt display of male genitalia. Consequently, we may assume that what is being placed in the foreground by such images is not the baseness of physicality as represented by the bared backside but, rather, an overtly stated masculinity. Ruth Mellinkoff has claimed that such displays – whether of male or female genitalia – should be considered as fulfilling an apotropaic function, 'driving away dark forces, including … demons',[9] but, as we shall see, the feared Other to which these carvings respond was something rather more tangible in the earthly realm than the infernal demons who are also to be found lurking in the shadows beneath the choir stalls. Such 'in your face' assertions of masculinity as may be seen at Ripon and elsewhere undoubtedly lack subtlety. Yet such broad strokes are far from uncommon on misericords – witness the monk with the bellows at Great Malvern Priory mentioned above – and this is particularly the case when treating of subjects pertaining to gender relationships in the Middle Ages, an observation which may be made not only of misericords but also of other visual media, along with various genres of contemporary literature.

Whilst the thirteenth century certainly witnessed a notable increase in the number of texts in circulation which offered praise of women and their virtues,[10] these nonetheless remained far outweighed by the vast body of misogynist writing which survives from throughout the medieval period, attesting to the widely propagated view that women more frequently followed the paradigm represented by Eve than that embodied by the Virgin Mary. These writings cite scriptural, classical, patristic and proverbial authorities in order to condemn women with charges of lust, greed, vanity

[8] This misericord is discussed in Jones, *Secret Middle Ages*, pp. 292–3.

[9] Ruth Mellinkoff, *Averting Demons: The Protective Power of Medieval Visual Motifs and Themes*, 2 vols. (Los Angeles: Ruth Mellinkoff Publications, 2004), I, 137. The central thesis of Mellinkoff's study is that demons formed the intended audience for much grotesque and other marginal art of the Middle Ages. Whilst certainly stimulating, the discussion frequently suffers from an approach which is as '[b]iased and subjective' (p. 124) as that of other scholars whom she dismisses, rather weakening the overall argument. An informed and balanced critical response may be found in Malcolm Jones's review of the book in *Profane Images in the Marginal Arts of the Middle Ages*, ed. Block *et al.*, pp. 339–63.

[10] C. M. Kauffmann, *Biblical Imagery in Medieval England 700–1550* (London: Harvey Miller Publishers, 2003), pp. 154–6, points to the influence of this upon biblical subjects illustrated in manuscripts.

and, perhaps most seriously of all, attempting to usurp the God-given role of men.[11] When we turn to themes relating to gender issues in misericord carvings, women fare even worse than they do in literature, finding even fewer defenders than in written sources; when we come to consider these images in the most sacred space of the church, it appears that we have, to appropriate the Wife of Bath's famous phrase, an even more restricted group of 'lion painters':

> Who peyntede the leon, tel me who?
> By God, if wommen hadde writen stories,
> As clerkes han withinne hire oratories,
> They wolde han writen of men moore wikkednesse
> Than al the mark of Adam may redress.[12]

> [Who painted the lion, tell me who? By God, if women had written stories like clerks have in their chapels, they would have written more of men's wickedness than all those in Adam's image may redress.]

Although specifically railing against widely circulated misogynist polemic by the likes of St Jerome and Theophrastus, Alison of Bath could well have made these same observations concerning contemporary male carvers and their male, clerical patrons, themselves, of course, steeped in this very same textual culture. Indeed, even on the rare occasions when we encounter what may at first seem to be a positive exemplar of women on misericords, interpretations are generally far from unequivocal. John Dickinson, for example, comments upon a misericord in St Mary, Nantwich – roughly contemporary with Chaucer's Wife of Bath – the main carving of which depicts a seated widow, identifiable by her head-dress, who studies an open book which she rests in her lap (fig. 21):

> What is clear is that she is a good and obedient woman. First because she is reading, itself still relatively rare among women, and primarily found among those who have had some interaction with a convent. Second, because in both the left and right hand supporters there are further examples of obedience; in the left a falcon waits patiently on a branch, while on the right a dog obediently sits up holding an object in its mouth.[13]

[11] An excellent introduction to these texts is Alcuin Blamires (ed.), *Woman Defamed and Woman Defended* (Oxford: Clarendon Press, 1992).

[12] Geoffrey Chaucer, *The Canterbury Tales*, III (D) 692–6, in *The Riverside Chaucer*, ed. Larry D. Benson (Oxford: Oxford University Press, 1988). A misericord in Chichester Cathedral, pre-dating Chaucer's *Canterbury Tales* by some half a century, shows a woman slaying a lion with a sword. Whilst the iconography most likely alludes to a reversal of 'natural' gender roles, one cannot help but wonder if Chaucer was familiar with the decoration of this south-east English church.

[13] John Dickinson, *Misericords of North West England: Their Nature and Significance* (Lancaster: Centre for North-West Regional Studies, 2008), p. 48. On the dating of the Nantwich stalls, see pp. 38–9.

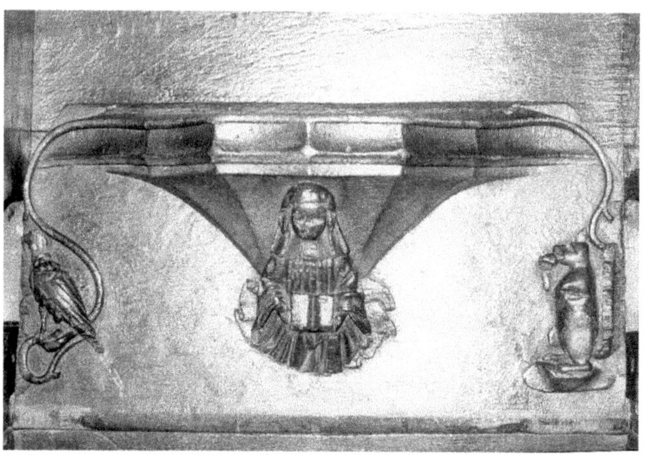

FIG. 21. ST MARY, NANTWICH MISERICORD.

This is a persuasive suggestion if the right-hand supporter is indeed a dog. However, such an identification is far from certain, the beast more closely resembling a fox, apparently dressed in some sort of clerical garb; in which case, this is a far from obedient creature who we shall meet again in chapter 5, where we shall also encounter devotional texts in which the falcon is employed as a symbol of the sort of prideful self-regard which should be shunned by good Christians.[14] As for the 'object' held in the beast's mouth, whilst this is now damaged, it seems to me that the remaining fragments suggest an unfortunate bird which, in common with a number of such hapless victims whom we shall also encounter later, has fallen prey to this wily predator. If, therefore, we accept this alternative reading, rather than seeing a pious, obedient widow poring diligently over her psalter or primer, we witness a proud, treacherous widow who is brazenly appropriating the authoritative texts which should be the sole preserve of the male clergy: the very model, in fact, of Chaucer's Alison of Bath. Likewise, an image in Winchester Cathedral of a reclining woman with a book, flanked in the supporters by Adam and Eve amongst oak leaves, can, as Paulette E. Barton observes, be interpreted as 'either disparaging the pursuit of knowledge or an approval of the pursuit of learning through reading on the part of women'.[15] Whilst the latter is a possibility, the explicit reference to the consequences of Eve's disobedient consumption of the forbidden fruit of the tree of knowledge – not to mention the image's occurrence in the all-male preserve of the Winchester choir – surely renders the former reading far more likely than the latter.

As we saw in chapter 2, very few unequivocally identifiable biblical or related scenes survive on English choir stalls. Of those which remain, only a surprisingly small number illustrate the perfidy of women.[16] Apart from

[14] Whilst the falcon indeed appears to be sitting patiently on a branch, I consider that its position – with its back to the central figure of the widow, even though an inward-facing stance would provide a more balanced overall composition – further militates against reading the image as one denoting obedience.

[15] Paulette E. Barton, *Mercy and the Misericord in Late Medieval England: Cathedral Theology and Architecture* (Lewiston: Edwin Mellen Press, 2009), p. 190.

[16] Indeed, as Elaine Block has noted, throughout Europe, 'men and beasts far outnumber the women depicted on … misericords': Elaine C. Block, 'Half Angel – Half Beast: Images of Women on Misericords', *Reinardus* 5 (1992), 17.

the images of Adam and Eve which have already been mentioned, in Gloucester Cathedral we may see Delilah taking her shears to the hair of the sleeping Samson, and on a misericord in Ely Cathedral may be found a sequence of scenes across the supporters and the main console in which Herodias's daughter performs her notorious dance at the banquet, is handed the head of John the Baptist by his gaoler, and finally presents the severed head to her mother on a platter. Such examples of the ways in which great men of the past have met their ends through the wiles of evil women are familiar from contemporary misogynist polemic both within and outside of the Church. Although openly acknowledging that he has been duped by the fox, for example, King Noble in Caxton's *History of Reynard the Fox* may nonetheless assert that 'my wyf is cause therof',[17] whilst Gawain's sudden rude awakening to his imperfect nature at the Green Chapel at the climax of *Sir Gawain and the Green Knight* prompts a largely unprovoked vituperative outpouring concerning the 'wyles of wymmen':

> For so was Adam in erde with one bygyled,
> And Salamon with fele sere, and Samson eftsones –
> Dalyda dalt hym hys wyrde – and Davyth therafter
> Was blended with Barsabe, that much bale tholed.
> Now these were wrathed with her wyles, hit were a wynne huge
> To luf hom wel and leve hem not, a leude that couthe.[18]
>
> [For so was Adam in truth beguiled by one, and Solomon with a great many, and Samson afterwards – Delilah dealt him his fate – and afterwards David was blinded by Bathsheba, enduring great misery. Now as these were brought low by their wiles, it would be a great gain for a man who knew how to love them well and not believe them.]

Gawain's examples drawn from scripture are representative of a repertoire of stock characters from which the polemicist could pick, apparently at random, in order to demonstrate the ways in which women are invariably the root cause of the unwary man's inevitable downfall. Such use, we may imagine, would have been made of the women carved beneath the choir stalls.

As noted above, biblical exemplars on misericords, as far as surviving evidence suggests, were in short supply. Even if we extend our scope to include apocryphal stories such as the ale-wife carried to Hell in St Lawrence, Ludlow, which we encountered in chapter 1, pickings are still slim. Yet the opportunities offered for misogynist extemporisation by the relatively small number of wicked biblical women depicted on misericords are considerably increased when one casts one's net further afield and, indeed, more specifically when one casts one's net over the side of a boat.

[17] William Caxton, *The History of Reynard the Fox*, ed. Edward Arber (London: English Scholar's Library, 1878), p. 53.
[18] *Sir Gawain and the Green Knight*, in *Sir Gawain and the Green Knight, Pearl, Cleanness, Patience*, ed. J. J. Anderson (London: J. M. Dent, 1996), ll. 2416–21.

For, of the multitude of fantastic creatures which inhabit English choir stalls, few are represented with such frequency as the siren, whether in the form of a cross between a woman and a bird or as the much more common woman/fish hybrid.[19] The forms were largely interchangeable by the fourteenth century, and the conflated image of the avian temptress of Greek legend and the half-fish figure of the mermaid is graphically displayed in MS Bodley 764, in which sirens are described as 'deadly creatures, which from the head down to the navel are like men, but their lower parts down to their feet are like birds', whilst the accompanying illustration depicts sailors lulled to sleep by fish-tailed mermaids.[20] This mutability between the two already hybrid forms may also be seen on a misericord in Carlisle Cathedral, on which a siren is carved with both claws and feathers as well as the tail of a fish (fig. 22). Whatever form she took, however, the siren symbolised the lure of vain pleasures which conspire to draw 'ignorant and imprudent men to their death'.[21] In medieval visual representations of the siren, this is a lure which is explicitly sexualised,[22] and Anthony Weir and James Jerman have gone so far as to suggest a kinship between the twin-tailed mermaids of the kind which may be found in Cartmel Priory and the splayed-legged, vulva-exposing Sheela-na-gig carvings which enigmatically inhabit the lofty reaches of numerous medieval church exteriors.[23] Even in the much more common examples of the mermaid with a single tail, the bared breasts and unbound hair attest to the temptation offered by the female, whilst the frequently depicted comb and mirror speak of both feminine vanity and the deliberate artifice of the deceptive surface beauty which lures the unwary

[19] Of more than forty sirens carved on misericords throughout the country, around three-quarters depict mermaids. On the conflation of the two forms in the later Middle Ages, see Beryl Rowland, *Animals with Human Faces: A Guide to Animal Symbolism* (London: George Allen and Unwin, 1973), pp. 139–41. A comprehensive discussion of the development of the siren/mermaid symbol may be found in Jacqueline Leclercq-Marx, *La Sirène dans la pensée et dans l'art de l'Antiquité et du Moyen Age: Du mythe païen au symbole Chrétien* (Brussels: Académie Royale de Belgique, 1997).

[20] See Richard Barber (ed. and trans.), *Bestiary, Being an English Version of the Bodleian Library, Oxford MS Bodley 764* (Woodbridge: The Boydell Press, 1999), p. 150.

[21] Ibid., p. 150.

[22] On the evolution of the siren as a sexual temptress, see Luuk Houwen, 'Sex, Songs and Sirens: A New Score for an Old Song', *The Profane Arts of the Middle Ages* 5.i (1996), 103–21.

[23] Anthony Weir and James Jerman, *Images of Lust: Sexual Carvings on Medieval Churches* (London: B. T. Batsford Ltd., 1986), pp. 51–3. As Terry Pearson notes, whilst the two-tailed mermaid is more common in mainland Europe, it is extremely rare on English misericords, with the only survival other than Cartmel Priory being in the church of Mary Magdalene, Leintwardine: Terry Pearson, 'The Mermaid in the Church', in *Profane Images in the Marginal Arts of the Middle Ages*, ed. Block *et al.*, p. 119. The Sheela-na-gig carvings (none of which appear on English misericords) have themselves suggested numerous, often mutually exclusive, interpretations from pagan fertility goddess to Christian symbol of lust: these are addressed in Barbara Freitag, *Sheela-na-gigs: Unravelling an Enigma* (London: Routledge, 2004), esp. pp. 16–51. As Michael Camille notes, representations of women exposing themselves are much less common than those of men: Michael Camille, 'Dr Witkowski's Anus: French Doctors, German Homosexuals and the Obscene in Medieval Church Art', in *Medieval Obscenities*, ed. Nicola McDonald (Woodbridge: York Medieval Press, 2006), p. 20.

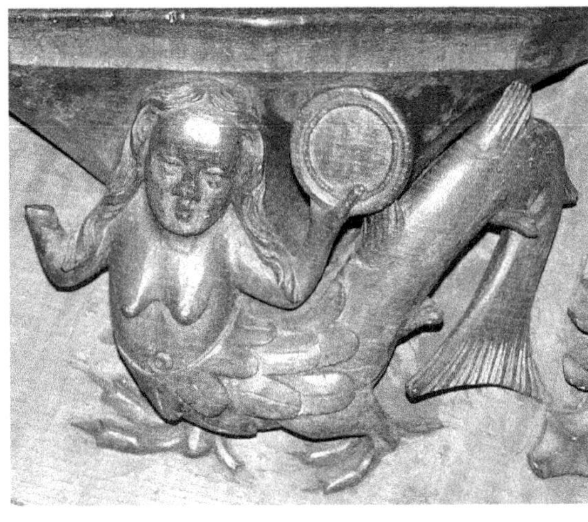

FIG. 22. CARLISLE CATHEDRAL MISERICORD.

and which has subsequently become the prime focus of the mermaid of secular folklore.[24] The didactic, admonitory import of this alluring seductress within the specifically male confines of the liturgical choir is probably clear enough to require no further elaboration.

A frankly unequivocal scene of the lure of the flesh may be seen on a misericord in King Henry VII's Chapel, Westminster Abbey, whereon an old man is depicted paying for the sexual favours of a young woman in a low-cut dress.[25] In this scene, derived from an engraving by Albrecht Dürer,[26] the would-be lover embraces the woman with his right arm whilst he plunges the fingers of his left hand suggestively into his purse, the purse being a common metaphor for the vulva in many European vernaculars.[27] This direct and unadorned image of prostitution is perhaps indicative of the seriousness of the subject, a seriousness which is reflected in the fifteenth-century French *Danse Macabre des Femmes*, a variant of the *Dance of Death* tradition we encountered in chapter 2, in which, as the title suggests, the moralisations are specifically applied to different categories of women. Of all the women who are addressed in this text, ranging across the social spectrum from queen to commoner, the witch and the whore are the only two figures to whom Death speaks in an admonitory tone, chiding the whore:

Femme de petite value
Mal vivant en charnalite
Mene avez vie dissolue
En tout temps yver et este
Aiez le cueur espouente
Car vous serez de pres tenue
Pour mal faire on est tourmente
Pehe nuist quant on continue

[24] On the mermaid in English folklore, see Jennifer Westwood and Jacqueline Simpson, *The Lore of the Land: A Guide to England's Legends, from Spring-Heeled Jack to the Witches of Warboys* (London: Penguin Books, 2005), especially pp. 120–1

[25] As well as representing prostitution, this image may also be considered as an example of the broad strain of satire aimed at the follies of the old, which is discussed in Christa Grössinger, 'The Foolishness of Old Age', in *The Playful Middle Ages*, ed. Hardwick.

[26] Grössinger, *The World Upside-Down*, pp. 67–8.

[27] Michael Camille, *The Medieval Art of Love: Objects and Subjects of Desire* (New York: Harry N. Abrams, 1998), pp. 18 and 64–5.

[Worthless woman
Living in carnal sin,
You have led a dissolute life
In every season, winter and summer.
Feel terror in your heart,
For you will be held tight.
One is tormented for doing bad things.
When one keeps doing it, sin is harmful.][28]

However, whilst women were seen as constantly presenting a temptation to be resisted by man, it was of course widely accepted – particularly, we may assume, amongst a celibate male clergy – that it was because of woman's own susceptibility to temptation that mankind had initially been cast out from the Garden of Eden. In consequence, all women were considered to be Eve's direct descendants and, therefore, tainted with her flaws, from the lust and vanity represented in the image of the mermaid to the gossiping and rebelliousness to which we shall shortly turn. The significance of this Fall from Paradise as a result of Eve's womanly weakness and wilfulness is reflected in the fact that, as noted above, it is one of the few biblical narratives of which there is more than one depiction to be found on English misericords;[29] and because of Eve's initial temptation by the Devil, woman was seen as perpetually susceptible to further diabolic manipulation. This is strikingly represented on a misericord in Ely Cathedral, on which we once more meet the devil Tutivillus, whom we encountered earlier leading Mankind astray (fig. 23).[30]

FIG. 23. ELY CATHEDRAL MISERICORD.

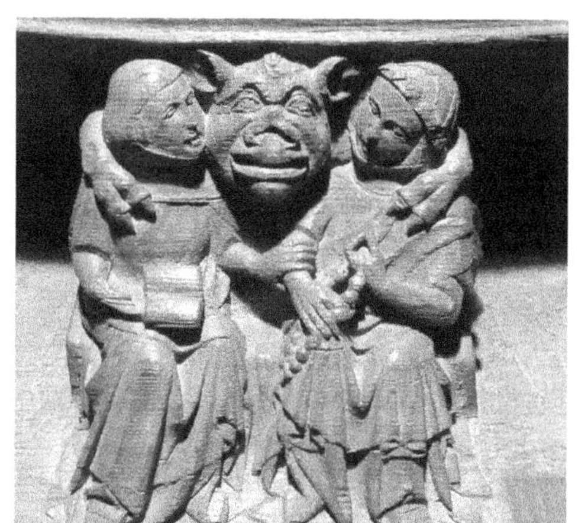

The first mention of this then-unnamed devil occurs in Jacques de Vitry's *Sermones Vulgares*, written in the first quarter of the thirteenth century, in which we are told that:

[28] Text and translation from *The Danse Macabre of Women: Ms. Fr. 995 of the Bibliothèque Nationale*, ed. Ann Tukey Harrison with a chapter by Sandra L. Hindman (Kent, OH: Kent State University Press, 1994), p. 102.

[29] As well as the Winchester Cathedral example discussed above, the Temptation also appears in: St Mary's, Blackburn; Bristol Cathedral; Ely Cathedral; and Worcester Cathedral. All except Bristol Cathedral also show the Expulsion, whilst Ely and Worcester additionally have images of Adam digging and Eve spinning.

[30] The spelling of the devil's name varies between Titivillus and Tutivillus; rather than attempt to impose consistency, I shall adopt the spelling used in whichever source is currently under discussion.

> A certain holy man, while in the choir, saw the devil loaded down with a full sack. He adjured the devil to tell him what he was carrying, and the devil replied that the sack was full of syllables and words and verses of the psalms abbreviated or omitted by the clergy during that service.[31]

As we can see here, Tutivillus's original victims were the clergy, and he was not initially responsible for leading his victims astray, merely being responsible for collecting the 'abbreviated or omitted' words of negligent clerics as they rushed carelessly through the Mass. This concern with the suitability of clerics to carry out their duties had recently been explicitly addressed in the tenth decree of the Fourth Lateran Council of 1215, which asserted that:

> generali constitutione sancimus, ut episcopi viros idoneos ad sanctæ prædicationis officium salubriter exequendum assumant, potentes in opere & dermone, qui plebes commisias, vice ipsorum, cum per se idem nequiverint, solicite visitantes, eas verbo ædificent & exemplo, quibus ipsi, cum indiguerint, congrue necessaria ministrent, ne pro necessariorum defectu compellantur desistere ab incæpto.[32]
>
> [We by a general constitution decree that bishops are to choose men effective in action and speech, suitable for executing the office of sacred preaching to advantage, to visit zealously the peoples committed to them in their place when they themselves cannot and edify them by word and example, and they are to furnish these men, when they need them, with what is appropriate and necessary lest for lack of the things necessary they be forced to abandon an undertaking.[33]]

It is appropriate, then, that we should find representations of Tutivillus located in the very devotional heart of the church, offering a tangible reminder of the need for effective speech in discharging clerical responsibilities.[34] However, although he was initially a figure of clerical self-admonishment and correction, the role of Tutivillus soon expanded into that of collector of all inappropriate words spoken in the church, in

[31] *The Exempla or Illustrative Stories from the 'Sermones vulgares' of Jacques de Vitry*, ed. and trans. Thomas F. Crane (London: Nutt, 1890), ch. Xix, fol. 20r.

[32] *Concilium Lateranese* IV, p. 998.

[33] Translation from Harry Rothwell (ed.), *English Historical Documents: 1189–1327* (London: Eyre and Spottiswoode, 1975), pp. 650–1.

[34] As Christa Grössinger notes, the first known representation of Tutivillus is on a carved arm-rest at the entrance to the choir of Bonn Minster, where he is already depicted as writing on a scroll – the activity which, as we shall see below, was to become his usual attribute. This carving is dated c.1220, very close to the composition of Jacques de Vitry's *Sermones Vulgares*. Christa Grössinger, 'Tutivillus', in *Profane Images in the Marginal Arts of the Middle Ages*, ed. Block *et al.*, p. 49. It is interesting to note that in the carving of the ale-wife being carried to Hell in St Lawrence, Ludlow, a supporter shows Tutivillus and his scroll – in this case longer than his body – presumably bearing his record of the countless sins for which she cannot be pardoned.

particular, as time progressed, those spoken by women.[35] In addition to matters relating to clerical reform, a major emphasis of the decrees of the Fourth Lateran Council had been upon the promotion and examination of lay piety. In carrying out this programme, thereby broadening the scope of lay religious understanding, encouraging a direct, affective religious experience, and promoting the spiritual self-awareness necessary for thorough confession, the Church unwittingly empowered what has been characterised as a 'new and cantankerous type of educated or half-educated laity'.[36] As we have seen throughout this study, by the fourteenth century, elements of the laity knew too much to accept the Church as it stood, fuelling vernacular anticlericalism and, ultimately, the Lollard heresy and later reform movements. This effective lay appropriation of devotional discourse was perhaps at its most threatening when it spread to that most marginalised sector of late medieval society: women. Indeed, as Alcuin Blamires has noted, at its most extreme, a dissociation of oneself from 'the disparagement of women implicit in orthodoxy' could in itself be considered a hallmark of heterodoxy.[37] Thus the proliferation of wall paintings, stained glass and misericords depicting Tutivillus – particularly in relation to women – throughout the church may be read as evidence of growing anxiety at the threat posed by the laity to clerical authority, with the original iconography of clerical self-correction becoming recast in a defensive 'closing of ranks' against mounting external pressures.

The Ely misericord depicts Tutivillus embracing two women who gossip when they should be attending to their prayers, as is indicated by the book and rosary that lie unattended in their laps. It has been suggested that the right supporter shows the devil recording their gossip on the scroll which became his prime iconographic attribute, in order that it may be presented as evidence on Judgement Day, while the left supporter illustrates an exemplary anecdote recorded by, amongst others, Robert Mannyng, in which a priest explains why he has laughed while reading the gospel. As Mannyng's version of the story in his *Handlyng Synne* explains:

> As y redde þat yche tyde,
> Twey wymmen iangled þer bysyde.
> Bytwyxe hem two y sagh a fende
> Wyþ penne & parchemen yn hende,
> And wrote al þat eure þey spak
> Pryuyly byhynde here bak.
> Whan hys rolle was wryte al ful,
> To drawe hyt out he gan to pul,

[35] For a discussion of the development of the figure – along with his representation in the visual arts – see ibid., pp. 47–62.
[36] W. A. Pantin, *The English Church in the Fourteenth Century* (Cambridge: Cambridge University Press, 1955), p. 161. On the examination of the laity, see Thomas N. Tentler, *Sin and Confession on the Eve of the Reformation* (Princeton: Princeton University Press, 1977).
[37] Blamires (ed.), *Woman Defamed and Woman Defended*, p. 250.

Wyþ hys teþe he gan to drawe
And hard for to togge and gnawe,
Þat hys rolle to brast & rofe,
And hys hed agens þe wal he drofe
So hard and so ferly sore,
Whan hys parchemen was no more.[38]

[As I read that particular time, two women chattered next to each other. Between them two I saw a devil with a pen and parchment in its hand, writing all that they ever spoke secretly behind their backs. When his roll was full with writing he began to pull to stretch it out. With his teeth he began to pull on it, tugging and gnawing so hard that his roll burst and tore, and he drove his head against the wall so hard and marvellously painfully when his parchment was no more.]

The rather smug superiority inherent in the humour here is typical of contemporary misogynist polemic against the stock character of the chattering woman. However, the visual representation of the episode on the Ely misericord adds a further dimension that is not present in the written narratives as, in this vigorous scene, the devil appears not only to be stretching the parchment with his teeth, but also to be drawing forth the words from his own mouth.[39] The implicit suggestion, therefore, is that the women's speech is not simply recorded by the devil; rather, it is to the devil that it owes its origin. In gossiping rather than performing their devotional duties, then, the women are effectively carrying out the devil's actions – a process of succumbing to Tutivillus's blandishments akin to that which we have observed in *Mankind*.[40]

The misogynist theme is again addressed in St Mary, Minster-in-Thanet, in a carving that depicts the bust of a woman who proudly luxuriates in an ostentatiously decorated, horned head-dress (fig. 24). As Françoise Piponnier and Perrine Mane have noted, 'in the fifteenth century female headgear developed some extraordinary constructions',[41] and such examples of sartorial extravagance given free rein as that which is depicted in the

[38] Robert Mannyng of Brunne, *Handlyng Synne*, ed. Idelle Sullens (Binghamton, NY: Medieval and Renaissance Texts and Studies, 1983), ll. 9282–95. This association is made in Grössinger, *The World Upside-Down*, p. 80.

[39] Unfortunately, if there were ever words painted on the scroll they are now lost and were never recorded.

[40] See also a carving in the choir of St Mary, Nantwich, in which the bat-winged Tutivillus stands behind the head of a young woman, his long fingers holding her mouth open, again suggesting that he is both placing the words in her mouth and drawing them out. It is interesting to note that the earliest known carving of Tutivillus – that in Bonn Minster – whilst showing the devil in his principal act of recording, also has him with widely gaping mouth, possibly in order to bring to mind the mouth of Hell through which transgressors will be led, but equally likely, I suggest, to highlight this same aspect of devilish origin for the speech which he ultimately records.

[41] Françoise Piponnier and Perrine Mane, *Dress in the Middle Ages*, trans. Caroline Beamish (New Haven and London: Yale University Press, 1997), p. 81.

Minster-in-Thanet carving had long been focused upon in criticisms of women. A particularly lurid example may be found in an early fifteenth-century record of an anonymous woman's vision of Purgatory, in which she describes the sufferings of a nun named Margaret with whom she had been acquainted. The sufferings are inflicted upon Margaret as punishment for the vanity to which she had succumbed in life:

> And then the same devell tok wormes and pykk and tarre and made lokkes and sete tham appon hir hede, and he toke a grete longe neddir and putt all abowte hir hede and that, me thoghte, hissed in hir hede, as it had bene hote brining iryn in the colde water; and me thoghte scho cryed when scho was so arrayed, als me thoghte that alle the werlde myghte hafe herde hir.[42]

> [And the same devil took worms [serpents] and pitch and tar and made locks and set them upon her head, and he took a great, long adder and set it all around her head, and I thought that it hissed in her head as if it had been hot, burning iron in cold water; and I thought she cried when she was thus arrayed, so that I thought all the world might have heard her.]

The woman goes on to recount a sequence of further horrific punishments, each of which addresses a specific aspect of Margaret's sinful worldliness in what is a strikingly vivid and violent account of her torments. Excessive though this particular description may be, the core message of the vision concerning the sinful vanity of women is far from uncommon. For example, a rather more succinct – and considerably less graphic – fourteenth-century satire against women, known as *The Follies of Fashion*, warns simply that:

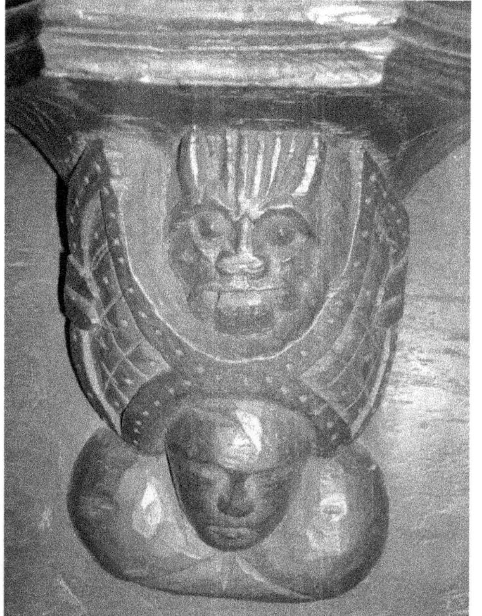

FIG. 24. ST MARY, MINSTER-IN-THANET MISERICORD.

> In helle
> Wiþ deueles he shule duelle
> For þe clogges þat cleueþ by here chelle.[43]

> [In Hell with devils she shall dwell
> because of the clumps (of hair)
> that cling to her head-dress.]

The Minster-in-Thanet carving expresses this dramatically, showing a grimacing devil of which the woman is apparently unaware nestling grimly between the horns of her

[42] *A Revelation of Purgatory*, in *Women's Writing in Middle English*, ed. Alexandra Barratt (London: Longman, 1992), p. 168.
[43] Thorlac Turville-Petre (ed.), *Alliterative Poetry of the Later Middle Ages: An Anthology* (London: Routledge, 1989), pp. 12–13, ll. 19–21.

head-dress. In making this explicit allusion to the evils inherent in concerning oneself overmuch with fashion and one's appearance, the devil is placed quite literally at the head of the woman, dominating her thoughts and actions.[44] Indeed, the horns of the head-dress themselves echo devil's horns, thereby suggesting an almost symbiotic relationship between the woman and the devil, as in the Ely carving of Tutivillus and the gossiping women discussed above.

Within the domestic sphere, of course, it was firmly believed that the head of the woman should be the man for, as the early fifteenth-century *Dives and Pauper* tells us, Eve may well have been created out of Adam's rib in order to be his equal companion,

> [b]ut when Eue synnyd, þan was woman maad soget to man, þat þe wyf schulde ben rewlyd by hyr housebound & dredyn hym & seruyn hym as felaw in loue & helper at nede & as nest solas in sorwe.[45]
>
> [but when Eve sinned, then woman was made subject to man, so that the wife should be ruled by her husband and respect him and serve him as a companion in love and helper in need and comfort in sorrow.]

This ideal, however, is rarely to be found depicted on misericords, with only the contented couple at St Mary, Ripple, whom we met in chapter 1 sharing the warmth of the fire in the coldest month of the year, providing a rare – possibly unique – vignette of domestic concord. Indeed, it is perhaps the only exception to Dorothy and Henry Kraus's observation that, on misericords throughout Europe, 'at best, woman was an incorrigible scold, man her long-suffering victim'.[46] The images of household discord to which they refer reflect a view propounded in many philosophical and theological works which held contemporary currency in the medieval period. For example, in one of the key texts of medieval misogynist polemic, the fourth-century *Adversus Jovinianum* which is such anathema to Chaucer's Wife of Bath, St Jerome turns to the Old Testament, amongst other sources, to authorise his argument that the wise man should not marry, asserting that:

> 'It is better to dwell in the corner of the housetop, than with a contentious woman in a shared house' (Proverbs 21:9, 25:24). If a house common to husband and wife makes a proud wife and breeds contempt for the husband, how much more if the wife is the richer of the two, and the husband only a lodger in her house! She begins to be not a wife, but mistress of the house; and if she offends her husband, they must part. 'A continual dripping of

[44] See ibid., p. 89.
[45] *Dives and Pauper*, ed. Priscilla Heath Barnum, 3 vols, EETS o.s. 280 (Oxford: Oxford University Press, 1980), I.ii, 66.
[46] Dorothy and Henry Kraus, *The Hidden World of Misericords* (London: Michael Joseph, 1976), p. 25.

> water on a wintry day' (Proverbs 27:15) turns a man out of doors, and so will a contentious woman drive a man from his own house. She floods his house with her constant nagging and daily chatter, and ousts him from his own home, that is the Church.[47]

While the scenes to which we shall now turn are apparently secular in nature, expressing the fear inherent in the writings of Jerome and others that, given the slightest opportunity, women will usurp man's authority in the home, it is worth bearing in mind Jerome's broader application of this warning to the Church rather than purely to the domestic sphere. As we have seen above, it is after all within the church that the ever-vigilant Tutivillus waits to give loquacious wives their comeuppance for their 'constant nagging and daily chatter'.

A common motif, an example of which may be found on the supporter of a misericord in Beverley Minster, is that of the man who has clearly allowed his wife to gain the upper hand in the home. Here, this role reversal is signalled by the man kneeling in his apron to wash the dishes. This is surely related in some way to the main carving of the console, which depicts a woman warming her hands at the fire while a man chases a dog that has stolen food from the cooking pot. The precise connection between the two scenes, however, is not entirely clear. Are we to read the ignominy of the man's demotion to the realm of household chores as a punishment for his negligence in watching the pot or, rather, should we reverse this causal relationship and view the domestic calamity as having arisen as a result of orderly, 'natural' domestic gender roles having been inverted and the man having allowed himself to be forced into taking on the 'woman's work' in the home?[48] This is a question to which we shall return shortly. A nearby misericord, which may even have once been adjacent,[49] is very likely a precursor in a narrative sequence, showing the dog with its head in the pot while the woman seizes the man by his hair, threatening him with her distaff. There are many such scenes throughout the country and beyond, their frequency echoing Jacques de Vitry's warning that, 'some wives are unwilling to be subject: they would rather take precedence, and they don't just despise their husbands, they lash out and beat them'.[50] A similar scene to that in Beverley, for example, can be found in Bristol Cathedral, wherein the woman grasps the man by his beard and draws back her arm to strike him with an implement which is

[47] Quoted in Blamires (ed.), *Woman Defamed and Woman Defended*, p. 67.

[48] This carving, along with other examples of such domestic role-reversal, is discussed in Malcolm Jones, *Secret Middle Ages*, pp. 233–5.

[49] A number of clearly related groups of carvings, such as the crime and punishment of a fox preacher and the capture and display of a bear, are distributed randomly across the stalls, which strongly suggests that the misericords have been re-ordered at some point since their initial installation.

[50] From *Sermones Vulgares*, quoted in Blamires (ed.), *Woman Defamed and Woman Defended*, p. 145.

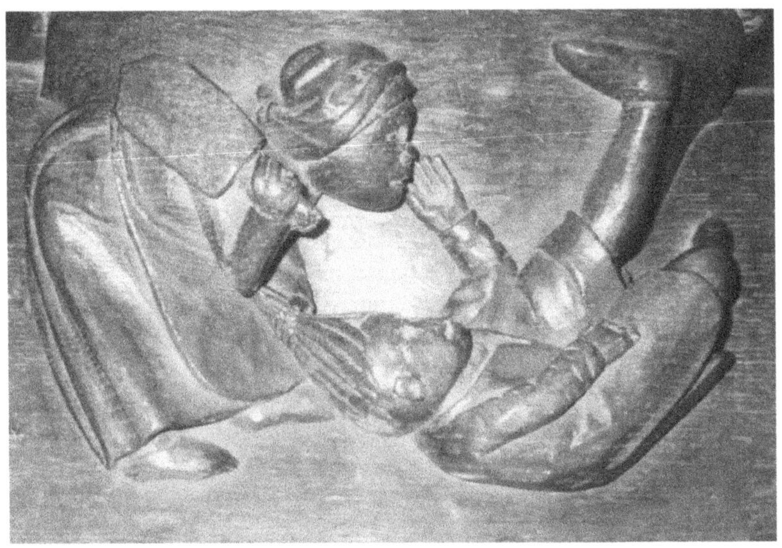

FIG. 25. ST MARY, FAIRFORD MISERICORD SUPPORTER.

now missing. The lost weapon may well, as in Beverley, have originally been a distaff – that ubiquitous iconographic signifier of domesticated medieval femininity – though elsewhere a washing beetle makes an effective weapon, as is the case in further marital altercations depicted in St Mary, Fairford (fig. 25) and Tewkesbury Abbey, in both of which the man lies prone and is firmly grasped by the hair as he helplessly takes a beating from his stern-faced mistress. The humiliation thus meted out to the man is taken to yet further extremes in a carving at Sherborne Abbey, in which the woman goes so far as to sit on her vanquished victim in a scene which, as Grössinger points out, is reminiscent of the story of Phyllis riding Aristotle, that lively and widely circulated – not to mention widely depicted – narrative demonstrating that even the wisest of men are not immune to the power of women.[51]

Whilst it is notable that it is almost always the woman who prevails when these contests are portrayed, it must be observed that the men do not always acquiesce as easily as those just described. On another carving in Ely Cathedral it certainly appears as if the woman has the upper hand in the conflict, as she is biting her opponent's thumb and apparently poking him in the eye, yet the man nonetheless possesses an air of grim determination in mounting his defence. Both figures remain resolutely upright and the contest looks far from being over. This ongoing battle of the sexes is nowhere more strikingly expressed than in an image which is not found on surviving English choir stalls, but which appears on misericords in France, Belgium and Spain, that is, the battle for who will

[51] Grössinger, *The World Upside-Down*, pp. 88–91.

wear the trousers in the household.[52] In scenes such as one which may be found in Rouen Cathedral, husband and wife appear to be locked in an equal struggle over this symbol of 'maistrie'. Elsewhere, at León Cathedral, the struggle is already over and we simply see the woman donning the hose. In keeping with the majority of representations of gender role inversion on choir stalls, when the contest is resolved these European sources invariably depict the outcome as being to the woman's advantage. Although there are no depictions of this battle for the trousers surviving in England, a related image may be found on a misericord in King Henry VII's Chapel in Westminster Abbey which we encountered in the last chapter. Here, the hapless husband, like the Beverley dish-washer we met earlier, takes on the woman's work; in this case he is winding wool as he cowers at his dominant wife's feet. It is significant that, in elaborating upon the images of domestic strife discussed earlier, this scene – itself derived from a Continental European model – shows the man's trousers pulled down, an undignified state of male humiliation which is surely a precursor to the dominant woman claiming the trousers for her own.[53] Just occasionally, however, the man may regain the upper hand, and this seems to be what happens on the Beverley carving discussed earlier. The scene of domestic chaos, flanked on the left by the man washing dishes, is flanked to the right by a supporter depicting a man pulling on his hose. We may, therefore, read the three images together as a sequential narrative, offering the viewer a cautionary reminder of the unavoidable disorder which will ensue if a man allows himself to become subservient to a woman, and thus providing a concomitant exhortation to reclaim the trousers.

In addressing these images of gender conflict, it would be reasonable to conclude that the kind of flagrant male genital display in the canopy at Ripon with which we began this chapter is indicative of male helplessness. There are most certainly no trousers in evidence on this clerical exhibitionist and it could convincingly be argued that in such a state men are not only behaving shamelessly but are also rendering themselves extremely vulnerable. However, the cleric's smiling expression appears far from threatened and he seems – unlike the grovelling and beaten husband in Westminster Abbey – fully in control of his garment. An image noted by Malcolm Jones may modify any perceptions concerning the figure being humiliated and help in the search for alternative explanations. A fifteenth-century lead badge excavated in Bruges shows two women

[52] On this motif, see Pierre Bureau, '"La dispute pour la culotte": variations littéraires et iconographiques d'un thème profane (XIII<sup>e</sup>–XVI<sup>e</sup> siècle)', *Le miroir des misericords (XIII<sup>e</sup>–XVII<sup>e</sup> siècle)*, Les Cahiers de Conques 2 (1996), 95–120, and Elaine C. Block, 'A Note on Another Fight to Wear the Pants in the Family', *The Profane Arts of the Middle Ages* 8.2 (1999), 90–9. The motif may also be found in other media: see, for example, Lène Dresen-Coenders, 'Witches as Devils' Concubines', in *Saints and She-Devils: Images of Women in the 15th and 16th Centuries*, ed. Lène Dresen-Coenders (London: The Rubicon Press, 1987), pp. 64–6.

[53] On the source of this image, see Grössinger, *The World Upside-Down*, p. 67.

flanking a huge, erect phallus, all contained within the waistband of a pair of trousers.[54] While we could read this on a superficial level as being overtly sexual, we should heed Michael Camille's warning against making the common modern mistake of 'seeing a body part as a purely sexual rather than social sign'.[55] With this caveat in mind, we may consider the phallus on the Bruges badge to carry a broader social significance, metonymically representing masculinity in general. The women, each with one hand on the phallus and the other raised with the fist clenched as they turn their heads to confront the viewer, have triumphantly gained the trousers, along with all that goes with them.[56] If we accept this reading, we may see our Ripon cleric as brazenly asserting his masculinity and, consequently, his authority. This in turn may help to explain a rather shocking image which may be found in the Priory Church of St Mary, Lancaster. Flanking a badly damaged scene which apparently depicts a meeting or confrontation between a man and an elegantly dressed woman are supporters which show: on the right, a contorted female form who, clad in nothing but a head-dress, gestures towards her backside; on the left, a seated angel who is touching his genitals or even masturbating. It has been reasonably suggested that these supporting figures could be fallen angels,[57] yet we should perhaps look beyond this to explore the possibility that – as is often the case on English misericords – they should be read as extensions of, or commentaries upon, the central scene. Indeed, each of the figures in the supporters faces the viewer and uses their free hand to gesture towards the central carving, adding weight to the suggestion that we should read them as offering interpretation of the main scene. As Caroline Walker Bynum has noted, in the Middle Ages woman was commonly seen as representing 'the physical, lustful, material, appetitive part of human nature, whereas man symbolized the spiritual or mental'.[58] So, although this main scene is damaged beyond recognition, the female grotesque could fall into the tradition which has already been noted, commenting upon the baseness of the elaborately attired woman's pride in fashion, while the angel's gestures could refer to the holy authority of the male.

Whilst speculative, such readings do find corroboration in contemporary written sources. Chaucer's Wife of Bath, for example, while superficially expounding upon the purely secular concern of marriage, commences her Prologue by taking on the unequivocally masculine role of the preacher:

[54] Jones, *Secret Middle Ages*, pp. 29 and 233.
[55] Camille, 'Dr Witkowski's Anus', p. 23.
[56] While these enigmatic badges may, as Jones suggests, be 'broadly apotropaic', I believe that this particular example may address issues relating to power and authority rather than 'sexual opportunity'. See Jones, 'Sexual and the Secular Badges', p. 200.
[57] Grössinger, *The World Upside-Down*, p. 111.
[58] Caroline Walker Bynum, *Fragmentation and Redemption: Essays on Gender and the Human Body in Medieval Religion* (New York: Zone, 1991), p. 147.

Experience, though noon auctoritee
Were in this world, is right ynogh for me
To speke of wo that is in mariage.[59]

[Experience, though there were no written authorities in this world, is surely enough for me to speak of the woe that is in marriage.]

If we accept the view that the Wife's Prologue follows the Man of Law's Epilogue,[60] she adopts her preaching stance immediately after the 'Shipman' has denied the right of the Parson, accused by the Host of Lollardy, to preach.[61] Leaving aside questions of the Wife of Bath's possible Lollardy,[62] the way in which she claims authority through personal experience, rather than through written validation, is paradoxically reminiscent of the doctrinally authoritative strategies employed in contemporary preaching, in which 'comen experiens' could be cited in order to augment scriptural and patristic 'authorities'.[63] Certainly, Chaucer's Friar tacitly acknowledges the Wife's appropriation of masculine, clerical authority in his riposte to her *Tale*:

'Dame,' quod he, 'God yeve yow right good lyf!
Ye han heer touched, also moot I thee,
In scole-mater greet difficultee.
Ye han seyd muche thyng right wel, I seye;
But, dame, heere as we ryde by the weye,
Us nedeth nat to speken but of game,
And lete auctoritees, on Goddes name,
To prechyng and to scoles of clergye.
But if it lyke to this compaignye,
I wol yow of a somonour telle a game.'[64]

['Madam,' he said, 'God give you an exceptionally good life! You have here touched upon, as I may thrive, difficult points of scholarly debate. You have expressed many things astutely, I declare; but,

[59] Chaucer, *Canterbury Tales*, III (D) 1–3.
[60] See N. F. Blake, *The Textual Tradition of the Canterbury Tales* (London: Edward Arnold, 1985), p. 195 for a summary of the occurrences of this exchange in surviving manuscripts. For further discussion of the placing of this passage, see *Riverside Chaucer*, p. 862. I feel that the appropriateness of this interlude to the issues of authority raised in fragment III lends weight to the argument for placing it immediately before this group.
[61] For manuscript variants which attribute this speech to the Wife of Bath, the Summoner or the Squire, see *Riverside Chaucer*, p. 1126, and Blake, *Textual Tradition*, p. 195. It may be significant in this case to note that the portraits of the Wife of Bath and the Parson are placed side by side in the *General Prologue*, suggesting that the reader should be attuned to comparisons between these two pilgrims.
[62] This subject is discussed in Alcuin Blamires, 'The Wife of Bath and Lollardy', *Medium Ævum* 58 (1985), 224–42.
[63] D. M. Grisdale (ed.), *Three Middle English Sermons from the Worcester Chapter Manuscript F.10* (Leeds: Leeds School of English, 1939), p. 77. Further instances are given in Siegfried Wenzel, 'Chaucer and the Language of Contemporary Preaching', *Studies in Philology* 73 (1976), 151–2.
[64] *Canterbury Tales*, III (D) 1270–9.

> madam, here as we ride along our way we do not need to speak of anything but game, and leave the quoting of authorities, on God's name, to preaching and to schools of clerks. But if this company likes, I will tell you a light-hearted story about a summoner.']

The Friar clearly recognises a skilled professional rival. In his measured response, the Wife's erudition is acknowledged but deemed inappropriate, as such topics should be left to 'prechyng and to scoles of clergye', effectively, self-proclaimed 'maisters' such as the Friar himself.[65] Indeed, in spite of his expressed views upon the inappropriateness of preaching in the current circumstances, he readily adopts the role of the preacher at the close of his own *Tale*, thereby evincing an anxious haste to reclaim this role for himself.[66]

Tellingly, it is the ambiguously gendered Pardoner, that immoral 'noble ecclesiaste',[67] who voices his approval of the Wife of Bath. Their exchange, where he commends her in strikingly similar terms to those in which he himself is described – '[y]e been a noble prechour in this cas' – carries an air of good-natured complicity.[68] Questions of the Pardoner's much debated sexuality may be left to others,[69] but it should be noted in passing that the nearest we have to a contemporary reader's response to the Pardoner, the so-called *Canterbury Interlude* that prefaces *The Tale of Beryn* in a fifteenth-century continuation of the *Canterbury Tales*, depicts him as unequivocally heterosexual as he is comically thwarted in his schemes for a nocturnal tryst with Kit the tapster.[70] For this continuator, at least, Chaucer's description of the Pardoner as 'a geldyng or a mare' is overlooked in terms of his sexual preferences and activities,[71] yet he is nonetheless markedly unsuitable for the clergy. Indeed, the reader is more likely to be reminded of the Pardoner's own self-revelation of performing in church '*lyk* a clerk';[72] like the Wife of

[65] Of course, in the *General Prologue*, I (A) 261, Friar Huberd is said to be '*lyk* a maister or a pope', suggesting inappropriate pretensions above his station. Such ambiguities acknowledged, however, I believe that his discomfort at the Wife's encroachment upon his territory remains symptomatic of wider clerical concerns which are scrutinised by Chaucer through his characteristic twin lenses of acuity and ambiguity.

[66] Chaucer's use of a quotation from Psalm 10 – 'The leoun sit in his awayt always / To sle the innocent, if that he may': *Canterbury Tales*, III (D) 1657–8 – at the close of the *Friar's Tale* is surely intended as an echo of, and riposte to, the Wife's earlier reference to the painting of lions.

[67] *Canterbury Tales*, I (A) 708.

[68] *Canterbury Tales*, III (D) 165. Frank V. Cespedes, 'Chaucer's Pardoner and Preaching', *English Literary History* 44 (1977), 1–18, while defining both characters as 'noble prechours', argues that there is an implied conflict between the two. In view of the dramatic interaction within the fragment, I feel that the absence of a contesting *Pardoner's Tale* at this point lends support to the reading of complicity.

[69] The most influential discussion is Monica E. McAlpine, 'The Pardoner's Homosexuality and How It Matters', *PMLA* 95 (1980), 8–22. See also Robert S. Sturges, *Chaucer's Pardoner and Gender Theory: Bodies of Discourse* (London: Macmillan, 2000).

[70] The *Canterbury Interlude* may be found in John M. Bowers (ed.), *The Canterbury Tales: Fifteenth-Century Continuations and Additions* (Kalamazoo: TEAMS, 1992), pp. 55–79.

[71] *Canterbury Tales*, I (A) 691.

[72] *Canterbury Tales*, VI (C) 391. My emphasis.

Bath, he claims inappropriate 'maistrie' and authority. Could the jibe at the Pardoner's biological masculinity, then, be a comment not upon his relationship to women, but rather upon his failings with regard to divinely ordained masculine authority?

Alcuin Blamires has noted that '[i]t is an exaggeration, but not a crazy one, to assert that "in the misogynistic thinking of the Middle Ages, there can, in fact, be no distinction between the theological and the gynaecological"'.[73] Taking this into consideration, then, the ostensibly sexual aspects of Chaucer's discussion of his Wife of Bath and Pardoner may be seen in fact as only a part of a wider discussion of, and concern with, (masculine) authority. We should remember that St Jerome, with whom the Wife of Bath takes such vehement issue, warns of the dominating woman ousting man 'from his own home, *that is the Church*'.[74] As Malcolm Jones has noted, '[t]he World Turned Upside Down in terms of gender roles was a common male fear in the Middle Ages',[75] and nowhere was this more so than in the Church, a situation which Chaucer clearly addresses in the Wife of Bath's Prologue and in her interaction with her fellow pilgrims. Away from the world of fiction, we may see this same anxiety expressed in responses to figures such Margery Kempe, who around August/September 1417 was accused by the Mayor of Leicester of being 'a fals strumpet, a fals loller, & a fals deceyuer of þe pepyl' – sexual impropriety apparently assumed to be part and parcel of her transgressive speech and behaviour – accusations which would later lead to demands by associates of the Archbishop of York that she should be burned as a heretic.[76] The threat posed by Margery is succinctly articulated by the archbishop's clerks, who acknowledge that:

> We knowyn wel þat sche can þe Articles of þe Feith, but we wil not suffyr hir to dwellyn a-mong vs, for þe pepil hath gret feyth in her dalyawnce, and perauentur sche myth peruertyn summe of hem.[77]
>
> [We know well that she understands the articles of the faith, but we will not permit her to live among us, for the people have great faith in her conversation, and perhaps she might lead some of them astray.]

Whilst it is right and proper for a woman to have the knowledge to be a good Christian, to speak of such things to others is potentially threatening to the *status quo*: as she is informed by the men she encounters on her subsequent journey to Beverley, it is altogether preferable that she should abandon her

[73] Blamires (ed.), *Woman Defamed and Woman Defended*, p. 3. Blamires is here qualifying a statement originally made in R. Howard Bloch, 'Medieval Misogyny', *Representations* 20 (1987), 20.

[74] Quoted in Blamires (ed.), *Woman Defamed and Woman Defended*, p. 67. My italics.

[75] Jones, *Secret Middle Ages*, p. 242.

[76] *The Book of Margery Kempe*, ed. Sanford Brown Meech and Hope Emily Allen, EETS o. s. 212 (Oxford: Oxford University Press, 1886), pp. 112 and 123–4.

[77] Ibid., p. 125.

peregrinations and 'go spynne & carde as oþer women don',[78] those quintessentially feminine activities to which our hen-pecked husbands on misericords have demeaningly lowered themselves. Whilst Margery was able to counter these accusations of heterodoxy through asserting that as she did not enter the pulpit, she did not actually preach,[79] others were still more outspoken, such as the Lollard Walter Brut, who went so far as to propose that, '"any Christian without sin, even a woman" could consecrate the body of Christ'.[80] These are but two of the more famous cases, but it is surely this anxiety about 'unruly' women which also lies behind the images of male genital display with which we began this chapter; they represent a 'naked', as it were, assertion of masculine dominance in the architectural centre of male clerical authority.

Such an assessment may even account for what is undoubtedly one of the most outrageous misericord carvings to be found in the country or, indeed, throughout Europe: a figure in Bristol Cathedral which is coyly described by Remnant as 'ape playing pipe',[81] though this description is clearly far from accurate. This seemingly naked and unmistakably human female figure, depicted from the waist upwards emerging from stylised foliage, holds and apparently takes into her mouth a large penis with prominent testicles (fig. 26). It has been suggested that this figure is 'in total command of the male organ and therewith man's virility, which she can destroy at will',[82] although it is difficult to detect even the subtlest hint of any destructive intent present in the scene. More plausibly, Malcolm Jones has suggested that the image is a literal representation of a woman drinking from a phallic vessel – the *phallovitrobolus* – of a type that is recorded from the Roman period and earlier. Indeed, a German example survives from around 1500 and court records from 1571 relate the usage of such a vessel in a West Ham brothel.[83] Whichever reading we take, we are drawn back once again to that nagging question which is raised by so many misericords and other apparently profane ecclesiastical decorations: what is such an image doing in a church? Perhaps a clue lies in comparison with the Ely image, considered earlier, of the devil Tutivillus stretching the scroll which he clasps

FIG. 26. BRISTOL CATHEDRAL SUPPORTER.

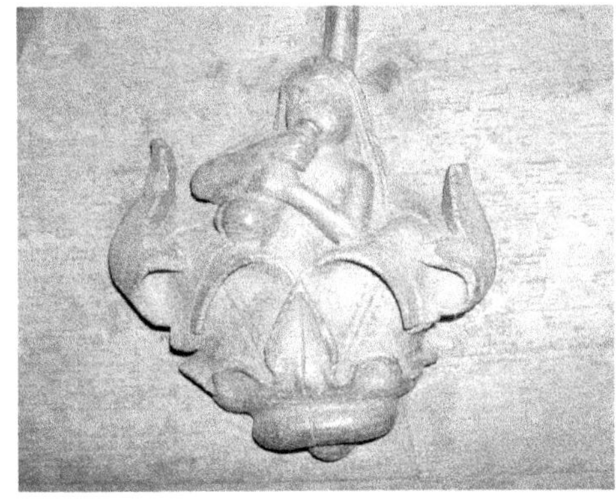

[78] Ibid., p. 129.
[79] Ibid., p. 126.
[80] On the trial of Brut, see Blamires (ed.), *Woman Defamed and Woman Defended*, pp. 250–60.
[81] G. L. Remnant, *A Catalogue of Misericords in Great Britain* (London: Oxford University Press, 1969), p. 46.
[82] Grössinger, *The World Upside-Down*, p. 112.
[83] Jones, *Secret Middle Ages*, p. 261. See also Koldeweij, 'Barefaced *Roman de la Rose*', p. 502.

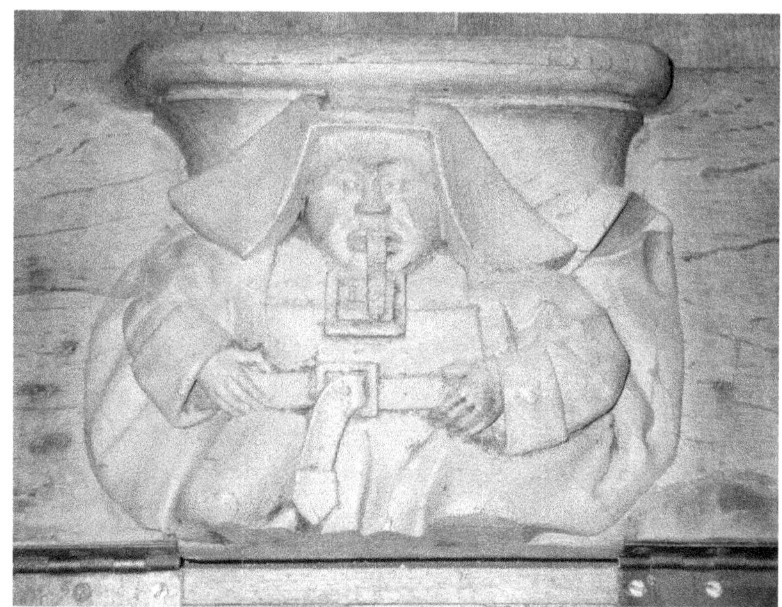

FIG. 27. SAINT-MAURILLE, PONTS-DE-CÉ MISERICORD.

firmly in his mouth. If we read the Ely devil as a condemnatory reference to women's speech, the similarly posed figure in Bristol may surely be read in the same way. Whether the object here is a drinking vessel or an actual phallus, we may look beyond what to a modern viewer may appear an overtly sexual subject and detect in this collocation of the woman's mouth and exaggerated phallic symbol the familiar clerical anxiety concerning women's appropriation of authoritative masculine discourse.[84]

Before finally returning once again to the clerical exhibitionist of Ripon, there is one more image that neatly draws together the elements which we have surveyed in this chapter. On a misericord at Saint-Maurille, Ponts-de-Cé, on the Loire, we find an image in which, somewhat uncharacteristically, a man has most assuredly asserted his authority. There can be no more frank representation of the silencing of women than this carving of Sainte Babille – the spurious Saint Chatterer – who is here depicted with her mouth securely padlocked (fig. 27).[85] The padlocked mouth is a widespread visual trope of the admonition to women to remain silent throughout the Middle Ages and Early Modern periods. Indeed, in schematic representations of 'good women' throughout Europe – such as the German Anton Woensam's woodcut *The Wise Woman* of c.1525 – the locked lips combine with a whole range of unambiguous iconographic signs which promote piety, fidelity and

[84] It is interesting to note that the central carving of this misericord shows that master of devious speech Reynard the Fox as he is led to the gallows.

[85] On Sainte Babille, see Jacques E. Merceron, *Dictionnaire des Saints Imaginaires et Facétieux* (Paris: Seuil, 2002), pp. 349–51.

all the other desirable virtues thought appropriate to medieval woman.[86] The Saint-Maurille misericord, however, ostensibly shows only the command to silence. Yet of equal significance to the lock is the belt worn by the figure, the drooping end of which clearly recalls a limp phallus: if we can silence the virago, it seems to suggest, her appropriated virility will be lost. In this, of course, she is as far removed as it is possible to be from our Ripon cleric, high above the liturgical heart of the church which he proudly surveys, brazenly attesting to unequivocal masculine doctrinal authority.

In the light of the foregoing discussion we may, then, read these images of masculine genital display as coarse expressions of male power and authority within the Church at a time during which more lay women were gaining access to devotional texts, as satirised by Chaucer's Wife of Bath and depicted in the misericord carving of the reading widow at St Mary, Nantwich. Furthermore, some more extreme dissenters, crossing the line into heretical opinion, were expressing the view that these women had a status equal to that of the clergy. Such representations of masculine bravado, therefore, may – as is so often the case – stem from a real fear that this position of authority was not as unassailable as had previously been thought. If, as Mellinkoff suggests, the purpose of these images was apotropaic, their function being to 'driv[e] away dark forces',[87] it seems that the 'evil' against which they were employed was in fact no other demon than the ideologically demonised woman. As we have seen throughout our investigation of misericords so far, the turbulent state of late medieval England and its impact on the Church of the time informs not only those images which explicitly address matters of doctrine and devotion, but even those which to the modern viewer appear as unproblematic representations of contemporary life or even coarse humour. All of these carved scenes and figures acquire a symbolic resonance when we place them within a context of the concerns of their male, clerical patrons.

In both this chapter and foregoing discussions we have already been brought into contact with many images of a number of animals – such is the nature of their vigorous ubiquity on the choir stalls – and begun to see how their symbolic qualities may add a further dimension to our iconographic readings. It is, therefore, an apposite time to gather this menagerie more firmly together and, in our next chapter, focus more closely upon their important symbolic roles within the culture of the late medieval English Church.

[86] Woensam's woodcut is reproduced and discussed in Christa Grössinger, *Picturing Women in Late Medieval and Renaissance Art* (Manchester: Manchester University Press, 1997), pp. 43–5.
[87] Mellinkoff, *Averting Demons*, I, 137.

# 5 EXEMPLARY ANIMALS

As Terry O'Connor has noted, 'people's attitudes to animal bodies go right to the heart of the business of being human'.[1] To human society, animals may be workers or entertainers, pets or pests; the source of food, clothing or tools; objects of fear or comfort, revulsion or reverence. Consequently, our relationships with other species are immensely complex in a practical sense and, concomitantly, in a symbolic sense. Even today in the west, when dogs and cats are popular pets, to call someone a dog or describe them as catty is an insult, whilst a dogged determination or feline grace may be considered commendable. To consider these animals in the same class as cows or sheep – as sources for food and skins – provokes outrage. These attitudes are, as O'Connor goes on to explain,

> characteristically complex and range from the utilitarian to the highly conceptualised and culture-specific. When we consider medieval attitudes to animals ... therefore, we are tackling a fundamentally human and distinctly idiosyncratic behavioural trait.[2]

It is specifically to the 'highly conceptualised and culture-specific' aspect of man's relationship with animals that we shall now turn.

We have already encountered a number of animals and their symbolic status in our consideration of the doctrinal matters represented in misericord carvings, yet the menagerie which occupies the underside of choir stalls is far more extensive, ranging from the domestic to the exotic, the mundane to the mythical. We will consider this latter category of strange beasts more closely in the next chapter, but the current chapter shall focus upon the former category which includes the domestic dog and cat, farm animals such as pigs, sheep and cattle, the hunter's prey of hare and deer,

[1] Terry O'Connor, 'Thinking about Beastly Bodies', in *Breaking and Shaping Beastly Bodies: Animals as Material Culture in the Middle Ages*, ed. Aleksander Pluskowski (Oxford: Oxbow Books, 2007), p. 1.
[2] Ibid., p. 2.

and everyday pests such as rats and mice.[3] Of course, this does not preclude first-hand observation of less common beasts. An unusual instance of locally observed fauna, for example, is the series of carvings in Beverley Minster which show the hunt, capture and display of a bear (fig. 15). As Malcolm Jones has suggested, it is surely more than mere coincidence that the construction of the stalls in 1520 coincides with the visit of one John Grene and his tame bears to the town in the same year.[4] Whilst these animals are closely and carefully observed, other beasts of imported entertainment – those which are more exotic and less frequently seen – are rather less accurately rendered. It has been suggested, for example, that the carver of an elephant depicted in Exeter Cathedral had seen the beast presented by Louis IX to Henry III in 1255,[5] although Charles Tracy has subsequently argued that these misericords are in fact of an earlier date.[6] Regardless of specific occasion, however, if this beast was indeed based on observation, the carver – or whoever was responsible for the design from which he worked – was clearly too far back in the curious throng to get a clear view of the animal's feet, which are depicted as splayed and rather formless.[7]

What, however, is the significance of these beasts that crowd misericords in such profusion? As Luuk Houwen has observed, many animals may carry diverse, even contradictory, meanings – an observation he offers in support of his thesis that we should not look beyond the purely decorative function

[3] More than two dozen dogs appear on misericords throughout the country, attesting to their popularity, whilst the dozen surviving deer offer evidence of its status as both food and noble prey. The cat, whilst dwelling in the domestic sphere, was essentially there purely for its functional role as a mouser, although there is some evidence to suggest that it was beginning to take on some aspects of its modern status as household pet: see Katharine M. Rogers, *Cat* (London: Reaktion Books, 2006), for a broad overview of the animal's status in human society, whilst Douglas Gray, 'Notes on Some Medieval Mystical, Magical and Moral Cats', in *Langland, the Mystics and the Medieval English Religious Tradition: Essays in Honour of S. S. Hussey*, ed. Helen Phillips (Cambridge: D. S. Brewer, 1990), pp. 185–202, addresses some of the cat's symbolic qualities in the Middle Ages. Of farm animals, pigs occur on numerous sets of misericords, cattle on four (St Peter and St Mary Magdalen, Fordham; Norwich Cathedral; St Guthlac, Passenham; and St Gregory, Sudbury), and sheep on two (All Souls College Chapel, Oxford, and Wells Cathedral). The hare appears on six sets, including one in the decidedly un-naturalistic act of riding a fox (Beverley Minster) and another in which several hares roast their hunter on a spit. I have discussed the symbolic significance of the hare in my article, '"Hares on the Hearthstones" in Medieval England', *Reinardus* 20 (2007–08), 29–39.

[4] See Malcolm Jones, 'The Misericords', in *Beverley Minster: an Illustrated History*, ed. Rosemary Horrox (Beverley: Friends of Beverley Minster, 2000), p. 160.

[5] G. L. Remnant, *A Catalogue of Misericords in Great Britain* (London: Oxford University Press, 1969), p. 36.

[6] Charles Tracy, 'Dating the Misericords from the Thirteenth-Century Choir Stalls at Exeter Cathedral', in *Medieval Art and Architecture at Exeter Cathedral*, ed. Francis Kelly (Leeds: Maney, 1991), pp. 180–7.

[7] Elephants are one of the exotic beasts which, presumably because of the scarcity of actual sightings, are subject to many variations on the basic form, particularly with regard to feet, tusks and ears. On the lack of consensus concerning details of the elephant's physical appearance in medieval bestiaries, see Wilma George and Brunsdon Yapp, *The Naming of the Beasts: Natural History in the Medieval Bestiary* (London: Duckworth, 1991), pp. 89–90.

provided by representations of beasts on misericords.[8] Whilst this is certainly a valid approach, it seems likely that when animals found in the choir have known symbolic qualities, these associations were taken into consideration when images were chosen. Indeed, even the ambiguous, sometimes apparently contradictory, duality of signification to which Houwen refers could itself be an aspect of symbolism which was knowingly exploited.[9] Rather than being mere representations of nature, then, it is my contention that the beasts depicted on choir stalls belong to a rich strain of animal symbolism and allegory derived primarily, but not exclusively, from beast fables, animal epics and the bestiary tradition: 'the animal world', notes Beryl Rowland, 'was … a humanized world, with animals standing for qualities which were meaningful to man'.[10] Considering the symbolism associated with the animals mentioned above, for example, we find that in a complex allegory based upon the alleged mating behaviour of the elephant – itself a strange concoction of travellers' tale and folklore, in which the female seduces the male into the act of mating through offering him the fruit of the mandragora – these beasts were considered to represent Adam and Eve.[11] This is surely something that should be kept in mind when considering the elephant carvings in Exeter Cathedral and elsewhere. As for the bear, we are told that it 'signifies the devil, ravager of the flocks of our Lord'.[12] Consequently, whilst we may indeed see the sequence of images of the bear in Beverley Minster as offering a pictorial record of a popular contemporary entertainment, we should also be aware of its possible didactic function as a symbolic enactment of gaining mastery over the Devil. We may see, then, that the beasts which we find depicted on misericords offer a broad and illuminating scope for symbolic reading, and it is to this symbolic aspect of animal iconography that we shall now turn.

Although a commonly kept animal throughout the Middle Ages, the pig invariably attracts negative associations when we look to its symbolic use: '[i]n the spiritual sense the boar means the devil because of its fierceness and strength', whilst 'sows signify sinners, the unclean and heretics … [for] … the sow that has washed and returns to her wallowing in the mire is filthier than before'.[13] In some circumstances, the pig may even be employed

[8] Luuk Houwen, 'Bestiaries in Wood? Misericords, Animal Imagery and the Bestiary Tradition,' in *The Playful Middle Ages: Meanings of Play and Plays of Meaning. Essays in Memory of Elaine C. Block*, ed. Paul Hardwick (Turnhout: Brepols, forthcoming).

[9] See, for example, Hardwick, 'Hares on the Hearthstone', in which I argue that the hare's symbolic instability accounts for its occurrence as a figure to be feared in the domestic sphere, even to the extent of its becoming an apocalyptic indicator.

[10] Beryl Rowland, *Blind Beasts: Chaucer's Animal World* (Kent, OH: Kent State University Press, 1971), p. 10.

[11] Richard Barber (ed. and trans.), *Bestiary, Being an English Version of the Bodleian Library, Oxford MS Bodley 764* (Woodbridge: The Boydell Press, 1993), pp. 39–43.

[12] Ibid., p. 60.

[13] Ibid., pp. 87 and 84–6.

as a derogatory representation of the Jew.[14] One particularly curious representation of the pig, found in a number of northern English churches, is an apparently playful scene showing a sow standing erect on her hind legs, playing bagpipes for the entertainment of between two and four dancing piglets (fig. 16).[15] These are neither the only musical pigs to be found on English misericords – Winchester Cathedral has a pig playing the viol – nor are they the only pipers, but this recurring motif offers a particularly exuberant illustration of the 'world upside-down' through its lively subject matter and invocation of gleefully raucous music.[16] In a 1967 article, Kathleen Scott traced earlier analogues of the image in order to suggest that this iconography lay behind the description of Chaucer's Miller in his *General Prologue* to *The Canterbury Tales*,[17] and it will be illuminating here to consider further what such iconography may have meant to Chaucer's contemporary audience.

At the conclusion of Chaucer's *Knight's Tale*, the pilgrim narrator tells us that,

> Whan that the knyght thus his tale ytoold,
> In al the route nas ther yong ne oold
> That he ne seyde it was a noble storie
> And worthy for to drawen to memorie,
> And namely the gentils everichon.[18]

> [When the knight had thus told his tale, there was neither young nor old in all the company who did not say it was a noble story and one worth committing to memory, the nobles in particular.]

It is, in short, a worthy tale which makes a memorable impact and, in so doing, creates expectations, both within the company of pilgrims and within the poem's audience.[19] However, our expectations receive something of a

[14] See Elaine C. Block, 'The Jew on Medieval Misericords', in *Grant Risee? The Medieval Comic Presence: Essays in Memory of Brian J. Levy*, ed. Adrian P. Tudor and Alan Hindley (Turnhout: Brepols, 2006), pp. 73–99. See especially p. 88. Whilst Block cites only Iberian examples in this essay, it is very possible that the same connotations could pertain in the anti-Semitic climate of late medieval England.

[15] Beverley Minster; Bishop Tunstall's Chapel, Durham Castle; Manchester Cathedral; Ripon Cathedral; and St Mary, Richmond.

[16] As Elaine Block notes of representations of animal musicians on European misericords, 'On the continent, the pig is the major musician and his instrument is usually bagpipes, but sometimes a harp': Elaine C. Block with Frédéric Billiet, 'Musical Comedy in the Medieval Choir: England', in *Medieval English Comedy*, ed. Sandra M. Hordis and Paul Hardwick (Turnhout: Brepols, 2007), p. 222. Whilst bagpiping pigs may be found on misericords as far away as Spain – the Monastery of San Jerónimo, Yuste (Cáceres) and León Cathedral, both from around the later fifteenth century – as far as I am aware, the dancing piglets only appear in England.

[17] Kathleen L. Scott, 'Sow and Bagpipe Imagery in the Miller's Portrait', *Review of English Studies*, n.s. 18 (1967), 287–90.

[18] Geoffrey Chaucer, *The Canterbury Tales*, in *The Riverside Chaucer*, ed. Larry D. Benson (Oxford: Oxford University Press, 1988), I (A) ll. 3109–13.

[19] This point is made by Helen Cooper, *The Structure of the Canterbury Tales* (Athens, GA: Gerald Duckworth and Co., 1984), p. 65.

shock at this point. The Host, the 'governour' of the company,[20] has plans for how the storytelling contest should proceed: the Monk is urged to tell, '... if that ye konne, / Somwhat to quite with the knyghtes tale'.[21] The Host's choice of the Monk to make this attempt is perfectly reasonable – the highest-ranking member of the Church is best placed to follow the highest-ranking layman[22] – but the real 'governour' of proceedings, Chaucer himself, has very different plans: what he has lined up for the company (ourselves included) is a 'cherles tale',[23] and it is the drunken Miller who is chosen to deliver it.

This in itself is perhaps a little surprising. If opposition between high and low is called for,[24] who could be more socially at odds with the Knight than the Ploughman? What better 'cherl' could we ask for than the dung-carting labourer?[25] However, as we saw in chapter 1, Chaucer's Ploughman is clearly not one of the reluctant workers, 'idle and unwilling to serve', who are condemned by the Statute of Labourers and attacked in Gower's *Vox clamantis* as 'sluggish ... scarce, and ... grasping' [*tardi ... rari ... et auari*],[26] but, rather, a representative figure of Langlandian Christian ideals which transcend barriers of social status. The Ploughman having thus been disqualified from such churlish behaviour, therefore, the task of disruption falls to the Miller, a character who, after all, features prominently in the Langland-inflected 'peasant letters' of 1381.[27] The unruly Miller is certainly physically imposing enough to barge in – 'a stout carl for the nones; / Ful byg ... of brawn, and eek of bones'[28] – with a bulk that he uses both for wrestling and for less regulated exercise:

> He was short-sholdred, brood, a thikke knarre;
> Ther was no dore, that he nolde heve of harre,
> Or breke it at a rennyng with his heed.[29]

> [He was thick-necked, broad, a stout fellow; there was no door that he could not heave off its hinges, or break by running at it with his head.]

[20] Chaucer, *Canterbury Tales*, I (A) l. 813.

[21] Ibid., I (A) 3118–19.

[22] On the status of, and the relationship between, the Knight and the Monk, see R. E. Kaske, 'The Knight's Interruption of the Monk's Tale', *ELH* 24 (1957), 249–68; and Cooper, *The Structure of the Canterbury Tales*, 109–20.

[23] Chaucer, *Canterbury Tales*, I (A) l. 3169.

[24] *The Middle English Dictionary*, *s.v.* 'Cherl' 1: 'Any person not belonging to the nobility or clergy'.

[25] Chaucer, *Canterbury Tales*, I (A) l. 530.

[26] On the Statute of Labourers, see R. B. Dobson (ed.), *The Peasants' Revolt of 1381* (Basingstoke: Macmillan, 1983), pp. 63–8. John Gower, *Vox clamantis*, V.ix, l. 577 in *The Complete Works of John Gower* vol. 4, ed. G. C. Macaulay (Oxford: Clarendon Press, 1902), translated in *The Major Latin Works of John Gower*, trans. Eric W. Stockton (Seattle: University of Washington Press, 1962), p. 208.

[27] For the 'peasant letters', see Dobson (ed.), *The Peasants' Revolt*, pp. 379–85. The Langlandian influence is discussed in Anne Hudson, '*Piers Plowman* and the Peasants' Revolt: a Problem Revisited', *Yearbook of Langland Studies* 8 (1994), 85–106.

[28] Chaucer, *Canterbury Tales*, I (A) 545–6.

[29] Ibid., I (A) 549–51.

Presumably this striking physical prowess is employed for breaking and entering, with more than a hint of brutish intimidation. It may also suggest a lack of thought, although this is soon undermined by a description of his physiognomy which implies sharp animal cunning: 'His berd as any sowe or fox was reed'.[30] As Edward of Norwich's fifteenth-century treatise *The Master of Game* – itself essentially a translation of the late fourteenth-century *Livre de chasse* of Gaston de Foix – recounts, foxes are 'so cunning and subtle that neither men nor hounds can find a remedy to keep themselves from their false turns',[31] and the popular stories of Reynard and his brethren to which we shall turn later in this chapter attest to the fox's status as the cunning beast *par excellence*. There is no mistaking Chaucer's intention in invoking this simile for the Miller who knew how to 'stelen corn, and tollen thries'.[32] Yet the significance of the reference to the sow – in a simile which is repeated a mere four lines later – is perhaps less immediately grasped by the modern reader.

Given the Miller's pugnacious masculinity, we may readily expect a comparison with the boar, of which the bestiary tells us, '[i]n the spiritual sense the boar means the devil because of its fierceness and strength'.[33] The devilish aspect of such a comparison would chime particularly well with the Miller's 'forneys'-like mouth, suggesting the mouth of Hell as depicted so frequently in medieval art and, indeed, featuring in the mystery plays which underlie his tale.[34] Yet Chaucer chooses instead to employ the feminine simile of the sow, the apparent inappropriateness of which serves to draw our attention all the more closely to the symbolic significance of this surprising beast. Turning once more to the bestiary, '[s]ows', we are told, 'signify sinners, the unclean and heretics', for '[t]he sow that has washed and returns to her wallowing in the mire is filthier than before': she is also drawn to excess luxury and carnal desires, as well, of course, as being the watchword for greed in all its manifestations.[35] We may see, then, that these comparisons with the sow, rather than the boar, are heavy with specific significance, underlining the Miller's unrepentant self-interest. This does not, however, preclude more general negative associations held by the pig; for example, that its rapacious greed does not stop even at humans or, most shockingly, its own kind.[36]

In terms of his interruption of the Host's idea of how the contest should proceed, it is significant that, right from the *General Prologue*, the Miller has been explicitly sketched in terms which strikingly contrast with the Knight.

[30] Ibid., I (A) 552.
[31] Edward of Norwich, *The Master of Game*, ed. William A. Baillie-Grohman and F. N. Baillie-Grohman (Philadelphia: University of Pennsylvania Press, 2005), p. 67.
[32] Chaucer, *Canterbury Tales*, I (A) 562.
[33] Barber (ed. and trans.), *Bestiary*, p. 87.
[34] Chaucer, *Canterbury Tales*, I (A) 559.
[35] Barber (ed. and trans.), *Bestiary*, pp. 84–6.
[36] Beryl Rowland, *Animals with Human Faces: A Guide to Animal Symbolism* (London: George Allen and Unwin, 1974), p. 37.

Whilst the Knight is the consummate horseman who 'nevere yet no vileyne ne sayde / In al his lyf unto no maner wight'[37] [never spoke ill to anyone of any rank in all his life], the Miller is a 'janglere and a goliardeys'[38] [coarse story-teller and oaf] who is almost too drunk to stay on his horse. More significantly, perhaps, whilst the Knight is accorded precedence in both the company and the tale-telling contest, it is the Miller who effectively leads the company out of town:

> A baggepipe wel koude he blowe and sowne,
> And therwithal he broghte us out of towne.[39]

Much of the critical commentary on the Miller's bagpipe has concentrated on the possible sexual imagery of the instrument.[40] This, it should be noted in passing, explicitly references the male genitals, again throwing into relief the gender anomaly of the sow. Such coarse physicality may also be figured in what many have read as the 'unpleasant' sound of the Miller's bagpipes. However, Robert Boenig has drawn attention to contrasting, courtly and even angelic associations of the instrument in the Middle Ages. The chapel of the Royal Foundation of St Katharine, London, for example, has a fine, unique, late fourteenth-century misericord of an angel playing bagpipes.[41] Boenig suggests that if we read the portrait as referring to 'the soft, pleasing, courtly bagpipe', we have a subtly ironic portrait of the Miller who, boorish and gross as he is, can usurp an instrument more appropriate to the Knight than to himself.[42] Even if this is not the case, there is surely a deliberate comparison and contrast being made. We may see, then, that all aspects of the Miller's speech and behaviour point to a character who, although a churl, wishes to place himself in the position of the most noble. And the image with which Chaucer chooses to make this comment upon the events of 1381 is that of the piping sow, which would become a popular motif across a group of churches in the following century, once more suggesting that an apparently playful motif on misericords owes its iconography to the very real concerns of late medieval England.

Once it has been recognised that animals in the Middle Ages could never be fully separated from a web of lore and symbol, it comes as no surprise that the noble eagle and pious pelican are to be found on stalls throughout

[37] Chaucer, *Canterbury Tales*, I (A) 70–1.
[38] Ibid., I (A) 560.
[39] Ibid., I (A) 565–6.
[40] Scott, 'Sow and Bagpipe Imagery', 287–90. See also E. A. Block, 'Chaucer's Millers and their Bagpipes', *Speculum* 29 (1954), 239–43, and E. A. Block, 'History at the Margins: Bagpipers in Medieval Manuscripts', *History Today* 39 (1989), 42–8.
[41] This is illustrated and discussed in Block, 'Musical Comedy', pp. 218–19.
[42] Robert Boenig, 'The Miller's Bagpipe: a Note on the *Canterbury Tales* A565–566', *English Language Notes* 21 (1983): 6. On the variety of interpretations which may be accorded to medieval depictions of bagpipes, see Emanuel Winternitz, *Musical Instruments and their Symbolism in Western Art*, 2nd edn (London: Yale University Press, 1979), pp. 131–3.

the country,[43] their messages of steadfast devotion direct and unequivocal to the viewer and appropriate for this setting. Rather more surprising to the modern viewer, however, is the plethora of playful – even apparently irreverent – anthropomorphised animals, such as the piping sow, which jostle for position and, indeed, frequently crowd out their overtly pious neighbours. Of these seemingly scurrilous characters, by far the most common are the trickster fox and the mocking ape. The character of the fox in literature evolves throughout the Middle Ages, from the twelfth-century Latin *Ysengrimus*, through the accumulation of 'branches' of the *Roman de Renart*, and into popular tales throughout Europe, reaching England by the middle of the thirteenth century.[44] His literary popularity is reflected in his growing presence in art, including ecclesiastical decoration, with many scenes appearing on misericords. The ape, in contrast, is a more elusive figure. As we saw in chapter 2, the similarity to – but distinct difference from – the human form makes the ape an ideal vehicle for parody and satire, extending, at the farthest extreme, to the debased elements of human nature or even entering the realm of the diabolic.[45] On the other hand, sometimes an ape is merely an ape, enacting entertainments for the curious.[46] To understand the especial popularity of these two creatures on choir stalls, it is useful to look closely at two specific tropes which appear frequently on misericords and, indeed, in other media.

One often encounters St Paul's vivid metaphor of imperfect comprehension – 'for now we see through a glass, darkly'[47] – yet it seems particularly apposite for one particular problem of iconographic interpretation which quite literally involves peering through a glass: the interpretation of ape physicians. The primary iconographic symbol of the physician, whether human or animal, in the medieval period is the distinctive uroscopy flask (or 'jordan'), which was one of the most important diagnostic tools employed by the medieval medical doctor. Colour, quality, opacity, smell and sedimentary deposits of the patient's urine sample were all analysed, often with the help of elaborate reference charts.[48] Indeed, so ingrained is the iconography of the urine flask that it even occurs in the famous illustration of Chaucer's Physician in the Ellesmere manuscript of the *Canterbury Tales*. For whilst it is perhaps fitting for the Host to signal his approbation of the Physician's tale by exclaiming,

[43] Both the pelican and the eagle are seemingly ubiquitous in medieval art in general, with tens of carvings of each surviving on misericords. It should be noted that as well as gathering its own web of symbolic associations, the eagle is also the emblem of St John the Divine.

[44] A useful summary of this development may be found in Kenneth Varty, *Reynard the Fox: A Study of the Fox in Medieval English Art* (Leicester: Leicester University Press, 1967), pp. 21–4.

[45] See H. W. Janson, *Apes and Ape Lore in the Middle Ages and the Renaissance* (London: Warburg Institute, 1952), pp. 13–22.

[46] Ibid., pp.170–1.

[47] St Paul I Corinthians 13:12.

[48] On the practice of uroscopy in the Middle Ages, see Carole Rawcliffe, *Medicine and Society in Later Medieval England* (Stroud: Sutton, 1995), pp. 46–52.

> I pray to God so save thy gentil cors,
> And eek thyne urynals and thy jurdones,
> Thyn ypocras, and eek thy galiones,
> And every boyste ful of thy letuarie,[49]
>
> [I pray to god to protect your noble body, and also your urine flasks and glasses, your potions from Hippocrates and Galen, and every container full of your medicine.]

thereby drawing attention first and foremost to this most important of professional tools, it is still rather surprising to see the figure as illustrated engaged in the unlikely act of horseback uroscopy as he makes his way to Canterbury.

Unlikely though this equestrian diagnosis may be, the important point is that the iconography of the image should be unproblematic for the reader: the flask is a clear badge of professional calling, identifying this mounted figure as a physician. What, however, are we to make of the many images that occur, across a wide range of media, in which animals are portrayed as physicians? One of the most famous examples occurs as part of what appears to be a narrative sequence in the lower borders of the Smithfield Decretals (British Library, MS. 10. E. IV) of the second quarter of the fourteenth century. Here a fox is seen apparently administering to a sick wolf (f. 158v.), whilst earlier images in the manuscript illustrate both sick wolf and sick lion stories, analogous – though with significant differences – to surviving written texts such as the *Ysengrimus* and the *Roman de Renart*. As Kenneth Varty has noted, these images 'are not easy to interpret chiefly because they do not illustrate any one extant version of the fox-physician story'.[50] Furthermore, the fox holding the uroscopy flask before the sick wolf – the final picture in the sequence – is separated by more than a hundred folios from those which precede it. We may place the image firmly within an established tradition of fox fable, but interpretation remains tantalisingly out of reach. Our glass, as it were, has become slightly darker.

The glass through which we view these figures becomes darker still when we address single images without any broader narrative contexts in which to place them, such as the more common ape physicians which are found frequently not only in manuscripts, but also, as we saw in chapter 2, on misericord carvings, and even in ecclesiastical stained glass of the late medieval period. To return to the misericord carvings of Beverley Minster, for example, here we may see a wide variety of animal activities, including, as mentioned earlier, a now-disrupted sequence of scenes involving a captured bear, along with a number of scenes involving apes and other

[49] Chaucer, *Canterbury Tales*, VI 304–7.

[50] Kenneth Varty, *Reynard, Renart, Reinaert and Other Foxes in Medieval England: The Iconographic Evidence* (Amsterdam: Amsterdam University Press, 1999), p. 182. See also Kenneth Varty, 'Reynard the Fox and the Smithfield Decretals', *Journal of the Warburg and Courtauld Institutes* 26 (1963), 348–54.

creatures, both naturalistic and anthropomorphic.[51] Indeed, one of these scenes shows apes rifling the pack of a sleeping pedlar – a further incident which also appears earlier in the lower borders of the Smithfield Decretals.[52] However, there is no suggestion of a coherent narrative which encompasses the whole range of seats – individual scenes may well recall specific literary sources, but they exist in an interpretative vacuum. When we find the image of the ape physician as a supporter to a battle between a lion and a dragon in Beverley Minster, therefore, we may only guess at the significance.[53]

We have in chapter 2 explored the implications of the ape physician and the elevated Host in St Mary, Beverley, in the context of debates on transubstantiation. In another misericord carving in the same church, a fox's need for a physician is all too apparent as he is pierced through by an arrow shot by a pursuing Wild Man. Whilst, as Varty has noted, the inspection of the urinal is rather superfluous to diagnostic requirements in this case,[54] we may perhaps read the flask here as an iconographic token, like that in the Ellesmere *Canterbury Tales*, employed solely to signal the ape's professional role to the viewer. Further afield, at St Botolph, Boston, a late fourteenth-century misericord shows a fox consulting an ape doctor. The latter inspects the flask, whilst the fox holds a carrier which, it has been suggested, is a bucket containing a sample of droppings.[55] In both of these carvings, narratives are suggested, but neither scene has any obvious connection with adjacent carvings to offer clues, and the stories, once more, remain elusive.

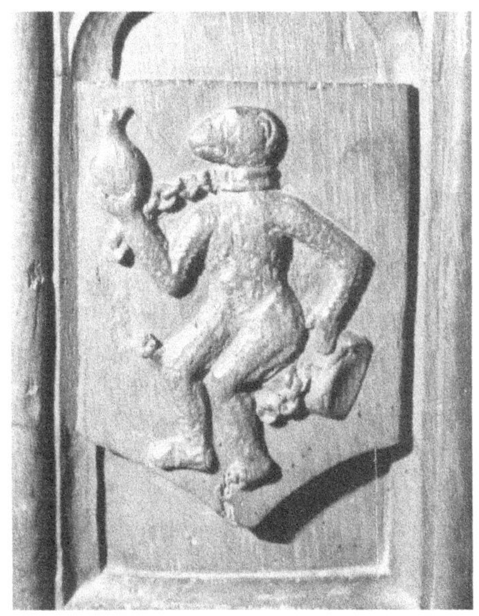

FIG. 28. ST HELEN, ABBOTSHAM BENCH-END. PHOTOGRAPH BY PAUL HARDWICK.

Perhaps the most enigmatic ape physician carving is to be found on a bench end of around 1500 at St Helen, Abbotsham in North Devon (fig. 28). In his essay on animal

[51] For a full discussion of the Beverley Minster misericords, see Malcolm Jones, 'The Misericords', pp. 157–74.

[52] This scene may also be found in carvings at Bristol and Manchester. For a discussion of this image, see Paul Hardwick, 'The Merchant, the Monkeys and the Lure of Money', *Reinardus* 19 (2006), 83–90.

[53] On the 'peculiarly English' motif of the fight between the lion and the dragon, see Malcolm Jones, 'The Misericords of Beverley Minster: a Corpus of Folkloric Imagery and its Cultural Milieu, with special reference to the influence of Northern European Iconography on Late-medieval and Early Modern English Woodwork', unpublished PhD thesis (Polytechnic of the South West, 1991), p. 193 and notes.

[54] Varty, *Reynard, Renart, Reinaert*, p. 206.

[55] Ibid., pp. 205–6; Christa Grössinger, *The World Upside-Down: English Misericords* (London: Harvey Miller Publishers, 1997), p. 101. In a personal communication, Elaine Block has suggested that this may be some sort of carrier for the flask to protect it from damage and possibly keep the sample warm.

physicians in the margins of medieval manuscripts, David Sprunger notes that '[u]nlike his human counterpart, the animal physician never appears in illustrations without a patient'.[56] Whilst this may be true of manuscript illustrations, it is not the case in other media, and the Abbotsham carving is an excellent example of a lone ape physician, chained to some sort of seat (possibly a tree-stump) as it examines its raised uroscopy flask. Once more, there is no relation to adjacent carvings, and in this case there is no obvious narrative within the carving itself. Consequently, the viewer is left with an unexplained image to which we must respond. One of the ways in which we may legitimately respond to any of these images is, of course, with laughter. Sprunger concludes his discussion by noting that,

> [t]hroughout its history, the parodic animal physician has always invoked laughter. The very audacity of the image suggests the *inversus mundi* in several ways: first, in the absurdity of depicting an animal engaging in one of the most complex human arts; and second, in showing an animal caring for the physical health of a traditional nemesis. It is this second aspect that goes beyond mere humor and reflects widespread suspicion of the physician–patient relationship, and thus the image of the parodic animal physician reminds us that truth can lie not at the center of things but at the edges.[57]

Surviving literary texts of the period certainly attest to this 'suspicion of the physician–patient relationship'. One of the most lively satires of the quack doctor appears in *The Simonie*, a vigorous attack on the abuses of the times, which ran to three versions in the second and third quarters of the fourteenth century:

> Anoþer craft Y se also  þat towcheþ þe clergie:
> Þat be þis fals fisicianes  þat helpeþ men to die.
> Þey wil wagge þe vryne  and vrynal of glas
> And suere þat he is sikerer  þan euer yit he was
>   And sayn,
> 'Dame, fore defaute of help,  þyn hosbonde is ney slayn.'[58]

> [I see another skill that touches upon the clergy: that is these false physicians who help men to die. They will wag the urine and its glass flask and swear that he is more sick than he ever was before, and say, 'Madam, for lack of assistance your husband is almost slain.']

After 'wagging the urine', the physician goes on to fleece the gullible wife,

[56] David A. Sprunger, 'Parodic Animal Physicians from the Margins of Medieval Manuscripts', in *Animals in the Middle Ages*, ed. Nona C. Flores (New York and London: Routledge, 1996), pp. 67–81 (p. 73).
[57] Sprunger, 'Parodic Animal Physicians', pp. 78–9.
[58] *The Simonie: A Parallel-Text Edition*, ed. D. Embree and E. Urquhart (Heidelberg: Carl Winter Universitätsverlag, 1991), B 259–64. All quotations are from this edition. On dating, see Embree and Urquhart's introduction, pp. 22–3.

force an evil concoction down the hapless patient's throat and take the best of the food for himself, before concluding his business:

> 'Dame,' he seiþ, 'drede þe noght, þe maister is wonne,'
>   And likket.
> But þus he bereþ awey þe siluer and þe wif beskikket.[59]

> ['Madam,' he says, 'don't worry yourself, the master is recovered,' and lies. But in this manner he carries away the silver and deceives the wife.]

Slightly later in the century, William Langland treats acquisitive doctors with the same scorn in *Piers Plowman*, as his figure of Hunger claims that '[t]hey do men deye thorugh hir drynkes er destynee it wolde' [they make men die by their potions before destiny would have it].[60]

In the light of such contemporary literary sources, then, it is easy to see images of animal physicians, as Sprunger suggests, within a broader context of distrust of the medical profession. This, however, seems to leave a familiar, important question unanswered: why should parodic, satirical images of physicians appear in church decoration? More prominent than any of the carvings considered so far are a number of examples in a still further 'dark glass' – the early fourteenth-century 'Pilgrimage Window' in the nave of York Minster, the main iconography of which is explicitly concerned with individual devotion.[61] Beneath an image of Christ suffering on the cross, we see male and female pilgrims flanking St Peter who, significantly, is here identified not only by his usual attribute of the key but also by the less ubiquitous symbol of the church that he holds – very apt in this case, as it is to him that the minster is dedicated. The unifying theme is one of individual devotional commitment placed beneath – and thereby ideologically overlaid with – the ultimate commitment to mankind of God made flesh. Interspersed throughout this major iconographic scheme are a number of lively and apparently unrelated marginal scenes, including a fox preaching to a cockerel and the famous monkeys' funeral, in which an apparent parody of the apocryphal funeral of the Virgin is acted out by apes.[62] The most frequently repeated motif in the glazing, however, is that of the 'delightful monkey doctors,'[63] which appear a number of times in the borders of the outer lights. Whilst we may at a stretch read these images in the context of contemporary satire when confined to the undersides of misericord seats,

[59] Ibid., B 292–4.

[60] William Langland, *The Vision of Piers Plowman: a Complete Edition of the B-Text*, ed. A. V. C. Schmidt (London: Dent, 1995), B VI 274.

[61] I have explored the complex iconography of this window in, 'Making Light of Devotion: The Pilgrimage Window in York Minster,' in *Medieval English Comedy*, ed. Sandra M. Hordis and Paul Hardwick (Turnhout: Brepols, 2007), pp. 61–82.

[62] This image is discussed at length in my article, 'The Monkeys' Funeral in the Pilgrimage Window, York Minster,' *Art History* 23 (2000), 290–9.

[63] David O'Connor and Jeremy Haselock, 'The Stained and Painted Glass,' in *A History of York Minster*, ed. G. E. Aylmer and Reginald Cant (Oxford: Clarendon Press, 1977), p. 357.

this is surely much less likely in a prominent part of the nave of what was at the time one of the most important ecclesiastical buildings in the country.[64]

In what remains the most thorough study of apes and ape lore, Horst Janson notes that representations of ape physicians begin to appear in the fourteenth century,[65] a date which may be significant for our reading of such images. As we have seen, throughout the thirteenth century the decrees of the Fourth Lateran Council relevant to the English Church – most notably those concerning lay piety and ecclesiastical reform – had become firmly embedded in devotional culture.[66] Turning to the twenty-first and twenty-second decrees, we find precepts which may lie behind some of these intriguing images in church decoration.

Canon 21, after prescribing annual confession for the laity, turns to the duty of the priest:

> As for the priest, he should be discerning and prudent so that like a practised doctor he can pour wine and oil on the wounds of the injured, diligently enquiring into the circumstances both of the sinner and of the sin, from which to choose intelligently what sort of advice he ought to give him and what sort of remedy to apply, various means availing to heal the sick.[67]

To use the medical doctor as a metaphor for one who tends to the well-being of the soul is a common device, which may even be used of Christ Himself, as may be seen in the preachers' manual *Fasciculus morum*, the widespread popularity and influence of which we have seen in chapter 1. The writer or compiler of *Fasciculus morum* employs an allegory of Christ as a 'good physician', beginning his account with a description of an activity which will by now be familiar:

> Christ acts like a physician in the following way. A doctor investigates the condition of the sick person and the nature of his sickness by such methods as taking his pulse and inspecting his urine. Thus when Christ visits a sinner, he first enlightens him with his grace to understand himself and his own sin ...[68]

After this initial diagnosis is carried out, the prescribed diet, medicine and fitness regime are all allegorised. Even *Piers Plowman* – so dismissive, as we have seen, of earthly doctors – refers to Christ's 'lechecraft', recounting how he,

[64] On the status of York Minster at this time, see Barrie Dobson, 'The Later Middle Ages: 1215–1500', in ibid., pp. 44–109.

[65] Janson, *Apes and Ape Lore*, p. 168.

[66] On the dissemination of the Lateran decrees in England, see M. Gibbs and J. Lang, *Bishops and Reform: 1215–1272: with Special Reference to the Lateran Council of 1215* (London: Oxford University Press, 1934), pp. 94–179 and C. R. Cheney, 'Legislation of the Medieval English Church', *English Historical Review* 50 (1935), 385–417.

[67] H. Rothwell (ed.), *English Historical Documents 1189–1327* (London: Eyre and Spottiswoode, 1975), p. 655.

[68] *Fasciculus morum: a Fourteenth-Century Preacher's Handbook*, ed. and trans. Siegfried Wenzel (London: Pennsylvania State University Press, 1989), p. 255.

> … dide hym assaie his surgenrie on hem that sike were,
> Til he was parfit praktisour, if any peril fille;
> And soughte out the sike and synfulle bothe,
> And salvede sike and synfulle,[69]
>
> [tried his surgical skills on those who were sick until he was a perfect practitioner, if any peril befell; and sought out both the sick and the sinful, and healed the sick and the sinful.]

Later in the same passage, Langland goes so far as to characterise Christ as the 'leche of lif'.[70] We may see here a paradox: within the same work, Langland can employ commonplace contemporary criticisms of doctors yet, at the same time, draw upon an independent tradition which allegorises Christ's works as 'lechecraft'.

Canon 22 of the Fourth Lateran Council goes on to emphasise the important distinction to be made between care of the body and care of the soul:

> As physical illness is sometimes the result of sin … we by the present decree ordain and strictly command doctors, when they are called to the sick, to warn and exhort them before anything else to call in doctors of souls, so that after his spiritual health has been seen to, the sick man may respond better to the bodily medicine – for when the cause ceases, the effect ceases.[71]

Here, in placing the soul firmly before the body, we see the clergy's role allegorised as that of spiritual 'lechecraft' – it is the healing work of Christ carried out by His representatives on earth.

Although it is often suggested that apes represent a fallen, bestial view of humanity,[72] this is by no means their only iconographic use. Indeed, they may in some instances be seen as a call to a positive 'aping' of the divine, such as in the York Minster Pilgrimage and Bellfounders' Windows; here they act as a pictorial gloss to the main iconography of the windows which encourages personal devotion and aspiration, whilst at the same time stressing the need for humility.[73] In this context, we may view the monkey physicians, rising up the outer borders of the Pilgrimage Window, not as laughter-provoking satires upon the medical profession, but as reminders of Christ's 'lechecraft' and of the need to 'ape' this in looking to the health of one's own soul whilst on earth.

In view of the more prominent location of the York apes, it is perhaps

[69] *Piers Plowman*, B XVI 106–9.

[70] *Piers Plowman*, B XVI 118.

[71] Rothwell (ed.), *English Historical Documents*, p. 655.

[72] Michael Camille, for example, suggests that 'medieval people felt themselves too close to beasts … to see the margins as anything other than the site of their wallowing, fallen co-existence': *Image on the Edge: the Margins of Medieval Art* (London: Reaktion, 1992), p. 38.

[73] Hardwick, 'Monkeys' Funeral', 297–8. A literary example of this positive aping may be found in Chaucer's *House of Fame*, III 1201–13, in which 'smale harpers with her gleës … ape' the playing of Orpheus, Glascurion and other legendary harpers.

tempting to argue for their uniqueness in providing a sharp contrast to the playful or satirical way apes are used elsewhere. However, consideration of the York glass may offer a new perspective on some of these other images. Turning once again to the Beverley St Mary's misericord we considered in chapter 2, if we indeed follow Grössinger's persuasive suggestion that the object held by the figure on the left is the Eucharistic Host, we may perhaps read this scene as an exhortation to turn one's back on one's physical health and focus instead first upon one's spiritual health, as prescribed in Canon 22 of the Fourth Lateran Council. And what, then, of our lone ape doctor at Abbotsham? Grössinger has suggested that a carving of a lone chained ape on a misericord in St Mary of Charity, Faversham, 'represents humanity tied to its animal instincts without thought for spiritual salvation'.[74] She does not comment, however, upon the upturned uroscopy flask clutched in the ape's left hand which, if my iconographic readings are valid, would add further support to her interpretation.[75] The grimacing ape looks down on that which is spilt rather than engaging in appropriate contemplative examination. The chained Abbotsham ape, on the other hand, represents the opposite – one who is presently bound to the earth, but who diligently attends to his spiritual health. We may note, in passing, that this bench end is nearest to the church's door, and would, therefore, be an image glimpsed upon leaving the church, perhaps acting as a reminder to remain scrupulously self-aware in the world outside.

As Sprunger has noted, in his observations cited earlier, 'truth can lie ... at the edges'. Yet our consideration of images of the ape physician should alert us to the fact that the truth so represented is not necessarily the same truth in each location. Some images undoubtedly refer to narrative sources and others may well reflect contemporary distrust of physicians. Nevertheless, as always, we must not overlook the allegorical strain in contemporary written sources, which reveals some of these apparently playful images in an altogether more serious, didactic light. If this is the case when considering the ape physician, however, we may perhaps feel ourselves to be on safer ground when dismissing many of the various misericord images of the fox, whom we have already met briefly disguised as a physician himself, as pure entertainment. After all, we have a rich source of medieval tales from the Reynardian tradition, and the undoubted entertainment value of many of them is in no small part due to the self-serving amorality of the protagonist. Yet, if we turn to English representations of a particular Reynardian motif – the encounter of the fox and the cock – we may be surprised to find that even this simple narrative is appropriated for a similar purpose to the image of the ape physician.

Whilst Europe boasts a rich and endlessly fascinating tradition of the

[74] Grössinger, *The World Upside-Down*, p. 101.

[75] Remnant refers to the 'urine-flask reversed' but does not offer an explanation of this unusual motif: *Catalogue of Misericords*, p. 71.

exploits of Reynard, Renart and Reinaert, the most famous medieval English fox is surely Chaucer's daun Russell, a name seemingly original to Chaucer for this renowned character. In *The Nun's Priest's Tale* daun Russell pits his wits against the regal Chauntecleer, the English epitome of the familiar put-upon cock, who inhabits the barnyard, going about his day-to-day business largely oblivious to the dangers at hand. Chaucer's masterfully lively and entertaining rendering of the tale perhaps supports the condemnation of 'the fabled intrigues of the fox and the cock', which are singled out for particular censure in *Pictor in carmine*, a thirteenth-century attack on the proliferation of apparently frivolous church decoration.[76] Pure, exuberant entertainment aside, however, by the close of the Middle Ages there is evidence to suggest that, at least in English churches, the episode was being employed for a serious didactic purpose.

Of course, long before Chaucer's retelling of the story of the fox and the cock, French versions were in circulation and, indeed, were being written in England for a French-speaking audience in the early thirteenth century.[77] Furthermore, from at least the late thirteenth century these tales were finding their way into ecclesiastical carvings and other media. As Varty has noted, however, in visual representations of the story the cock is frequently replaced by a goose, a bird which does not equate to the narrative but nevertheless, he suggests, is eminently suitable for the visual arts:

> There is a good reason why graphic and especially plastic artists should prefer the goose to the cock. For them, the long, slender neck of the goose had an attractive line which considerably enhances composition ... Conversely, the shorter neck of the cock, hen or duck can make for confused outlines when it comes to depicting a fox seizing a bird by its neck.[78]

This may well be the case, with aesthetic concerns taking precedence over a slavish adherence to narrative sources. The concomitant inference, however, is that when the less elegant cock is depicted, it is because it is deemed to be vital to the way in which the pictorial narrative is to be read, a point to which we shall return shortly.

Chaucer's sources are generally accepted as being Marie de France's *The Cock and the Fox* (*Del cok e del gupil*) and, perhaps to a greater extent, the second branch of the *Roman de Renart*.[79] The tale, in which the proud cock is beguiled by the wily fox only to turn the tables on his captor and escape, is widespread. Its popularity is easily understandable; the narrative is lively, the characters boldly and attractively painted, the cunning admirable and the moral – 'keep your mouth shut and your eyes open' – simple and

[76] M. R. James, '*Pictor in carmine*', *Archaeologia* 94 (1951), 141.

[77] On the development of the narrative in England, and its representation in the visual arts, see Varty, *Reynard, Renart, Reinaert*, pp. 31–54.

[78] Ibid., pp. 37–8.

[79] See S. H. Cavanaugh's introductory notes in *The Riverside Chaucer*, p. 936.

universally applicable. However, in Chaucer's version the story itself accounts for but a small part of his *Nun's Priest's Tale*, as the narrative is expanded almost ten-fold with digressions on dreams, authority, *exempla* and constipation, along with that rare direct Chaucerian reference to contemporary events in the form of 'Jakke Straw and his meynee'.[80] In doing this, Chaucer may be seen to be elaborating on the story, not only as it survives in written versions, but also as it is depicted on misericords.

In their comprehensive study of fox carvings on medieval choir stalls, Elaine Block and Kenneth Varty note the widespread distribution of Reynardian and other fox lore scenes.[81] Some scenes, such as the fox preaching or adopting other clerical roles, which we considered briefly in chapters 2 and 4, are found throughout Europe.[82] However, whilst depictions of a hunting fox seizing or making off with his prey are common throughout Europe, it is only in England where misericords survive showing the fox and his prey – be it a cock or a goose – chased by a woman wielding her distaff. Of these, only one misericord carving of the pursuit of the fox and his prey pre-dates Chaucer's *Nun's Priest's Tale*: the mid fourteenth-century carving at Ely Cathedral (fig. 29), which Block and Varty describe thus:

> The victim is clearly a cock which the fox seizes by the body and holds between his jaws. Towering over the fox is the good-wife wielding her distaff. On the right supporter, a mallet or stake over his shoulder, stands a man who may be Constant [the farmer in French versions], a farm hand or a serving man. To judge by their fierce expressions and open mouths, both man and woman are shouting loudly after the fox. The distaff is an interesting detail because it is not mentioned in the French epic tradition, but it is in both Chaucer and the popular lyrics.[83]

One element that is clearly not from the same narrative tradition as the chase, however, is the scene depicted in the left supporter which shows a cowled fox preaching to a cock and hens. We will return to this scene after first considering other representations of the chase.

Textual variants of the cock and fox stories may account for variations in details within the scene as it appears in different locations. A misericord

[80] Chaucer, *Canterbury Tales*, VII 3394.

[81] Elaine C. Block and Kenneth Varty, 'Choir-Stall Carvings of Reynard and Other Foxes', in *Reynard the Fox: Social Engagement and Cultural Metamorphoses in the Beast Epic from the Middle Ages to the Present*, ed. Kenneth Varty (New York: Berghahn Books, 2000), pp. 125–62.

[82] More than a dozen examples of the fox religious may be found on English misericords, but he is far from being confined to this location. As Kenneth Varty has noted (and illustrated), 'He is also to be found, appropriately, on pulpits. He struts round capitals, peers down from roof bosses, peeps up from paving stones, parades on friezes, high or low. He ornaments all kinds of church furniture. On rare occasions he penetrates into secular surroundings and may be seen by the paneling of a great hall or in the porch of a public house': Varty, *Reynard the Fox*, p. 57.

[83] Block and Varty, 'Choir-Stall Carvings', pp. 135–6, where early representations of this scene in other media are also noted.

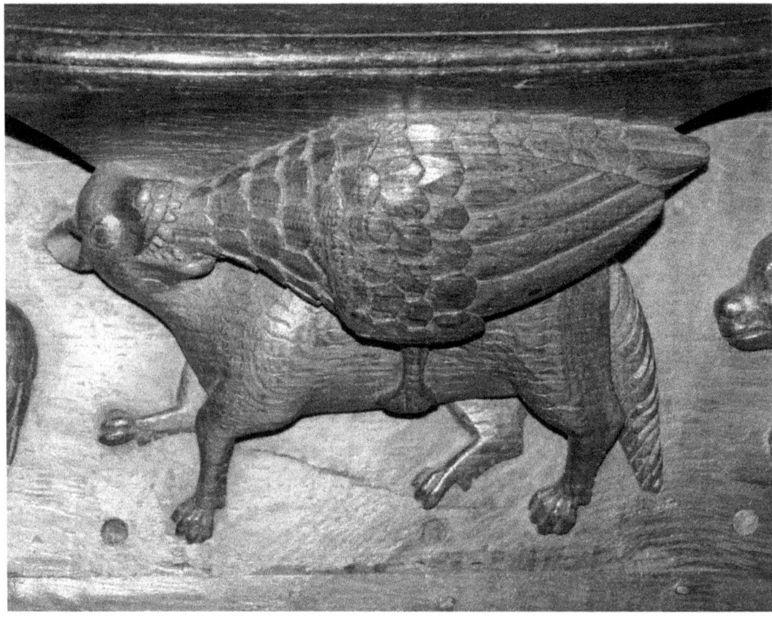

FIG. 29. ELY CATHEDRAL MISERICORD.

in St Botolph, Boston, is roughly contemporary with Chaucer, and conveys the same robust vigour as his version of the chase, as Dame Malkyn – 'with a dystaf in hir hand' – and her daughters cry:

> ... 'Out! Harrow and weylaway!
> Ha, ha! The fox!' and after hym they ran,
> And eek with staves many another man. . . .
> They yolleden as feendes doon in helle;
> The dokes cryden as men wolde hem quelle.[84]

> ['Out! Help and alas! Ha, ha! The fox!' and after him they ran, along with many other men with staves ... They cried as devils do in Hell; the ducks cried as if men would kill them.]

In carvings such as the one that may be found in Ripon Cathedral, the woman is seated – here in the left supporter – presumably prior to joining the chase.[85] Two closely related misericords of the early sixteenth century should also be noted, as they appear to be directly indebted to Chaucer's version of the tale. The earlier of the carvings, in Manchester Cathedral, shows the fox fleeing from a woman holding a broken object, presumably her distaff. The background shows a 'narwe cotage', as in Chaucer's tale, rather than the more opulent farm buildings encountered in the French

[84] Chaucer, *Canterbury Tales*, VII 3380–2 and 3389–90.
[85] Block and Varty, 'Choir-Stall Carvings', pp. 136–7, record similar scenes at St Mary and All Saints, Whalley, and St Mary's, Minster-in-Thanet.

tradition, at the door of which is a female figure whom we may take to be one of Malkyn's 'doghtren two'.[86] A later version of this scene, clearly influenced by the Manchester carving, may be found in Beverley Minster.[87] This latter carving elaborates the scene further to include the farmyard chaos as the 'dokes cryden as men wolde hem quelle'.

Whatever small variants may occur between the different carvings, it is nonetheless essentially the same scene that is depicted. Although spanning a period of approximately one hundred and thirty years in illustrating this popular tale, this body of English carvings invariably focuses upon the fox's flight with the cock or goose, rather than its earlier pursuit of its victim or, later, the point at which fox and cock ruefully contemplate each other. '[H]e that wynketh, whan he sholde see, / Al wilfully, God lat him nevere thee!' [He who wilfully blinks when he should see, God let him never thrive!], says Chauntecleer in Chaucer's version:

> 'Nay,' quod the fox, 'but God yeve hym meschaunce,
> That is so undiscreet of governaunce
> That jangleth whan he sholde holde his pees.'[88]
>
> ['No,' said the fox, 'but God give misfortune to he who is careless in self-governance that he chatters when he should hold his peace.']

It has been plausibly suggested that '[t]he isolation of [the] dramatic chasing of the fox within churches almost certainly means that it could be given a moral point'.[89] However, given the ecclesiastical setting of these carvings, it seems surprising that not one surviving instance shows the point at which the tale's explicit moral is delivered. That the tale was indeed used as a moral *exemplum* by preachers in Chaucer's lifetime is attested by its inclusion in the *Summa praedicantium* of the English Dominican John Bromyard, composed some time before 1354,[90] and it has been suggested that this version may have been known to Chaucer, either from a manuscript of the work or indirectly through its use in sermons.[91] Consequently, it is entirely plausible that this is the *raison d'être* for the episode finding its way into the decoration of church choirs. And it is to this sermon tradition that we shall now turn.

'Taketh the moralite, goode men',[92] advises the Nun's Priest at the close of his tale, and many modern critics have taken him at his word, seeking to find a coherent religious lesson embedded in the tale.[93] Whilst such readings

[86] Chaucer, *Canterbury Tales*, VII 2822 and 2829.

[87] On the relationship between Manchester and Beverley, already discussed in chapter 3, see Charles Tracy, *English Gothic Choir-Stalls 1400–1540* (Woodbridge: The Boydell Press, 1990), pp. 16–31.

[88] Chaucer, *Canterbury Tales*, VII 3433–5.

[89] Block and Varty, 'Choir-Stall Carvings', p. 139.

[90] See A. P. Shallers, '*The Nun's Priest's Tale*: an Ironic Exemplum', *ELH* 42 (1975), 325–7.

[91] Helen Cooper, *The Canterbury Tales*, 2nd edn, Oxford Guides to Chaucer (Oxford: Oxford University Press, 1996), p. 343.

[92] Chaucer, *Canterbury Tales*, VII 3440.

[93] The critical tradition of reading the *Nun's Priest's Tale* as a religious or moral allegory is usefully summarised in Derek Pearsall, *The Canterbury Tales* (London: Routledge, 1993), pp. 235–8.

are sometimes more ingenious than persuasive, what may be far-fetched when interpreting Chaucer is not necessarily so when addressing uses of the story of the fox and cock within the Church. As Helen Cooper observes, '[t]he appearance of the story in a preaching handbook underscores the deep association of fable with *moralitee* that Chaucer treats so equivocally at the end of the tale'.[94] Derek Pearsall further pursues the matter of Chaucer's equivocal stance towards his source material in the *Nun's Priest's Tale*:

> [t]he idea of the cock as a preacher, or of the fox as diabolical seducer, is certainly present in the tale by implication, as is the series of quite explicit allusions to the Fall. But the effect is not to set out for us a diagram of salvation, but to take us deeper into the comedy of the tale, and particularly to allow us to enjoy there the rich humour of the comedy of survival converted to the comedy of salvation.[95]

Chaucer generates his comedy through the multiplication of morals, caricaturing 'the absurdities of allegorised fable, of stories that have one point matched with allegories that have another'.[96] Yet even when framed to fit Bromyard's explicitly moral purposes, the *moralitee* is, as A. P. Shallers explains, far from simple:

> For Bromyard, the tale's moral is more far-reaching than we may perhaps expect:
> The cock is a victim, of course, and the victimizing fox is unquestionably hell-bound. But then so is the cock whose eye-closing stunt reveals not only credulousness but sinful irrationality ... Bromyard adds later that the cock merely blinds himself to his own spiritual weakness when he curses the fox at the end.[97]

As we have already seen, however, the extant English misericord carvings invariably depict an earlier point in the narrative, showing the cock still very much the victim of his own vanity and folly, but not yet compounding his flaws by cursing his captor or, indeed, resorting to deceit to effect his physical escape. We may, then, reasonably assume that these carvings carry a much simpler moral, as they stop short of the complications caused by mutual deception at the end of the tale. In order to explain this moral, we must turn now to medieval allegorisation of poultry and, in doing so, encounter a possible reason – other than the purely aesthetic – for the substitution of a goose for the cock on a number of carvings.

It is important to note that poultry do not always appear on misericords solely as victims of the hungry and duplicitous fox. Cocks crow in Beverley Minster and Wells Cathedral, take flight in St Gregory, Sudbury, fight each

[94] Cooper, *Canterbury Tales*, p. 343.
[95] Pearsall, *Canterbury Tales*, p. 237.
[96] Ibid., p. 238.
[97] Shallers, '*Nun's Priest's Tale*', p. 326.

other on a misericord now housed in London's Victoria & Albert Museum, or simply scratch in the barnyard with hens and chickens as in Beverley Minster and Tewkesbury Abbey. Although apparently purely naturalistic representations, rather than suggesting broader narratives, these scenes may usefully be considered in conjunction with those carvings already discussed. If one was to set about writing a beast fable concerning the perils of vanity, the cock may well be one of the first creatures to come to mind; as Kenneth Varty has noted, '[n]obody can observe a cock for long without imputing to it a vain and pompous character'.[98] Certainly, Chaucer's Chauntecleer, 'roial, as a prince is in his halle',[99] perfectly fulfils this role. Yet, perhaps surprisingly, this is not the defining trait of medieval beast allegory, which instead emphasises and allegorises the wakefulness engendered by the cock's crow:

> The crowing of the cock is a pleasant sound at night, and not only pleasant but useful, because, like a good neighbour, it wakes the sleeper, encourages the down hearted, and comforts the traveller, by charting the progress of the night with its melodious voice ... the devout go to their prayers at cock-crow, and can read their books once more. When the cock crew thrice, the rock of the Church was cleansed of the guilt he had incurred by his denial of Christ before cock-crow. Its song brings back hope to everyone, eases the pain of the sick, cools the fevered brow, brings faith back to those who have lapsed.[100]

Likewise, the hen also carries positive allegorical connotations:

> Hens are symbols of divine wisdom, as Christ Himself said in the Gospels: 'O Jerusalem, Jerusalem, thou killest the prophets, and stonest them which are sent unto thee, how often would I have gathered thy children together, even as a hen gathereth her chickens under her wings'[101]

The Christian virtues which may be demonstrated by poultry appear elsewhere in a particularly creative metaphor which may be found in *Fasciculus morum*. Addressing the subject of avarice, *Fasciculus morum* expands upon an observation which may be found in the thirteenth-century *De Proprietatibus Rerum* of Bartholomæus Anglicus which states of the goshawk that,

> þey beþ iloued of hire lordes and ibore on hondes and isette on perchis and istroked in þe brest and in þe taile and imade playne and smothe, and þey beþ inorischid wiþ grete besynesse and diligence. But whanne þey dyeþ, alle men holdiþ hem vnprofitable

[98] Varty, *Reynard, Renart, Reinaert*, p. 37.
[99] Chaucer, *Canterbury Tales*, VII 3184.
[100] Barber (ed. and trans.), *Bestiary*, pp. 172–3.
[101] Ibid., p. 174. The source is Matthew 23:37.

> and nought worth, and beþ noght I-ete but more iþrowe out on dongehilles.[102]
>
> [they are beloved of their lords and carried on hands and set on perches stroked on the breast and the tail and made clean and smooth, and they are fed with great fuss and diligence. But when they die, all men hold them valueless and worth nothing, and they are not eaten but thrown out onto dunghills.]

This comment upon the transitory usefulness of the bird to man is embellished in *Fasciculus morum* for allegorical effect:

> With respect to the evil consequences for those who scorn voluntary poverty, we must know that a greedy rich man and one who is voluntarily poor will have the same end as the chicken and the falcon. For during his life the falcon is carried on the fist, sits on a perch, and is fed fresh meat; while the chicken lives in the most vile places, such as ditches and dungheaps, seeks food of the same kind, and is put in a coop. But when they are dead, the falcon is tossed in a ditch, whereas the chicken is roasted and brought before the king and his noblemen in the high hall. In the same way, during his life here a rich man is fed with dainty dishes, is clothed in precious garments, and so forth. But to be sure, when he dies, there is reason to fear that he may be thrown into the ditch of hell. A poor man, however, gains his living with hardship and vexation, but when he dies, his soul is brought before the king and his saints in the high hall of heaven.[103]

Whilst in this case attractively elaborated, the kernel of this simile, expressed more concisely in a sermon of around 1400 as:

> Trewly birdes raue*ners*, when þei die þei be cast awey vppon þe myddyng*es* as no þinge of valew, bot þe birdes þ*at* þei dud þ*er* rau*ee*yn too ben born to lordes tables,[104]
>
> [Truly, birds of prey when they die are cast away on dunghills as being nothing of value, but the birds that they preyed upon are borne to lords' tables,]

is a sermon commonplace.[105] Thus, casting our net widely across contemporary moralisations, we can see that poultry carried connotations

[102] *On the Properties of Things: John Trevisa's translation of Bartholomæus Anglicus De Proprietatibus Rerum, A Critical Text*, ed. M. C. Seymour *et al.*, 2 vols (Oxford: Clarendon Press, 1975), I, 609. I would like to thank Baudouin Van den Abeele for drawing my attention to the example from Bartholomæus.

[103] *Fasciculus morum*, p. 393. I have translated the Latin *gallina* as *chicken*, rather than Wenzel's *hen*. On manuscript survival, see pp. 1–2.

[104] Woodburn O. Ross (ed.), *Middle English Sermons edited from British Museun MS. Royal 18 B. xxiii*, EETS o.s. 209 (London: Oxford University Press, 1940), p. 239.

[105] Wenzel draws attention to occurrences elsewhere in Bromyard and Holcot: *Fasciculus morum*, p. 397.

of spiritual wakefulness, comfort, wisdom and humility. These virtues, whilst appropriate to all Christians, are particularly apposite to members of the clergy whose explicit role may be defined as to 'wake the sleeper ... bring back faith to those who have lapsed' and 'gather their chickens under their wings'. Consequently, whilst we may read an image of a fox making off with a proverbially foolish goose as a generic warning against folly, the substitution of the rather less aesthetically pleasing cock surely carries a pointed reference to the clergy and the necessity of their humility as, indeed, exemplified by Chaucer's 'povre Persoun of a Toun'.[106]

That misericord carvings of the fox and the cock focus solely on the fox's escape with his hapless prey, then, is not surprising. To the purely clerical audience of such scenes, the important moral is to avoid the puff of pride and winking when one should be vigilant; to follow Chauntecleer's example and effect a physical escape after the fact through counter-deception would not be a suitable option. But why, in this case, do our carvings show the uniquely English feature of the chase? A clue to the answer may lie in Chaucer's description of the pursuit:

> They yolleden as feendes doon in helle;
> The dokes cryden as men wolde hem quelle;
> The gees for feere flowen over the trees;
> Out of the hyve cam the swarm of bees.
> So hydous was the noyse – a, benedictee! –
> Certes, he Jakke Straw and his meynee
> Ne made nevere shoutes half so shrille
> Whan that they wolden any Flemyng kille,
> As thilke day was maad upon the fox.[107]

> [They cried as devils do in Hell; the ducks cried as if men would kill them; the geese, for fear, flew over the trees; out of the hive came a swarm of bees. So hideous was the noise – ah, the Lord bless us! – certainly, Jack Straw and his company never shouted half so shrilly when they would kill any Fleming, as was made this day on account of the fox.]

For all the energy expended, the chase is in itself ineffective, merely providing an opportunity for Chauntecleer to deceive daun Russell, rather than to be rescued by his pursuers. Chaucer's apparently off-hand comparison of this barnyard lynch mob with the bloodthirsty rebels of the 1381 Revolt has been seen as 'very characteristic of the way he experiences political and social conflict, converting it into material for anecdotal humour, private and personal confrontations, and literary games'.[108] This, however, seems an unlikely response to the events of June 1381 from a civil servant living above Aldgate – the site of the rebels' entry into the city – and

[106] Chaucer, *Canterbury Tales*, I 478.
[107] Ibid., VII 3389–97.
[108] Derek Pearsall, *The Life of Geoffrey Chaucer* (Oxford: Blackwell, 1992), p. 147.

whilst, as Helen Phillips notes, '[t]here is no consistently worked out political allegory in the tale … it can, all the same, be read as a fictional attempt to contain awareness of new social forces and tensions ….'[109] Rather, the comparison may be indebted, at least indirectly, to the images of tension that we have been considering: in short, a failure of the clergy begets disorder. W. A. Pantin long ago suggested that the 'rise of the devout layman [was] one of the most important phenomena of the middle ages',[110] but this rise, coupled with the 'spread of literacy down the social scale, even to many women',[111] led to the challenges to the authority of the Church – and, indeed, government – which characterised late fourteenth-century England and which have, of necessity, informed our readings thus far. As Chaucer alludes to a recent popular uprising so, too, do our misericords refer to the threat or actuality of disorder within a turbulent period.

In our one carving that pre-dates 1381, on the choir stalls at Ely, the supporter to the main scene, in which the housewife looms threateningly over fox and cock, shows a cowled fox preaching to a congregation of poultry. Building upon my interpretations so far outlined, this carving would appear specifically to address the consequences of clerical failing; the hypocritical outward show preys upon the virtue that should reside within, and lay disorder ensues. Subsequent to 1381, such overt marginal commentary on the chase is no longer needed.

> But ye that holden this tale a folye,
> As of a fox, or of a cok and hen,
> Taketh the moralite, goode men.
> For Seint Paul seith that al that writen is,
> To oure doctrine it is ywrite, ywis;
> Taketh the fruyt, and lat the chaf be stille.[112]

> [But you who consider this tale a trifle of a fox, or of a cock and a hen, take the morality, good men. For Saint Paul says that all that is written is written for our edification, indeed; take the fruit and let the chaff remain.]

So the Nun's Priest advises us before he takes his leave, though it is, as many readers find, far from easy to discern precisely where the 'fruyt' may lie and what it may signify. However, when turning our attention to the fox and its prey on English misericords, there is a clear message that the viewer should not attempt to out-fox the fox but should, rather, follow the sound advice of *Fasciculus morum* and remain a lowly chicken until brought before the Lord.

Every image must, of course, be carefully considered in its own context,

[109] Helen Phillips, *An Introduction to the Canterbury Tales* (London: Macmillan, 2000), p. 194.
[110] W. A. Pantin, *The English Church in the Fourteenth Century* (Cambridge: Cambridge University Press, 1955), p. 253.
[111] Eamon Duffy, *The Stripping of the Altars: Traditional Religion in England c. 1400–1580* (New Haven and London: Yale University Press, 1992), p. 68.
[112] Chaucer, *Canterbury Tales*, VII 3438–43.

and the glass through which we view these images over half a millennium remains dark. Our apes and foxes – and, indeed, elephants, bears, poultry or any of the other beasts which abound on misericords – may possibly, on occasion, offer satirical commentary upon social ills or, as Houwen suggests, simply provide decoration. Yet when we think of the location, the audience and the culture in which these images were carved, a more serious message once again seems to arise. In consequence, we should always bear in mind – whatever first impressions may suggest – that 'the fabled intrigues of the fox and the cock' are not always mere 'folye', and that just because we see an ape with a uroscopy flask, it does not necessarily mean that it is taking the piss. When, however, the creatures that we encounter are not those which we may find in the natural world, our consideration of meaning is arguably further complicated with, as we shall see in the next chapter, potential meanings becoming multiplied as we move further into the realm of imagination and, indeed, away from the imaginative culture in which they were conceived and carved.

# THE MONSTERS AT THE MARGINS 6

'When I use a word,' says Humpty Dumpty in Lewis Carroll's fantasy world of White Rabbits, Gryphons and other curious hybrids, 'it means just what I choose it to mean.'[1] As modern viewers of misericords, as much as we may identify with Langland's constantly questioning Will, we may equally find ourselves in the position of Carroll's dream-narrative protagonist, Alice, asking questions of strange figures, always curious though sometimes sceptical of the answers as they appear to invent their own rules of meaning. As we have seen throughout our investigations, these figures, occupying that curious space which paradoxically draws attention to itself through its partial obscurity, act as enigmatic intermediaries between the devotional culture of the late Middle Ages and the present, with a frequently obtuse, Humpty-like self-confidence which we must negotiate. Carroll's own response to the misericords of Ripon Cathedral, to which he was a regular visitor when his father was a cathedral canon during the 1850s and 1860s, was to create the irascible White Rabbit who leads us into ever more baffling conundrums and the obtuse Gryphon who offers answers which clarify nothing at all,[2] a situation which neatly mirrors the mix of intrigue and frustration which often faces us today. Whilst this interpretative challenge is always present, it is perhaps most acute when we look to those fantastic creatures of the imagination – the legendary beasts, hybrids and semi-

[1] Lewis Carroll, *Through the Looking-Glass and What Alice Found There*, in *Alice's Adventures in Wonderland and Through the Looking-Glass: The Centenary Edition*, ed. Hugh Haughton (London: Penguin Books, 1998), p. 186.

[2] St Mary, Beverley, also makes claims for inspiration for Carroll's White Rabbit, citing the 'pilgrim rabbit' carved at the entrance to the sacristy. Whilst it is perhaps significant that the Ripon misericord depicts both rabbits and a gryphon, there is no reason to limit the figure to one particular source. Indeed, John Pudney suggests the pulpit of All Saints, Daresbury – the place of Carroll's birth – as a possible source for the gryphon: John Pudney, *Lewis Carroll and His World* (London: Thames and Hudson, 1976), p. 27. Elsewhere, Malcolm Jones has persuasively suggested that the Beverley stone sculpture is in fact a hare, with rather more in common with Carroll's messenger, Haigha, than his White Rabbit: see Malcolm Jones, *The Secret Middle Ages: Discovering the Real Medieval World* (Stroud: Sutton Publishing, 2002), pp. 137–8. The important point to note here is the imaginative response engendered across the centuries by the marginal arts of the later Middle Ages.

humans who populate the margins of the imagined medieval world with seemingly little differentiation from the people and beasts who could be encountered daily in town, village or, indeed, monastic life. It is to these we shall now turn, before addressing their place in the one part of the British Isles which we have not yet visited, a geographically and ideologically 'marginal' place in the Middle Ages, in which England and its influence was arguably most contentiously felt: Ireland.

In chapter 4 we have already seen how widespread the motif of the seductive bird/fish-woman hybrid is, yet an even more commonly represented fantastic creature on misericords is the Wild Man, otherwise known as a wodehouse or wodewose, whose human form is covered in coarse, shaggy hair. A popular motif of both ecclesiastical and domestic medieval art throughout Europe, more than forty Wild Men survive on English misericords, where they are often depicted alongside – and sometimes fighting – dragons or lions. In Hereford Cathedral, for example, a Wild Man subjugates a lion, that most noble of beasts, the carver drawing particular attention to the firmness of his grasp upon the lion's right flank. Whilst it is generally the Wild Man who gets the upper hand in these conflicts, he is not always so fortunate, and a carving in St Andrew, Norton, shows a less favourable outcome for the defeated Wild Man who is shown being eaten by the lion (fig. 30). Whoever the victor – or, indeed, if no combat is taking place, as in the scene of two Wild Men flanked by monumental dragons in St Mary, Beverley – the emphasis in these images is upon the Wild Man's strength, often stressed further by the addition of a substantial club or roughly hewn branch which he holds aloft. But to what purpose this strength is employed is something that is far from clear when considering his frequent appearances on misericords and elsewhere. Discussing a misericord from Chester Cathedral on which a Wild Man, arms raised triumphantly, rides on the back of a lion, Christa Grössinger suggests that 'the lion symbolises loyalty and strength, which the wodehouse has made his own by taming it',[3] yet in bestiary lore the lion is said to be a symbol of Christ. What are we to make of the Wild Man's triumphant bearing in this case? Further complicating possible readings, the lion is cited, somewhat surprisingly, as an exemplar of a placid

FIG. 30. ST ANDREW, NORTON MISERICORD.

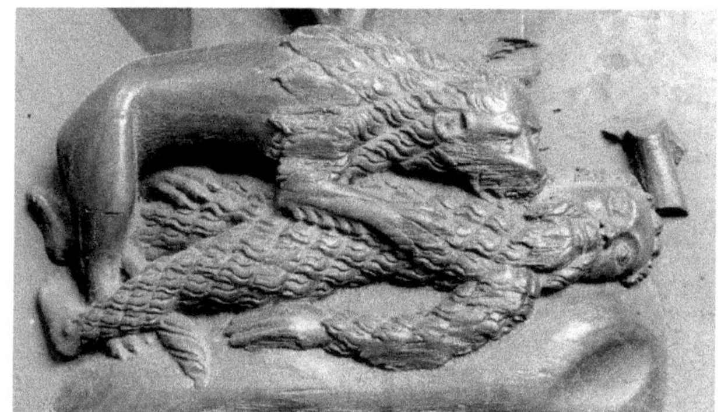

[3] In Jonathan Alexander and Paul Binski (eds), *Age of Chivalry: Art in Plantagenet England 1200–1400* (London: Weidenfeld and Nicholson, 1987), p. 433.

nature and even temper, with the advice that 'unreasonable men should learn by this example'.[4] In this context, then, the Wild Man may be seen as a representation of inappropriate, uncontrolled strength – quite literally 'unreasonable' wildness, possibly even threatening the autonomy of the Christian Church. Yet this is but one aspect of what is an intriguingly complex figure.

The Wild Man seems to owe his origins to the lore of the Germanic forest, possibly as a remnant of pre-Christian beliefs and practices,[5] although his traceable existence in the arts of Europe leads us back only as far as the twelfth century.[6] Whatever his origins, by the later Middle Ages he had become a part of both the literature of romance and urban festive culture. The fourteenth-century alliterative *Wars of Alexander*, for example, relates how Alexander is confronted by '[a] burly best & a bigg' [a great, burly beast] who:

> · was as a man shapen,
> Vmquile he groned as a galt · with grysely latis,
> Vmquile he noys as a nowte · as a nox quen he lawes,
> ȝarmand & ȝerand · a ȝoten him semed;
> And was as bristils as a bare · all þe body ouire …[7]

> [… was shaped like a man. Sometimes he grunted like a boar with dreadful voice, sometimes he made a noise like cattle, like an ox when he bellows, yelling and screaming, he seemed like a giant; and he was as bristly as a boar all over his body …]

Before the Wild Man can cause any harm, however, Alexander baits him with a 'comly mayden', which seductive distraction allows him to be captured and destroyed.[8] More commonly, however, the Wild Man's capture by the maiden is represented in terms of his uncontrolled sexual energy being appropriately tamed and focused upon licit desire, rather than merely distracted long enough to facilitate capture: the implicit message is that one's most powerful urges need not be negated but, rather, may be appropriately directed. This is nowhere more clearly expressed than on a misericord in St Mary, Whalley, in which a Wild Man reclines, his head supported on one hand as he gazes devotedly at a primly attired lady. The lady holds a scroll upon which is inscribed 'Penses molt et p(ar)les pou' [Think much and speak little]. Christa Grössinger comments on the appropriateness of the lesson:

[4] Richard Barber (ed. and trans.), *Bestiary, Being an English Version of the Bodleian Library, Oxford MS Bodley 764*. (Woodbridge: Boydell Press, 1993), pp. 23–5.

[5] The most comprehensive study of the origins and symbolism of the Wild Man remains Richard Bernheimer, *Wild Men in the Middle Ages: A Study in Art, Sentiment and Demonology* (Cambridge, MA: Harvard University Press, 1952).

[6] This is noted in Meg Twycross and Sarah Carpenter, *Masks and Masking in Medieval and Early Tudor England* (Aldershot: Ashgate, 2002), pp. 48–51.

[7] *The Wars of Alexander: an Alliterative Romance, Translated Chiefly from the Historia Alexandri Magni De Preliis*, ed. Walter W. Skeat, EETS e.s. 47 (London: N. Trübner and Co., 1886), ll. 4742–6.

[8] Ibid., ll. 4755–62.

> [The Wild Man] could not speak as he had no experience of civilization, whereas the Lady spoke the language of culture and romance, and his gesture of propping up his head with his hand is characteristic of deep melancholic thought probably brought about by his passionate yearnings which he must tame.

She goes on to suggest that the lady's damaged right hand may originally have held a birch, 'to reinforce her lesson'.[9] In view of the numerous images of dominant women that we encountered in chapter 4, this appears a strong possibility. Nonetheless, it seems to me that, in considering the lady's stance – paying no attention to the Wild Man but instead looking forthrightly at the viewer – it would be more likely that the raised right hand would have been making some sort of gesture aimed directly at the viewer, thereby signalling that this is not merely a scene of the maiden taming wildness but, rather, an admonition to the viewer to take heed and employ purity and innocence in order to tame his own wildness in favour of a more contemplative life.

When translated into the festive culture of the medieval court or, indeed, street, the Wild Man became a figure of misrule and licence, particularly, as we may expect from the foregoing discussion, of a sexual nature, with the phallic aspects of his club/branch exploited to the full, in rather the same manner as the fool's phallic *marotte*.[10] Phyllis Siefker goes so far as to suggest that the traditional fool was in fact a descendant of the Wild Man,[11] although the co-existence of the two figures throughout the medieval period suggests kinship rather than lineage, the Wild Man possessing an element of unbridled nature which is not part of the composition of the essentially social fool.

Most commonly, then, we may think of the Wild Man as a figure broadly encompassing mankind's uncontrolled natural urges which need to be tamed – or in a festive context, indulged, albeit within carefully regulated parameters. Perhaps the most famous enactment of the opportunities offered for misrule by the Wild Man disguise is that of the tragic 'Bal des Ardents' masking of 1392, recorded by Froissart, in which four courtiers, who 'appeared like savages, for they were covered with hair from head to foot', died when their

[9] Christa Grössinger, *The World Upside-Down: English Misericords* (London: Harvey Miller Publishers, 1997), p. 146.

[10] For the theatrical aspect of the Wild Man, see Bernheimer, *Wild Men in the Middle Ages*, pp. 49–84. On the incorporation of the Wild Man as a symbol of sexual desire in courtly circles, see Michael Camille's comments on the decorative motifs on a number of German gift caskets from the fourteenth century: Michael Camille, *The Medieval Art of Love: Objects and Subjects of Desire* (New York: Harry N. Abrams, 1998), pp. 66–7. Another example in a different medium is the tapestry showing Wild Men hunting, now in the Musée Historique de Bâle, which, significantly, was made to commemorate the marriage in 1468 of a former Mayor of Basle, Hans von Flachslanden, to Barbara von Breitenlandenberg of St Gall. Such examples in a number of media, frequently associated with betrothal and marriage, may be found throughout Europe.

[11] Phyllis Siefker, *Santa Claus, Last of the Wild Men: The Origins and Evolution of Saint Nicholas, Spanning 50,000 Years* (Jefferson: McFarland, 1997), p. 123.

costumes caught fire from the hall torches.[12] A fifth reveller, King Charles VI of France himself, was only saved because he had separated himself from the group in order to present himself to the watching ladies, 'as was natural to his youth'[13] – a phrase which Meg Twycross and Sarah Carpenter interpret as indicative of youthful irresponsibility,[14] but it should also be borne in mind that this behaviour is more generally an example of the kind of irresponsibility in keeping with the licence afforded by the Wild Man disguise. Yet when this force of nature is tamed, associations with reckless misrule give way to positive connotations of strength. The narrator of the mid-fourteenth-century poem *Wynnere and Wastoure*,[15] for example, describes an emblem of a Wild Man amidst the king's panoply of noble display: 'Vpon heghe one the hale ane hathell vp stondes, / Wroughte als a wodwyse alle in wrethyn lokkes' [High on the tent a noble man stands up, fashioned like a Wild Man all in tangled hair].[16] Such associations with nobility may be found on a misericord in St Paul, Bedford, which depicts a castle occupying the central console flanked in the supporters by a knight with a crossbow and a Wild Man carrying, in addition to his familiar club, a shield bearing the town's arms. Such heraldic employment of the Wild Man, along with perhaps some of the scenes of combat considered above, attests to his symbolic status as a figure of resolutely harnessed strength to be both admired and depended upon.

The Wild Man's iconographic possibilities are further compounded when we consider the similarity of his furred body to the shaggy devils which proliferate in the art of the period.[17] Richard Bernheimer, in his seminal study, finds no explicit European written association of the Wild Man with devils until the second quarter of the sixteenth century, although he offers persuasive evidence to suggest that such connections were made at least as early as the late fifteenth century.[18] Scarcity of written evidence, however, should not detract from the implications of close physical similarity in visual

[12] John Froissart, *Chronicles of England, France, Spain and the Adjoining Countries*, trans. Thomas Johnes, 2 vols (London: William Smith, 1839), 2.550.

[13] Ibid.

[14] Twycross and Carpenter, *Masks and Masking*, p. 145.

[15] On the date of *Wynnere and Wastoure*, see Thorlac Turville-Petre (ed.), *Alliterative Poetry of the Later Middle Ages: an Anthology* (London: Routledge, 1989), pp. 38–9. Dating, however, remains contentious: see, for example, David A. Lawton, 'The Unity of Middle English Alliterative Poetry', *Speculum* 58 (1983), 80–1, in which a case is made for the poem post-dating Langland's *Piers Plowman*.

[16] *Wynnere and Wastore*, in Turville-Petre (ed.), *Alliterative Poetry of the Later Middle Ages*, ll. 70–1. In his notes to the poem, Turville-Petre explains that for *holt*, wood', in l. 70 of the ms, he has emended the text to read *hale*, 'tent', in order to make sense of the passage. Whilst 'holt' does render the sense obscure, if it is indeed the correct reading it indicates not a heraldic symbol but, rather, an actual knight dressed as a Wild Man, a disguise which was not unknown at contemporary tournaments: see T. H. Bestul, *Satire and Allegory in Wynnere and Wastoure* (Lincoln, NE: Nebraska University Press, 1974), p. 103.

[17] Of the hundreds of medieval devils across all media throughout the country, perhaps the most remarkable array is to be found in the stained glass of St Mary, Fairford, although neither Wild Men nor devils appear on the earlier misericords.

[18] Bernheimer, *Wild Men in the Middle Ages*, pp. 59–61.

representation which suggests that there could indeed be a diabolic aspect to the Wild Man. To further confuse matters, however, Malcolm Jones draws attention to a tradition of religious folktale known as 'The Hairy Anchorite', in which the protagonist, after perpetrating a particularly brutal crime – the emphasis in these narratives is very much on transgressions of the body – flees to the wood and becomes a Wild Man, later attaining sanctity.[19] We may discern in this a symbolic use of the Wild Man which signifies the descent into the most bestial aspects of humanity. Yet, at the same time, this descent is also a necessary stage of the protagonist's reconstitution as a saint, seeming to suggest that he cannot rise to sanctity without first relinquishing all humanity. In a perplexity of meaning every bit as tangled as the wild wood which he inhabits, then, we may see in the figure of the Wild Man both licence and control, the devil and the saint. Placed, as he so frequently is, within the church, we may then consider the Wild Man as a simultaneous embodiment of a multiplicity of sometimes apparently mutually exclusive attributes. Like his frequently depicted distant cousin, the Green Man, whom we considered in the introduction, the Wild Man is neither of nature nor of humanity, neither demonic nor sanctified, but instead occupies the border between virtue and vice, the physical and the spiritual. As such, he provides a mirror for the experiential choice open to the viewer, in which human will alone can decide which way to turn: either to immoral licence or moral strength. Consequently, whilst M. W. Tisdall's suggestion that the Wild Man is 'God's bouncer' may initially appear somewhat frivolous, he certainly seems to act as a deterrent against entering into that which one should not.[20]

The Wild Man is thus, like the closely related fool, one of the embodiments *par excellence* of the margins, manifesting not only Otherness, but also potential mutability for good or ill. This ambiguous duality is something which may also be seen as applicable to perceptions of the inhabitants of the geographical margins of the western medieval worldview, whether located in the exotic 'East' or in locations rather closer to home. That the margins of the known world need not be drawn too far away can be illustrated with reference to an anecdote recorded by Bede. In AD 634, Bede tells us, Pope Honorius wrote to the Scots – that is, the Irish – concerning their 'error' about the observance of Easter:

> He earnestly warned them not to imagine that their little community, isolated at the uttermost ends of the earth, had a wisdom exceeding that of all churches ancient and modern throughout the world.[21]

[19] The folktale motif is outlined in Jones, *Secret Middle Ages*, pp. 65–6; specific examples, including St John of Beverley who was said to have raped and murdered his sister before entering his self-imposed exile of madness, are discussed on pp. 24–5.

[20] M. W. Tisdall, *God's Beasts: Identify and Understand Animals in Church Carvings* (Plymouth: Charlesfort Press, 1998), p. 158.

[21] Bede, *A History of the English Church and People*, trans. Leo Sherley-Price, revised edn (Harmondsworth: Penguin, 1968), p. 136.

We are in the present study concerned with a much later period, yet one to which Honorius's acidic comments are, as we shall see, no less pertinent. We will shortly take a close look at the late fifteenth-century choir stalls in St Mary's Cathedral, Limerick, which possess the only surviving set of misericords in Ireland, depicting a range of figures which represents a broad spectrum stretching from the divine to the bestial. By virtue of this unique location, the primarily devotional nature of the carvings beneath the Limerick stalls is explicitly compounded and, indeed, complicated by concerns of geographical, political and ideological marginality to a particularly acute degree. Before turning to this fascinating body of carvings, however, it is appropriate to place Ireland within the thought of the Christian Middle Ages, in which Honorius's derogatory classification of it as 'the uttermost ends of the earth' provides something of an early, concise summary of a lasting and more widely held view.

Gerald of Wales, towards the end of the twelfth century, prefaces his *History and Topography of Ireland* from a similar perspective to that expressed in those earlier comments by Honorius. Visiting Ireland at the behest of Henry II, Gerald was chosen to undertake the trip because of his family ties with some of the first Anglo-Norman conquerors. Thus, whilst his personal political bias may frustrate or even anger later generations of readers, his account perfectly articulates the Anglo-Norman perspectives held by Ireland's near neighbours.[22] 'What secret things', asks Gerald, 'not in her usual course [has] nature hidden away in the farthest western lands?'

> For beyond those limits there is no land, nor is there any habitation either of men or beasts – but beyond the whole horizon only the ocean flows and is borne on in boundless space through its unsearchable and hidden ways.
>
> Just as the countries of the East are remarkable and distinguished for certain prodigies peculiar and native to themselves, so the boundaries of the West also are made remarkable by their own wonders of nature. For sometimes tired, as it were, of the true and the serious, she draws aside and goes away, and in these remote parts indulges herself in these secret and distant freaks.[23]

[22] Gerald, of course, was himself culturally marginal, being part Welsh and part Norman. However, although decidedly Welsh in his discussion of matters pertaining to Wales, '[e]arly in his career Gerald learned to allay his ambivalence of origin by becoming an enthusiastic colonizer of Ireland, a place distant enough for him to construct an unambiguous other whose dispossession and eradication allowed him to forget for a while the similarly violent history of colonization that produced him': Jeffrey Jerome Cohen, 'Hybrids, Monsters, Borderlands: The Bodies of Gerald of Wales', in *The Postcolonial Middle Ages*, ed. Jeffrey Jerome Cohen (New York: Palgrave, 2001), pp. 93–4. On Gerald's 'hybridity', see also, Asa Simon Mittman, 'The Other Close at Hand: Gerald of Wales and the "Marvels of the West"', in *The Monstrous Middle Ages*, ed. Bettina Bildhauer and Robert Mills (Cardiff: University of Wales Press, 2003), pp. 97–112.

[23] Gerald of Wales, *The History and Topography of Ireland*, trans. John J. O'Meara (London: Penguin, 1982), p. 31.

Gerald, naturally, takes great delight in recounting 'these secret and distant freaks' at length, devoting much of the Second Part of his work to recording such prodigies as strange beasts and unnatural births. When it comes to describing the inhabitants, they, too, are firmly located outside the norm:

> This people is, then, a barbarous people, literally barbarous. Judged according to modern ideas, they are uncultivated, not only in the external appearance of their dress, but also in their flowing hair and beards. All their habits are the habits of barbarians. Since conventions are formed from living together in society, and since they are so removed in these distant parts from the ordinary world of men, as if they were in another world altogether and consequently cut off from well-behaved and law-abiding people, they know only of the barbarous habits in which they were born and brought up, and embrace them as another nature.[24]

In Gerald's narrative, then, we find the disdainful language of the conqueror – elsewhere, for example, we find that the 'flowing hair and beards are not the sole domain of the men', attributing to the inhabitants the characteristics of Wild Men and Women – exotically mixed with the loquacious extravagance of the traveller's tale so beloved in the period. As we see above, Ireland is specifically compared with the mysterious East of works such as the famous *Travels of Sir John Mandeville* – we may recall, for example, the unnamed, savage island in the domain of Prester John, 'where the folk be all skinned rough hair, as a rough beast, save only the face and the palm of the hand … And they eat both flesh and fish all raw'[25] – locating it at the utmost remove from the civilised centre of 'well-behaved and law-abiding people'.

Incidences of this classification of Ireland as being at the edge of the world multiplied throughout the Middle Ages,[26] whether from the political perspective of the Anglo-Normans whose twelfth-century conquest of the country never managed to achieve full control, or as a result of a wider European perspective that located Ireland at the furthermost western reaches of Christendom. As one may expect from such circumstances, Colum Hourihane's work in the hitherto under-represented field of Gothic art in Ireland has located Irish art of the later Middle Ages firmly within a culture of marginality and instability.[27] He points out that within the intensely politicised history of Gothic forms – which are generally

[24] Ibid., pp. 102–3.

[25] John Mandeville, *The Travels of Sir John Mandeville*, ed. A. W. Pollard (London: Macmillan, 1900; repr. Mineola: Dover Publications, 1964), p. 196. As John Block Friedman notes, the hairy people recorded in the Middle Ages have many antecedents in Pliny and the legends of Alexander the Great. See John Block Friedman, *The Monstrous Races in Medieval Art and Thought* (Syracuse: Syracuse University Press, 2000), pp. 15–16.

[26] For further examples, see Seán Duffy, *Ireland in the Middle Ages* (London: Macmillan, 1997), pp. 7–10.

[27] Colum Hourihane, *Gothic Art in Ireland 1169–1550: Enduring Vitality* (New Haven and London: Yale University Press, 2003).

characterised as being introduced into Ireland by English invaders in the twelfth century and rejected during the 'Gaelic Revival' of the fifteenth century – there is a complex interplay of native and more broadly European forms.[28] Thus the art of the late Middle Ages in Ireland may be termed 'marginal' in many senses, and few works can be considered more so than those chance survivals in the 'most fertile of marginal genres',[29] with which we are concerned, the misericords in St Mary's Cathedral, Limerick.

The Limerick stalls can be dated to the late fifteenth century – probably during the renovation and enlargement of the cathedral by Bishop Folan (1489–1521)[30] – a period in which England, its attentions recently occupied by the Wars of the Roses, was losing its hold in Ireland, particularly in the west. By this time, the English craftsmen who had spearheaded the introduction of Gothic art into Ireland had largely been superseded by native craftsmen,[31] whose skill may be clearly seen in the surviving carvings, which compare favourably with contemporary work carried out in England. Of the twenty-three stalls, twenty contain identifiable carvings on misericords, with one defaced beyond recognition and two having modern seats. The misericords are no longer located in their original sequence, having been rearranged in 1906,[32] and a study from 1893 makes mention of twenty 'modern' stalls, suggesting that there had been at least one earlier reordering.[33]

In common with many English sets, the misericords display a broad range of subjects, ranging from the human to the monstrous, and from the bestial to the celestial. Five of the main motifs are repeated twice, although the work of different hands is suggested by variations in treatment of the square, foliate supporters which are common to all of the misericords. Even allowing for possible thematic relationships which may have been obscured by past rearrangement, it is initially difficult to posit any coherent overriding scheme across the carvings. One notable design, depicting an angel with clasped hands, rising from a ducal coronet, is the crest of the Harolds,[34] 'one of the most ancient families in the city of Limerick', whose line throughout the later Middle Ages included twelve mayors, eighteen bailiffs

[28] See especially ibid., pp. 19–34 on the politics of artistic form both in the late medieval period and in subsequent historiography.

[29] Michael Camille, *Image on the Edge: The Margins of Medieval Art* (London: Reaktion Books, 1992), p. 93.

[30] The dating offered in D. Alleyne Walter, 'Ancient Woodwork IV: The Misericords in the Cathedral Church of Limerick', *The Reliquary*, n. s. 7 (July 1893), 129, has not subsequently been challenged. On Bishop Folan, see Maurice Lenihan, *Limerick: Its History and Antiquities, Ecclesiastical, Civil, and Military, from the Earliest Ages* (repr., Cork: The Mercier Press, 1967), pp. 577–8.

[31] Hourihane, *Gothic Art in Ireland*, pp. 140–4.

[32] G. L. Remnant, *A Catalogue of Misericords in Great Britain* (London: Oxford University Press, 1969), p. 200.

[33] In summer 2002, the stalls were temporarily on display in the north transept during restoration work in the choir.

[34] J. A. Haydn, *Misericords in St Mary's Cathedral Limerick*, revised M. J. Talbot (Limerick: Treaty Press, 1994), p. 10. The Harold family motto is 'formitas in caelo'.

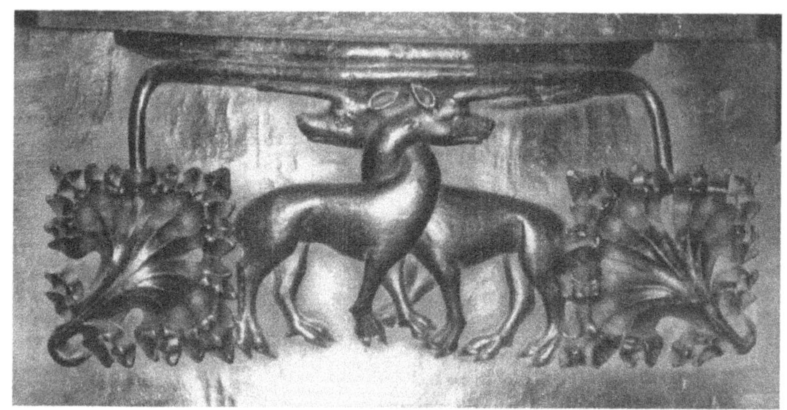

FIG. 31. LIMERICK CATHEDRAL MISERICORD.

and sheriffs, and a bishop.[35] Whilst the exact nature of this commemoration/patronage is clarified by no surviving documentary evidence, it does, however, place the only explicitly religious image on the stalls firmly into the sphere of earthly commemoration. Once this is taken into consideration, we may initially view all the carvings as representing decidedly physical concerns. Apart from two scenes depicting a battle between a lion and a wyvern, and one showing two horned beasts – variously identified as unicorns (Remnant), antelopes (Haydn) or yales (Hourihane) – all of the carvings show simple portraits without any suggestion of narrative content (fig. 31).[36] Indeed, even those which show two beasts cannot really be said to suggest a narrative as such but are, rather, self-contained scenes. Consequently, the Limerick carvings appear to represent a mere picture gallery of men, animals and fabulous beasts; and it is to these two latter categories that we shall now turn.

As we saw in the last chapter, in medieval beast lore all animals, both real and fantastic, could be subject to elaborate and ingenious allegorisation, and it is useful to consider this background to those which are depicted in Limerick. If we commence with the real animals, the antelope's serrated horns are likened by the bestiary to 'the two Testaments … with the help of which you can fell and root out all bodily and spiritual vices'; in particular, the snares of drunkenness and the consequent descent into lust,[37] '[f]or wine and women make men forsake God'.[38] The eagle was believed in old age to consume itself in the fire of the sun before plunging three times into the water of a clear fountain, thereby renewing itself through the fire of the sun's rays. This the bestiary uses in order to exhort those 'whose clothes are old

[35] Lenihan, *Limerick*, pp. 141–2.

[36] Remnant, *Catalogue of Misericords*, p. 199; Haydn, *Misericords in St Mary's Cathedral*, p. 11; Hourihane, *Gothic Art in Ireland*, pp. 91–2.

[37] Barber (ed. and trans.), *Bestiary*, p. 34.

[38] Willene B. Clark, *A Medieval Book of Beasts. The Second-Family Bestiary: Commentary, Art, Text and Translation* (Woodbridge: The Boydell Press, 2006), p. 126.

and the eyes of whose heart are darkened' to turn to 'the spiritual fountain of the Lord' in order to renew their own spiritual vigour.[39] We have already encountered the 'wild and unruly' boar in chapter 5, where we saw how, 'in the spiritual sense [it] means the devil'.[40] We may expect the elegant swan – which, as Hourihane observes, is rather less common than the other Limerick beasts in medieval Irish art[41] – to have more positive connotations: Edward I, after all, chose the swan as his heraldic device. Contrary to these expectations, however, the bestiary offers it as yet another admonitory example, asserting that it 'represents successful deception' through its concealment of black flesh under white feathers, and pride and delight in earthly things which lead ultimately to damnation.[42] If we consider the way in which these diverse images, and that which they each individually signify, are combined within the choir of Limerick Cathedral, we may perhaps discern a generic message of virtuous living coupled with sharp reminders of the consequences of falling into vice. Indeed, this supposition is reinforced if we interpret the carvings of combat between the lion and the wyvern as signifying the battle between good and evil – a very common trope of late medieval Irish art.[43]

But what are we to make of the fantastic beasts that outnumber representations of 'real' animals by about two to one? Following the conclusions drawn from our cursory look at the moralisations of the birds and beasts that the carvers and patrons would recognise from the natural world, we may reasonably apply the same technique to the fantastic beasts which accompany them beneath the choir stalls. As Pamela Gravestock has observed of creatures as they are depicted in bestiaries:

> In general, the imaginary animals are not treated in a more fantastic manner or given any special attributes or qualities that would serve to separate them from living animals, except of course for those features that identify them as a particular imaginary 'species' (such as the unicorn's horn or the griffin's beak, wings and paws) … In fact, in the bestiaries, the imaginary animals are given the same treatment – both pictorially and textually – as those animals that were known to exist.[44]

The same observation may be made of the fabulous creatures carved on the misericords at Limerick, and indeed elsewhere, in which one may discern nothing in the style of representation to delineate classes of beasts. Consequently, there is no reason to believe that they were in any way intended to be read differently from their natural counterparts. Whether a

[39] Barber (ed. and trans.), *Bestiary*, pp. 118–19.
[40] Ibid., p. 87.
[41] Hourihane, *Gothic Art in Ireland*, pp. 79 and 97–8.
[42] Barber (ed. and trans.), *Bestiary*, pp. 134–5.
[43] Hourihane, *Gothic Art in Ireland*, p. 92.
[44] Pamela Gravestock, 'Did Imaginary Animals Exist?', in *The Mark of the Beast*, ed. Debra Hassig (New York and London: Routledge, 2000), p. 120.

creature is observed from life or is the product of the medieval imagination, it is, therefore, given equal weight on what is seen as the broad spectrum of God's creation, which stretches from the familiar to the monstrous.

As late as 1573, the French royal surgeon Ambroise Paré sought to explain incidences of the monstrous – ranging from human birth abnormalities to fantastic beasts – in rational terms. His compendious study bears all the hallmarks of a scientific catalogue, with biblical and classical authorities invoked in order to set a precedent for contemporary cases, with names, dates and locations frequently cited in order to add veracity to even the most outlandish prodigies, none of which are dismissed or even questioned. Paré's introductory table of 'the causes of monsters' reveals a fascinating mix of the medical and the superstitious, with equal weight given to 'hereditary or accidental illness' as to 'the artifice of wicked spital [spiteful] beggars'.[45] The primary causes of monstrosity are, however, clearly identified as, 'first … the glory of God. The second, his wrath.'[46] Even at so late a date, then, we can see that monstrosity is perceived first and foremost as providing further evidence of the frequently mysterious workings of God. This is not, of course, to suggest that the inhabitants of the medieval west necessarily held an unquestioning belief in fantastic creatures. In discussing the monstrous races, those humanoid prodigies who occupy the unknown reaches of the world in accounts from Pliny onward, John Block Friedman makes an observation that can be applied equally to all forms of monsters and marvels, noting that even first-hand experience of exotic locations did not result in the abandonment of tales of the monstrous races said to inhabit these regions, for:

> there appears to have been a psychological need for [the monstrous races]. Their appeal to medieval men was based on such factors as fantasy, escapism, delight in the exercise of the imagination, and – very important – fear of the unknown.[47]

The psychological resonance of monsters is certainly attested by their proliferation across the choir stalls, amongst many other decorated surfaces, of late medieval churches. In terms of humanoid or part-humanoid prodigies, we have already encountered green men, sirens and Wild Men in their symbolic roles. To these we may add a number of others, including centaurs, the classical horse/man hybrid which was adopted to signify Christ's vengeance on his betrayers,[48] and that staple of the medieval world

[45] Ambroise Paré, *On Monsters and Marvels*, trans. Janis L. Pallister (Chicago: University of Chicago Press, 1982), p. 4.

[46] Ibid., p. 3.

[47] Friedman, *The Monstrous Races*, p. 24.

[48] M. D. Anderson, in his introduction to Remnant, *Catalogue of Misericords*, draws particular attention to the centaur in Exeter cathedral which is represented shooting an arrow from a short bow, which he interprets as 'the soul of Christ departing to deliver souls from Hell' (p. xxxvi), an interpretation deriving from Philippe de Thaon: see Beryl Rowland, *Animals with Human Faces: A Guide to Animal Symbolism* (London: George Allen and Unwin, 1974), p. 54.

map, the blemmyae,[49] along with creatures with only a trace of the human, such as the manticore, to which we shall return later in this chapter. Sometimes clearly composed of elements of other creatures, at others pure creations of the imagination, fantastic beasts without any elements of the human – particularly those which are based upon serpentine forms – may be found as commonly on misericords as they are in other media of architectural and manuscript decoration where they abound. These monstrous forms were, as Asa Simon Mittman observes, equal to images of Christ and the saints as

> images of God and his heavenly hosts for the medieval viewer, whose universal spectrum was broad enough to contain at one end holy perfection and at the other the most wretched and abject, the vile and the absolutely evil. Medieval English viewers would likely have located themselves somewhere between these two extremes, and the lower end of the scale was no less important than the higher end in this process of identity formation.[50]

Within this spectrum, the part-human hybrids may well interrogate the very definition of the line between man and beast.[51] When these hybrids are present in a devotional context, whether that be a misericord or a manuscript, it is surely their symbolic function which is paramount, and the same is undoubtedly true of those creatures which bear no resemblance to the human or, in some cases, any other living beast.

The beast which appears most frequently on the Limerick misericords is also the most common fabulous beast to be found across the corpus of British choir stalls, the wyvern, being twice depicted on its own and twice in combat with a lion.[52] As already noted, this may be a figure of the battle between good and evil; the lion commonly represents Christ,[53] whilst the wyvern is a variety of dragon and, consequently, 'is like the devil, the fairest of all serpents … deceiving fools with hope of vainglory and human pleasures', [54] its powerful tail equating to the duplicity which 'binds the way of sinners to Heaven by the knots of their sins and kills them by strangling them, because if anyone entangled by a chain of offence dies, beyond doubt he is damned to Hell'.[55] Such a reading certainly conforms to the theme of moral admonishment that, as we have seen, is suggested by the iconography of the real animals throughout the stalls. It may be significant in this particular

[49] Curiously, sciopods, the other fantastic race most frequently illustrated on medieval maps, do not appear on English misericords.
[50] Asa Simon Mittman, *Maps and Monsters in Medieval England* (London: Routledge, 2006), p. 5.
[51] This is persuasively suggested by Joyce E. Salisbury, *The Beast Within: Animals in the Middle Ages* (London: Routledge, 1994), p. 149.
[52] Wyverns may be found on more than thirty misericords.
[53] Barber (ed. adn trans.), *Bestiary*, pp. 23–7.
[54] Ibid., p. 183.
[55] Clark, *A Medieval Book of Beasts*, p. 195.

instance to note that the wyvern may sometimes be found representing the more specific subject of pestilence. Given the generally accepted dating of the Limerick carvings to the closing years of the fifteenth century, it is tempting to read prophetic, apocalyptic significance into the recurrence of this beast, as the closing years of the fifteenth – and early years of the sixteenth – century marked a time of widespread famine and natural disaster, as well as pestilence, in Ireland.[56] Read in this light, the successful outcome of the battle between the forces represented by the lion and the wyvern would appear to be more vital still for the stalls' designer and original occupants.

Whilst in these two carvings of its struggle with the wyvern the lion appears to have the upper hand – perhaps revealing a degree of hope for the faithful concerning the possible outcome of contemporary difficulties, whether in this world or in the next – the proliferation of fantastic beasts throughout the stalls suggests that the ongoing battle is nonetheless against alarming odds. The manticore, with its lion's body, scorpion's sting and face of a man with a triple row of teeth, is another figure which is associated with the Devil.[57] Alison Syme, referring specifically to an illustration in Bodley 764 which shows a leg clutched in the manticore's fearsome mouth, has drawn particular attention to the connotations of cannibalism which derive from the creature's human physiognomy.[58] There are no limbs protruding from the manticore's mouth on the Limerick misericord, but the moralising tradition would undoubtedly suggest a reading of figurative human consumption by the Devil with, perhaps, further connotations of humans' concomitant 'unnatural' desires.[59] Two further fantastic creatures found on the misericords are closely related to the wyvern. The lindworm is essentially a wyvern without wings and may, therefore, be assumed to carry similar connotations.[60] The amphisbæna – a creature very rarely depicted in Irish art[61] – is likewise of the same family, although its having a head at each end specifically emphasises the characteristic of deception, as it is literally two-faced.

[56] Lenihan, *Limerick*, records the famine of 1497–98 and the depredations of extreme weather conditions in 1502 (p. 69), as well as the 'terrible pestilence, which prevailed all over the city' in 1521–22 (pp. 73–4).

[57] Rowland, *Animals with Human Faces*, p. 126. The only other manticore to be found on British stalls is in St George's Chapel, Windsor, where it is flanked in the supporters by hybrid creatures.

[58] Alison Syme, 'Taboos and the Holy in Bodley 764' in *Mark of the Beast*, ed. Hassig, pp. 165–6.

[59] Syme goes on to draw attention to what she terms the 'well-recognized and close relationship between cannibalism and incest' (ibid.). Whilst I do not consider that pursuing such an association at length would add to the present discussion, it is nonetheless worth noting this further possible dimension of the manticore's symbolic representation of transgressive, 'unnatural' behaviours.

[60] I know of no other lindworms on misericord carvings.

[61] Hourihane, *Gothic Art in Ireland*, p. 79. See also, Clark, *A Medieval Book of Beasts*, p. 141. Although uncommon in all media in medieval Irish art, a number of amphisbænae are to be found on English misericords: Carlisle Cathedral; Chichester Cathedral; St Mary the Virgin, Godmanchester; Royal Foundation of St Katharine, Stepney; Tewkesbury Abbey; St George's Chapel, Windsor; and the Victoria & Albert Museum, London.

A much more ambiguous creature which we find beneath the Limerick stalls is the griffin (fig. 18). Whilst on the one hand this oft-depicted hybrid may be taken to symbolise 'both the divine and the human element in Christ',[62] by the early sixteenth century it could also be used to signify corruption within the Church, as in the anticlerical satire known as *The Ploughman's Tale*,[63] which we considered in chapter 2. Indeed, this negative interpretation of the half-lion, half-eagle which, as the bestiary warns us, 'if it comes face to face with a man ... will attack him',[64] is perhaps more immediately comprehensible than its positive interpretation.[65] Other than the battling lion and the eagle, then, the only beast on the Limerick stalls which potentially carries an unequivocally positive association is that which has been identified as either a yale, an antelope or a unicorn, this latter being a common allegorical figure of Christ Himself, for:

> Our Lord Jesus Christ is the spiritual unicorn of whom it is said: 'My beloved is like the son of the unicorns' [Song of Songs 2:9]; and in the psalm: 'My horn shalt thou exalt like the horn of an unicorn' [92:10]; and Zacharius said: 'He hath raised up an horn of salvation for us, in the house of His servant David' [Luke 1:69]. The single horn on the unicorn's head signifies what He Himself said: 'I and my Father are one' [John 10:30]; according to the Apostle, 'The head of Christ is God' [I Corinthians 11:3] ... [N]either principalities nor powers, nor thrones nor lordships could capture Him; the underworld could not hold Him, and not even the most cunning devil could understand Him. But by the will of the Father alone he descended into the Virgin's womb to save us.[66]

This latter point, of course, refers to the legend that the unicorn, like the Wild Man who we considered earlier in this chapter, may only be trapped by a virgin. Yet in view of the negative connotations of the other beasts amongst which it resides, Hourihane's identification of this ferocious creature as a yale, a fearsome beast with movable horns and a glance that can kill, seems more likely, thus adding to the ranks of symbolically dangerous creatures to be encountered beneath the stalls.[67]

[62] Richard Barber and Anne Riches, *A Dictionary of Fabulous Beasts* (Woodbridge: Boydell, 1971), p. 75. There are more than two dozen griffins on British misericords.
[63] *The Plowman's Tale: The c.1532 and 1606 Editions of a Spurious Canterbury Tale*, ed. Mary Rhinelander McCarl (New York and London: Garland, 1997).
[64] Barber (ed. and trans.), *Bestiary*, p. 39.
[65] This interpretation seems most appropriate also when considering a misericord in St John, Halifax, on which a Wild Man is shown spearing a griffin.
[66] Barber (ed. and trans.), *Bestiary*, pp. 36–7. The unicorn, like the griffin, is common on misericords, with more than twenty surviving, a number of which are depicted at their point of capture.
[67] On account of the range of possible identifications of somewhat generic horned beasts, this may be a unique occurrence of the yale although, for precisely the same reason, the case may well be made for other creatures to be thus classified.

Taken all together, then, we could read the assembled beasts on the Limerick misericords – both real and fantastic – as together comprising a unified and devotionally appropriate iconographical scheme that exhorts the viewer to vigilance against sin which, whilst seemingly overwhelming in its multifarious forms, may nonetheless be overcome by constant moral fortitude and Christ's aid. Furthermore, when one takes into account the extensive re-ordering and the significant repetition of motifs on the surviving carvings, it would not be far-fetched to posit an original scheme in which the iconography of the north side of the choir mirrored that of the south side.[68] This would perhaps be bracketed at one end by one of the carvings of human heads in order to anchor the reading firmly in the human sphere, and at the other by the Harold family crest with which we began this analysis, in order to indicate patronage and, by virtue of its emblem, the transcendence of worldly concerns that comes with spiritual victory. Alternatively, the sequence could have enacted that spectrum of existence with 'at one end holy perfection and at the other the most wretched and abject'.[69]

Such a sequence would provide a valid reading of the misericords in Limerick Cathedral, regardless of the church's location. However, a further consideration of geographical location seems to me to invite a more complex reading. We have seen earlier how Ireland was considered to be at the 'uttermost ends of the earth', with all the negative connotations that such a designation entails. We may recall, for example, the words of Gerald of Wales:

> Just as the countries of the East are remarkable and distinguished for certain prodigies peculiar and native to themselves, so the boundaries of the West also are made remarkable by their own wonders of nature.[70]

As Pamela Gravestock has observed, to the compilers of bestiaries and their antecedents, 'many animals are located in India or Ethiopia, but these two place names were almost used generically to refer to anywhere far away or exotic. That is, "India" and "Ethiopia" were more ideas than actual places.'[71] As the above quotation from Gerald reveals, for the late medieval inhabitant of England, the idea of the western edge of Christendom is constructed in exactly the same manner as 'the East'.[72] Thus, when we read that '[i]n India there is a beast called the manticore', or that the dragon is a native of 'Ethiopia and India',[73] we may just as easily substitute Ireland as the strange location at the edge of the known world where, in Gerald's words, nature

[68] This is suggested in John Hunt, 'The Limerick Cathedral Misericords', *Ireland of the Welcomes* 20.3 (1971), 12–16.

[69] Mittman, *Maps and Monsters*, p. 149.

[70] Gerald of Wales, *History and Topography of Ireland*, p. 31.

[71] Gravestock, 'Did Imaginary Animals Exist?', p. 123.

[72] On the emphasis to this viewpoint provided by maps on a number of manuscripts of Gerald's *Topography*, which show Ireland reduced to a marginal position in representations of the British Isles, see Mittman, 'The Other Close at Hand', pp. 106–8.

[73] Barber (ed. and trans.), *Bestiary*, pp. 63 and 183.

'indulges herself in … secret and distant freaks'.[74] Could the menagerie of strange beasts in the Limerick choir, then, carry a direct reference to the marginal nature of Ireland as it sits at the 'uttermost ends of the earth', where the battle of a few worthy men against almost overwhelming dark forces is at its most fraught with peril?

Kathy Lavezzo has explored the way in which England in the early Middle Ages saw itself as defined by its isolation, a sense of national identity being created and reinforced by a perception of self as both separate and different from Europe and beyond. In both writing and map-making, argues Lavezzo:

> [t]he English were not simply self-conscious of their marginality during the Middle Ages; English writers and cartographers actively participated in the construction of England as a global borderland.[75]

She goes on to note, however, that by the later Middle Ages England had more consciously aligned itself with Europe, in particular the historically powerful centre of Rome. As a consequence, and first finding expression in the writings of Gerald of Wales, the positive connotations of marginality which had been employed by the English in constructing their sense of self gave way to a sense of belonging to an international Christian community. English writers, in turn, drew attention to the marginality of Ireland in order to diminish their own: 'If not for Ireland,' notes Lavezzo, 'the marginality of the English would be absolute and hence insurmountable.'[76] As we saw earlier, by the close of the fifteenth century the English hold over Ireland was weakening. However, as Maurice Lenihan notes in his history of Limerick, Henry VIII, upon ascending to the throne in 1508 – in the middle of the period to which the misericords have been dated – was rather more concerned than his predecessors with the government of Ireland, to the extent of intervening directly in the affairs of Limerick.[77] Indeed, in 1536 a series of sumptuary laws were enacted, including the stipulation that:

> no woman [should] wear any coat or kirtle tuck'd up, or embroider'd with silk or laid with *Usker*, after the *Irish* fashion; and none to wear any *mantles*, *coat* or *hood*, made after the *Irish* fashion.[78]

The human figures portrayed on the misericords most certainly cannot be accused of dressing specifically 'after the *Irish* fashion', for they wear the bag-like chaperon which originated in Burgundy and became common throughout Europe in the fifteenth century (fig. 32). Popular with the

[74] Gerald of Wales, *History and Topography of Ireland*, p. 31.
[75] Kathy Lavezzo, *Angels on the Edge of the World: Geography, Literature, and English Community, 1000–1534* (Ithaca: Cornell University Press, 2006), p. 7.
[76] Ibid., p. 54.
[77] Lenihan, *Limerick*, p. 70.
[78] Ibid., p. 74.

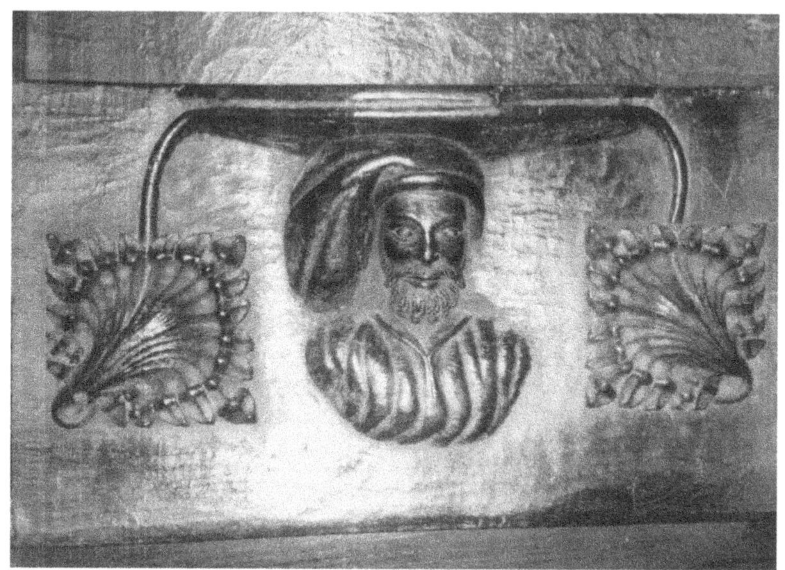

FIG. 32. LIMERICK CATHEDRAL MISERICORD.

wealthy classes, it is far from being 'uncultivated' apparel,[79] and may be found on contemporary misericord carvings throughout England and Europe.[80] Could this assertion of non-Irishness in the human figures, then, suggest a reading of the misericords which not only imparts the moral lessons outlined above, but also offers a coarse political statement of English dominance over the troublesome 'barbarians' of the world's edge? If, as suggested by John Hunt, we take the carvings of the boar and the collared antelope as representing Yorkist insignia – the badges of Richard III and Henry VI respectively – this may well be the case.[81]

Yet, of course, all such tentative suggestions, however plausible they may be, are equally susceptible to converse interpretations. In spite of his concerted efforts, Henry VIII failed to prevail upon the pope to name his own choice, Walter Wellesley, as successor to Bishop Folan in Limerick; the post went instead to the Dominican friar John Coyn, or Quin.[82] As already mentioned, by the late fifteenth century native craftsmen had largely taken over from their English antecedents in Ireland, and in a climate of renewed English interest in the city it is perhaps more persuasive to suggest that the Irish bishop and his Irish craftsmen may have used the didactic scheme across the choir stalls to introduce a secondary iconography of resistance to English meddling in their affairs. Such a reading would see the would-be

[79] Gerald of Wales, *History and Topography of Ireland*, p. 102.
[80] See Grössinger, *The World Upside-Down*, pp. 158–9. See also, James Laver, *Costume and Fashion: A Concise History*, revised edn (London: Thames and Hudson, 1995), pp. 70–1.
[81] Hunt, 'Limerick Cathedral Misericords', p. 16.
[82] Lenihan, *Limerick*, p. 578. Wellesley was Prior of Conal and was later elevated to the see of Kildare.

dominant English firmly trapped in the liminal, marginal space of the misericords, tellingly placed amidst the beasts and monsters.

When I visited Limerick to study the misericords early in the summer of 2002, repair work was being undertaken in the cathedral choir and the stalls had been moved for safety into the north transept. Consequently, the misericords were – however temporarily – in yet another configuration following that most recently recorded by Remnant in 1969. And as I looked at them and made notes, it seemed that the losses and subsequent re-orderings within the cathedral have been, however unintentionally, entirely appropriate to the iconography of the stalls. The array of images carved thereon represents a sequence of both commonplace allegorical symbols of the Middle Ages and the unusual, even unique, combining together to offer a familiar perspective on man's place within God's creation. Yet in this marginal location – not just in the half-hidden but tantalisingly attractive regions of the choir which we have explored throughout this study, but at the unstable edge of English dominion and, indeed, of Christendom itself – they suggest more, hinting at a political resonance which is, nonetheless, impossible to pin down with any certainty. Their ambiguity encourages the viewer to make his or her own interpretation, but, ultimately, as we do so we find ourselves entering into – in the words of Gerald of Wales – 'unsearchable and hidden ways'.[83] And such, of course, is always the case when we engage with the misericords of the late Middle Ages: as we stoop and raise the seat, we find ourselves face to face with a lost, frequently inscrutable past in which they did indeed 'do things differently'. And sometimes, as we look down upon the 'fair feeld ful of folk' revealed by the tipped-back seat,[84] with all its variety of forms from the human to the bestial and, indeed, from the divine to the damned, and its dizzying multiplicity of possible meanings, perhaps the only appropriate response – which is no less pleasurable for its unavoidability – is to exclaim with Carroll's Alice: 'Curiouser and curiouser!'[85]

[83] Gerald of Wales, *History and Topography of Ireland*, p. 31.
[84] William Langland, *The Vision of Piers Plowman: a Complete Edition of the B-Text*, ed. A. V. C. Schmidt (London: Dent, 1995), B Prologue 17.
[85] Carroll, *Through the Looking-Glass*, p. 16.

# CONCLUSION: LOOKING BOTH WAYS

Lewis Carroll's imaginative approach to the misericords of Ripon Cathedral may at first appear to have little bearing upon the readings that have been posited throughout the present volume. However, just as Carroll could appropriate these images for his own creative purposes within a few years of Wildridge's assertion concerning their near neighbours in Beverley Minster that they are 'the most important and instructive of [medieval ecclesiastical] ornaments'[1] – and, indeed, contemporary creative writers may use choir stall carvings as a stimulus at the same time as medievalists assay their original signification[2] – so it is perhaps unwise to assume a singularity of meaning for the original audience. We have seen throughout that the carvings on misericords – whether of naturalistic flora or fanciful fauna, of devout piety or brazen sexuality – belong to a complex web of symbol and allusion that threads its way throughout late medieval culture, both connecting and, at the same time, blurring the distinctions between the sacred and the profane. The literature of popular entertainment, from heroic romances of Alexander to the amoral wiles of Reynard (or Russell) could be employed in order to make serious points concerning pride or resistance to temptation, just as Caesarius of Heisterbach could focus flagging attention by invoking King Arthur before moving on to serious matters of devotion. Likewise, the bawdy physicality that we expect from the fabliau could be employed in order to figure the 'natural' order of masculine ecclesiastical superiority as well as to provide an admonishment against the temptations of the flesh. This latter can be further articulated by the seductive hybrid of the mermaid, whilst other hybrids may signify anything from the infinite variety of God's creation to the 'secret and distant freaks' in which nature indulges herself in the remote areas of the Christian world.[3] And, as we saw in chapter 3, without clear explanation and

[1] T. Tindall Wildridge, *The Misereres of Beverley Minster: A Complete Series of Drawings of the Seat Carvings in the Choir of St John's, Beverley, Yorkshire; with Notes on the Plates and Subject* (Hull: J. Plaxton, 1879), p. 2.

[2] See, for example, the title poem of Tony Flynn's *The Mermaid Chair: New and Selected Poems* (Market Rasen: Dream Catcher Books, 2008) or Oz Hardwick's 'The Fairford Mermaid' in his collection, *Carrying Fire* (Bristol: bluechrome, 2006), p. 41.

[3] Gerald of Wales, *The History and Topography of Ireland*, trans. John J. O'Meara (London: Penguin, 1982), p. 31.

close supervision, misinterpretation was a very real possibility even during the late medieval period in which the carvings were made.

When the modern scholar looks to the margins, there is a temptation to view them solely as the habitation of 'ejected forms',[4] a refuge for that which is cast out from the centre – a centre which in the later Middle Ages was explicitly Christian. Yet, as hinged misericords may show two aspects, so the margins themselves can be viewed in different ways, not merely as the extreme limits of a superior centre, but also as places of transition through which we pass from the earthly concerns of our everyday lives in order to reach the spiritual truths found at that centre. When considering medieval misericords, therefore, we should perhaps abandon our customary centrifugal perspective in favour of one which is centripetal, focusing from wider cultural, devotional and doctrinal concerns of the period into the greater truth to which the carved images pertain. I hope that the foregoing chapters have presented a case for taking such an approach, offering a persuasive web of cultural threads which is strong enough to bear the weight of my readings of these misericords as expressions of the rich and dynamic devotional culture of late medieval England. As Chaucer's Nun's Priest advises, following the teaching of St Paul: 'al that written is, / To oure doctrine it is ywrite, ywis.'[5] So, too, I believe we should view the misericords which survive in English churches as testaments to the way in which the apparently profane, playful or scandalous may stand alongside more explicitly devotional images as reminders that all things are created by God and should inform the way we perceive – and make our way through – God's world.

Whilst acknowledging this, it must be admitted that, as we saw in chapter 5, even when we recognise the truth of St Paul's words, it is often a far from simple matter to separate the 'fruyt' from the 'chaf' and, with the passing of some six hundred years since the installation of the later misericords we have considered, this winnowing process has become increasingly difficult. This being said, I believe that, like the Lincoln ploughman, we should nonetheless apply ourselves diligently to the labour at hand, however much 'labour and pein in [the] brayn' it may sometimes cause us.[6] The present volume has sought to relocate the study of misericords firmly within the profoundly Christian context in which they were designed, made and initially viewed, and from which they have so often been separated in modern scholarship. I hope that the explorations which we have taken into the enigmatic world presented thereon may provide a stimulus for further, variant, and even opposing interpretations. For, however certain one may be of one's own readings, nothing would do this fascinating corpus of medieval carvings a greater disservice than to deny its enticing ambiguity.

[4] Michael Camille, *Image on the Edge: The Margins of Medieval Art* (London: Reaktion Books, 1992), p. 9.

[5] Geoffrey Chaucer, *The Riverside Chaucer*, ed. Larry D. Benson (Oxford: Oxford University Press, 1988), VII 4631–2.

[6] Reginald Pecock, *The Repressor of Over Much Blaming of Clergy*, 2 vols, ed. Churchill Babington (London: Longman, Green, Longman and Roberts, 1860), I, 212.

# GAZETTEER

The most complete guide to misericords in the British Isles remains G. L. Remnant's *A Catalogue of Misericords in Great Britain* (London: Oxford University Press, 1969). Whilst containing numerous errors of detail,

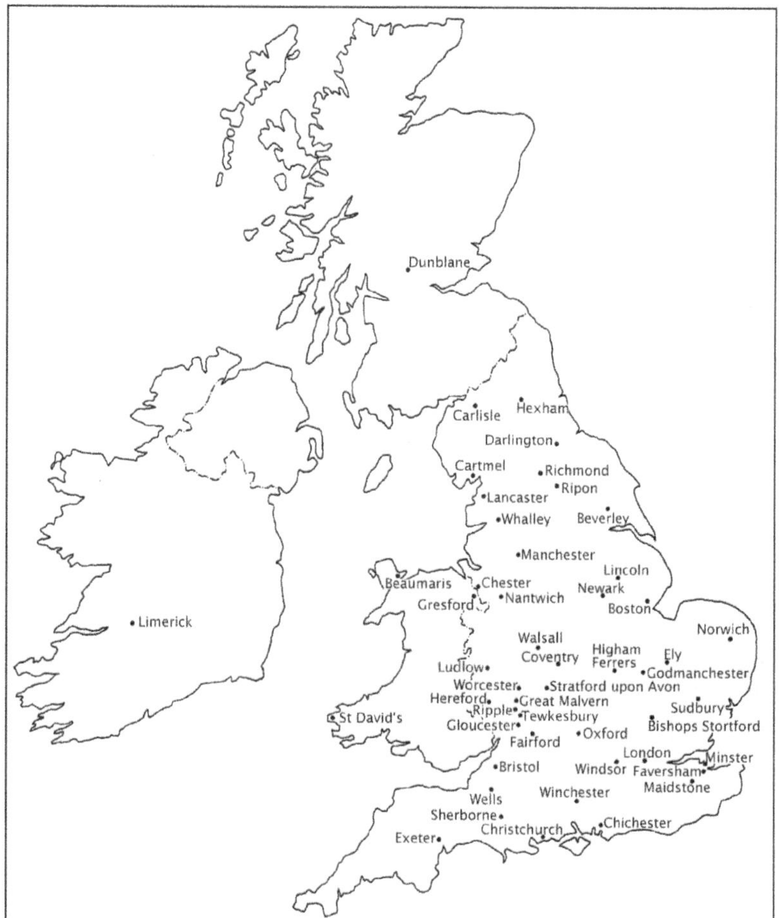

it nonetheless still provides the best available companion for explorations beneath the choir stalls. In due course, the late Elaine C. Block's *Corpus of Medieval Misericords in Great Britain* (Turnhout: Brepols) will offer a more accurate, illustrated account. As these two volumes demonstrate, any serious attempt to catalogue all British misericords would require a complete book in itself. It is the intention of this section, therefore, to provide an annotated gazetteer of the surviving sets which are of particular interest because of the number of surviving misericords and/or the richness of design. At most of the churches listed, individual guides may be purchased. As Block and Remnant order their catalogues by county (Remnant's now inaccurate on account of subsequent boundary changes), I offer the alternative of a single alphabetical list by place name, which may perhaps prove more manageable for the armchair misericordian unfamiliar with British counties.

### BEAUMARIS, ST CATHERINE

All twenty of these late fifteenth-/early sixteenth-century misericords depict angels bearing shields as the main motif, whilst the supporters show a variety of head and portrait busts.

### BEVERLEY MINSTER

Dated 1520 on the precentor's seat, the sixty-eight misericords in Beverley Minster are amongst the most varied in the country. Of particular note are three carvings relating to the capture of a bear. A fox preaches from a pulpit to a congregation of geese, another is chased with his prey; further foxes are ridden by hares and apes, hunted by men and, ultimately, hanged by a party of geese. Other aspects of 'the world upside-down' include a sow playing pipes and the cart going before the horse whilst, at the opposite end of the spectrum, we may see the traditional pelican in her piety and the biblical figures of Joshua and Caleb. Domestic scenes, foliate heads, flora and fauna all contribute to the interest of these misericords, the designs of a number of which may be traced to Continental prints which were becoming popular in Britain in the early sixteenth century.

### BEVERLEY, ST MARY

The most fascinating of these twenty-three mid-fifteenth-century misericords shows two foxes singing from a book held upon a lectern in the form of an eagle. This is of particular interest in being one of very few misericords to which paint is applied – in this case musical notation on the pages of the book, showing it to be the *Magnificat*. A number of other foxes appear across the misericords, two of which are in clerical garb – the first as a preacher, the second carrying a goose in his hood. A further fox, penetrated by an arrow, seeks help from an ape physician. A further ape physician may be found administering to a man holding the Eucharistic Host. The misericords also depict a number of Wild Men, knights attacking dragons and boars, bear baiting and other animals.

## BISHOP'S STORTFORD, ST MICHAEL

These eighteen fifteenth-century misericords mainly depict an array of individual human heads. Of the scattering of other creatures that punctuate these portraits, the most interesting depicts a monstrous fish, baring its teeth and sporting a serrated ridge on its back.

## BOSTON, ST BOTOLPH

Although somewhat coarsely carved and suffering from cracking of the timber, these sixty-two late fourteenth/early fifteenth-century misericords retain a rare vigour. In the variety of subjects carved, too, there is an earthy vitality. These include: Sir Yvain's horse caught in the castle portcullis; a failed hunter beaten by his irate wife; a distaff-wielding woman in pursuit of the fox and his prey; another fox preaching to a congregation of birds; a schoolmaster birching a tardy pupil; fools playing cats like bagpipes; bears playing the pipe organ; a Wild Man battling a lion; and a mermaid tempting two sailors.

## BRISTOL CATHEDRAL

Dating from the first quarter of the sixteenth century, the twenty-eight misericords are particularly vigorous. Of note are the six lively scenes relating to Reynard the Fox, depicting the beguiling of Bruin and Tybert, Tybert's escape, the ubiquitous fox preacher, and two scenes at the gallows. Biblical characters, Adam and Eve and Samson, may be found, but more immediately striking is the unusual proliferation of nude figures – seated, wrestling or being led into the mouth of Hell. Scenes from everyday life are interspersed with such undoubtedly symbolic oddities as a sleeping pedlar robbed by apes, a man leading a giant snail like a horse, and a man and woman, seated on a pig and a bird respectively, jousting with domestic implements. Such enigmatic scenes make the iconography of the Bristol misericords particularly fascinating.

## CARLISLE CATHEDRAL

These forty-six misericords, probably dating from the early years of the fifteenth century, depict a number of angels, either playing musical instruments or carrying shields. Other clearly religious iconography includes the Coronation of the Virgin, St Michael and the dragon, the pelican in her piety, and a scene which has variously been interpreted as Judas in the jaws of Satan and St Margaret of Antioch being swallowed by a wyvern – it being difficult to make a precise identification when the figure is only visible from the waist down. Amongst the scenes may also be found such favourites as griffins, mermaids, the fox and the goose, and a scene of fireside marital conflict.

## CARTMEL PRIORY

Dating from around 1440, many of these misericords show foliate designs. Of the figural designs, the Flight of Alexander, a fine elephant and castle, and an ape physician are of particular note.

## CHESTER CATHEDRAL

The iconography of the forty-four late fourteenth-century misericords in Chester Cathedral is particularly varied. Whilst overtly religious subjects are unusual in England, a number occur in Chester, including the emblems of the Passion, the Virgin and child, the Coronation of the Virgin and a scene from the life of the local St Werburgh. Such images, however, are balanced by romance scenes of Yvain, Tristan and Iseult, and Richard Cœur de Lion, as well as bestiary-derived scenes such as the capture of the tiger and the fox feigning death. With monsters, Wild Men and the Green Man, in addition to more naturalistic creatures and scenes, the Chester misericords are striking in their vigorous diversity.

## CHICHESTER CATHEDRAL

Dating from the second quarter of the fourteenth century, the thirty-eight misericords in the cathedral display a marked vigour, both in subject and execution. A viol player kissing a dancing woman exudes energy, whilst a seated harpist and piper play a more sedate music. Elsewhere, a fox, too, plays the harp, to a goose and an ape. Many grotesques, monsters and hybrids lurk beneath these stalls, some of which contend with human assailants.

## CHICHESTER, ST MARY'S HOSPITAL

Although not as imaginatively extravagant as their neighbours in the cathedral, the thirteen late thirteenth-century misericords in St Mary's Hospital feature a number of hybrids, including an awkwardly contorted merman.

## CHRISTCHURCH PRIORY

Most of the thirty-nine misericords are from the early sixteenth century, although three earlier carvings have been inserted, including mid-fourteenth-century symbols of St Mark and St John. Most of the later carvings show expressively carved human figures, with a proliferation of fools and acrobats. A supplicant beggar offers a rare misericord image of poverty.

## COVENTRY, HENRY VIII'S GRAMMAR SCHOOL

These fifteen misericords date from the fifteenth century and were originally located in the Carmelite friary. Many show heraldic devices, whilst two are apparently survivals of a sequence representing the months. Whilst the carving is very good, the condition is poor.

## COVENTRY, HOLY TRINITY

The twenty fine-quality carvings in Holy Trinity were also originally located in the Carmelite friary. Amongst foliage and heraldic devices are a number of foliate masks and Wild Men, the latter accompanied by – or overcoming – lions. A further reference to the forest may be found in a carving of a hound attacking a stag, flanked by a hunter and a hare.

## DARLINGTON, ST CUTHBERT

Probably dating from the second quarter of the fifteenth century, the dozen misericords include the Flight of Alexander and three scenes which, it has been suggested, relate to the life of the local St Godric.

## DUNBLANE CATHEDRAL

Eighteen misericords survive, apparently from three different programmes from the fifteenth century or possibly earlier. The majority of carvings are foliate and rather angular in execution. Other designs include a leopard, a bat and a Green Man.

## ELY CATHEDRAL

Sixty-five misericords, dating from the second quarter of the fourteenth century, provide one of the most varied selections of motifs to be found in the country. Biblical motifs, such as the Temptation and Expulsion of Adam and Eve and Noah's Ark, mix with images of clerics and the stock symbol of the pelican in piety. A less positive image of the clergy may be found in the cowled fox preaching to a congregation of poultry, which provides a supporter to the fox's capture of a goose. Royalty and commoners, hunters and dicers, saints, angels, devils, men and monsters all jostle for position across these lively carvings.

## EXETER CATHEDRAL

Although the stalls in which they are mounted date only as far back as the nineteenth-century restoration by Gilbert Scott, most of the fifty misericords are from the first half of the thirteenth century, making them the oldest large set in the country. This in itself warrants a visit, but amongst the sinuous, sometimes rather crude depictions of fauna and flora – and hybrids thereof – are a number of fascinating scenes not found elsewhere. A crowned figure – possibly Herod – apparently rages whilst sitting in a basin. The Swan Knight of Anglo-French romance is unique to Exeter, and accompanies two other similarly helmed knights who battle monsters, neither of which, it must be admitted, appears to be a particularly worthy adversary. Male and female centaurs display their prowess in archery, and there is an unusual proliferation of mermaids and sirens.

## FAIRFORD, ST MARY

The figures on the thirteen misericords from the late fifteenth century are particularly robust in execution. Men reap and women pluck poultry; both a fox and a hawk prey on water fowl; a married couple engage in domestic violence – the latter a possible consequence of the heavy drinking which is seen elsewhere, as perhaps is the dog scrabbling in the cooking pot and the man sleeping, possibly under the table.

## FAVERSHAM, ST MARY OF CHARITY

Twelve late fifteenth-century misericords include two Wild Men (one battling a griffin), a chained ape, a wolf, a camel, and a fox making off with a goose.

## GLOUCESTER CATHEDRAL

The forty-six misericords from the middle of the fourteenth century show an unusual degree of conflict: men fight dragons, men fight men, lions fight dragons, dragons fight dragons and hybrids fight hybrids, a lion stalks a fox, a fox abducts a goose. Youths playing a ball game offer a less destructive mode of competition, whilst hunters and knights both gallop by, in keeping with the vigour of most of the scenes depicted. Scenes of particular note include the Flight of Alexander and Samson and Delilah.

## GODMANCHESTER, ST MARY THE VIRGIN

Most of the twenty, rather coarse, later fifteenth-century misericords depict animals and birds, including cats (one with a mouse), apes, lions, a dog and a hare.

## GREAT MALVERN PRIORY

Of particular interest is the now incomplete series depicting the labours of the months, dating to the third quarter of the fifteenth century. These are interspersed with earlier carvings – the original arrangement having been disrupted in the nineteenth century – possibly from the late fourteenth century. Amongst the seemingly unrelated earlier carvings are some striking unique images, such as: a monk inserting a pair of bellows into the behind of an ape-like creature; a physician visiting a patient; and a particularly lively 'world upside-down' scene of a cat being hung by rats.

## GRESFORD, ALL SAINTS

The eleven misericords from around 1500 have not fared well; some are now all but indecipherable. However, an acrobat suspended from a pole and the ubiquitous preaching fox offer testament to the quality of what has been lost.

## HEREFORD CATHEDRAL

The thirty-eight early fourteenth-century misericords predominantly show paired figures, sometimes engaged in combat – a wyvern and a horse, two half-human hybrids, two pigs, a griffin and a ram, etc. – others in apparent contentment. These latter include male and female sirens, a goat lutist accompanying a cat on a viol and a mermaid suckling a lion. An interesting 'world upside-down' motif shows a fox attacked by geese.

## HEREFORD, ALL SAINTS

The sixteen late fourteenth-century misericords depict a number of male faces, one foliate, and a number of fantastic creatures.

## HEXHAM ABBEY

Many of the thirty-two boldly carved, early fifteenth-century misericords depict an array of animal and human (two foliate) heads and a number of foliate designs. A number of the other misericords depict hybrid creatures.

## HIGHAM FERRERS, ST MARY

Of particular interest amongst the twenty early fifteenth-century misericords is a depiction of Christ's face on the veil of St Veronica. More common images include the pelican in her piety and a foliate mask, whilst portrait heads and hybrids account for most of the remainder. The portrait of an archbishop no doubt relates to the Chichele arms located opposite, pertaining to the locally born Archbishop of Canterbury who was invested in 1422.

## LANCASTER, ST MARY'S PRIORY

Remaining details of the twelve fourteenth-century misericords hint at a number of finely carved, elaborate scenes which, as a result of serious damage (much of it apparently deliberate), are now impossible to decipher with any certainty.

## LIMERICK CATHEDRAL

With twenty-three examples, dated c.1480–1500, this is the westernmost set of misericords in Europe and the only survival in Ireland. Of most interest is the array of beasts, both natural and fantastic, ranging from eagle and swan to wyvern and amphisbaena.

## LINCOLN CATHEDRAL

The ninety-two late fourteenth-century misericords would assure Lincoln's significance even if they were not so varied in subject matter. Biblical subjects include the Nativity, the Ascension, the Coronation of the Virgin and the Resurrection; romance scenes are taken from *Yvain*, *Tristan and Iseult* and *Alexander*; a ploughman tills his field; knights fight dragons; apes enact a funeral; a maid captures a unicorn; and myriad men, women and beasts – naturalistic and fantastic – inhabit the remainder of this remarkable assembly.

## LONDON, ROYAL FOUNDATION OF ST KATHARINE, STEPNEY

Thirteen late fourteenth-century misericords include Tutivillus listening to two women, an angel playing bagpipes, the pelican in her piety, an elephant and castle, a woman riding a half-human hybrid, the battle between a lion and a dragon, and a number of portrait heads, both human and grotesque.

## LONDON, VICTORIA & ALBERT MUSEUM

As well as a number of early sixteenth-century Netherlandish misericords which are outside the scope of the present volume, the museum houses thirteen English misericords of varied date and provenance. Of these, a man and woman loading harvested sheaves onto a cart and a scene from a carver's workshop are of particular interest.

## LONDON, WESTMINSTER ABBEY, HENRY VII'S CHAPEL

Of the forty early sixteenth-century misericords, a number are derived from Continental prints. Biblical scenes are represented by Samson and the lion, the Judgement of Solomon, David and Goliath and, it has been suggested, Balaam and the ass. The need for proper devotion is emphasised by two carvings depicting clerics being seized by devils. Amongst the fantastic creatures present both Wild Men and a mermaid may be found.

## LUDLOW, ST LAWRENCE

The dishonest ale-wife being cast into Hell is the most famous of these twenty-eight misericords, dating from the late fourteenth and early-to-mid-fifteenth century. Alongside this, a bridled scold attests to the misogyny common during the period. A taverner and a man warming himself by a winter fire offer glimpses of everyday life, whilst the common motif of the preaching fox is here elevated to the status of a bishop. A selection of flora and fauna punctuates the historiated carvings.

## MAIDSTONE, ALL SAINTS

The twenty early fifteenth-century misericords consist largely of foliage and heraldry. Of the others, particularly unusual is the scene of a cook going about his business.

## MANCHESTER CATHEDRAL

A number of hunting scenes – some derived from Continental prints – are of particular interest in this set of thirty early sixteenth-century misericords. The hunters are not only human: the not uncommon image of a fox making off with a goose appears, as does the unique scene of a fox riding a dog whilst carrying a hare on a pole over his shoulder. Other noteworthy scenes include Joshua and Caleb, two men playing a board game in an ale house, an elephant and castle, a sleeping pedlar robbed by apes, and a number of compositions featuring Wild Men.

### MINSTER-IN-THANET, ST MARY

From the first quarter of the fifteenth century, the misericords carry a number of heraldic devices. Of the historiated scenes, of particular interest is the woman with her distaff, presumably preparing to chase the fox who makes off with a bird in the left-hand supporter, offering a different focus on this fairly common narrative. Other notable scenes show a devil settling in a woman's elaborate head-dress and a cook stirring a large pot.

### NANTWICH, ST MARY

Dating perhaps to the earlier years of the fifteenth century, the set consists of twenty misericords. Conflict may be found in fights between a lion and a wyvern, Samson fighting the lion, two men wrestling, St George battling the dragon, a wyvern attacking a curious winged figure, a griffin triumphing over a knight, and a woman beating her husband with a ladle. Other scenes of particular interest include hunters skinning a deer, a virgin entrapping a unicorn, the bestiary fox playing dead to lure birds, and a devil – most likely Tutivillus – pulling open a woman's mouth.

### NEWARK, ST MARY MAGDALEN

The twenty-six misericords date from 1521–24. There is a particular profusion of birds and animals, perhaps the most notable being an owl catching a mouse. Note also the unusually fine foliate head or 'Green Man'.

### NORWICH CATHEDRAL

Most of the sixty-one misericords are dated to the fifteenth century, with a few additions from the early sixteenth century. Samson battles the lion and St Michael slays a dragon, joining a number of angels, evangelists' symbols and the pelican in her piety in the array of overtly religious subjects, which also includes the Coronation of the Virgin. Nobility is commemorated by a number of figures who are identified by clear heraldic devices. A noteworthy scene shows a schoolroom in which four scholars read whilst a fifth is birched by the master; another carving, perhaps iconographically linked, depicts an ape birching a dog that is held by a second ape. Elsewhere an ape beats a beast on which it rides, whilst another beats two others who push him on a cart. It has been suggested that a number of scenes, including an armed man riding a boar and a man riding a sow whilst carrying a tankard in each hand, symbolise specific sins: whether or not this is the case, they certainly challenge the viewer's interpretation.

### OXFORD, ALL SOULS COLLEGE CHAPEL

Stalls display more than forty misericords, including numerous portrait heads and naturalistic animals. Hybrids include a mermaid and a goat with a man's face.

## OXFORD, MAGDALEN COLLEGE CHAPEL

The twenty-nine fifteenth-century misericords in Magdalen College are notable for the array of grotesque masks, amongst more naturalistic animals such as the hare, horse and swan. An owl with a mouse is particularly striking.

## OXFORD, NEW COLLEGE CHAPEL

More than sixty misericords from the late fourteenth century cover a broad range of subjects, with a number suggesting noble concerns, such as heraldic devices, stag hunting and romance – this is one of the sites at which the popular image of Yvain may be found. Other misericords refer to penitence, including renunciation of the Seven Deadly Sins, represented as a hydra.

## RICHMOND, ST MARY

The dozen early sixteenth-century misericords were originally from Easby Abbey. Of note are the sow playing bagpipes for two dancing piglets and a dragon making off with a goose.

## RIPON MINSTER

From the last decade of the fifteenth century, the thirty-five finely carved misericords offer a wide variety of subjects, some of which derive from Continental prints. Of note are biblical scenes: Joshua and Caleb, Samson and the gates of Gaza, and two scenes of Jonah and the whale. A number of foxes are depicted: preaching to fowl, making off with geese, and being caught by hounds. Amongst conventional subjects, such as a mermaid with comb and mirror and the pelican in her piety, may be found a man wheeling a woman in a barrow, two piglets dancing to a bagpiping sow, and an oak-crowned figure with a club which, it has been suggested, may depict Orson.

## RIPPLE, ST MARY

The fifteenth-century Ripple stalls are unique in boasting a complete series of the labours of the months amongst the sixteen misericords.

## ST DAVID'S CATHEDRAL

Of the twenty-eight misericords from the third quarter of the fifteenth century, of particular interest are two relating to boats: one shows boatbuilders at work, whilst the second shows four men in a boat at sea, one of whom appears to be suffering from sea-sickness – possibly representing an incident from the life of the local St Govan. Other noteworthy carvings include two dogs fighting over a bone, a couple setting themselves to a meal involving a calf's head on a platter, pigs attacking a fox, an animal (damaged – possibly a fox) seizing a bird, and a wyvern swallowing a man.

### SHERBORNE ABBEY

Ten fine-quality mid-fifteenth-century misericords survive. The pious subjects of the Last Judgement and St Margaret overcoming the dragon are balanced by a man birching a boy and a woman birching a man. A scene showing boys engaged in archery and riding a hobby-horse and a lion may record some form of dramatic entertainment.

### STRATFORD-ON-AVON, HOLY TRINITY

The twenty-six late fifteenth-century misericords include a number of interesting scenes amongst a number of grotesques and monsters: a rare pairing of mermaid and merman, the capture of a unicorn, a naked woman riding a stag, and a particularly violent scene of domestic disharmony.

### SUDBURY, ST GREGORY

The eighteen misericords from the second quarter of the fourteenth century predominantly depict human or animal heads.

### TEWKESBURY ABBEY

The sixteen fourteenth-century misericords have suffered some damage, rendering a number of the carvings illegible. There is a scene of marital disharmony with the woman beating the man and there are a considerable number of fantastic creatures and hybrids.

### WALSALL, ST MATTHEW

The seventeen mid-fifteenth-century misericords display a particular fondness for hybrids and grotesque masks.

### WELLS CATHEDRAL

What is perhaps most striking about the sixty-four Wells misericords, dated to the second quarter of the fourteenth century, is that a dozen remain unfinished – this is very uncommon in any location. Many of the carvings show individual animals, whilst common motifs include a mermaid, the pelican in her piety, and a preaching fox – this latter no doubt related to a further carving of a fox with a captured goose.

### WHALLEY, ST MARY

Eighteen mid-fifteenth-century misericords survive, though with much damage. Of particular interest are the three carvings – one of a woman with a Wild Man, one of the proverbial 'shoeing the goose' motif, and one of a vine – which carry inscriptions, in French, English and Latin respectively. Other carvings of note show the pursuit of a fox with a bird in its mouth, a man being beaten by his wife, a dragon carrying a swaddled child, and the pelican in her piety.

## WINCHESTER CATHEDRAL

The sixty-six early fourteenth-century misericords are notable for their range of entertainers: fools, grimacing acrobats and the occasional musician – some of which are animals. Many of the carvings show single animals, although amongst the notable exceptions are an owl and ape, a cat and mouse, and a wolf attacking a man. A particularly curious carving shows an ape carrying eggs. One carved head has a movable tongue – a very unusual feature which may also be found in St John, Halifax.

## WINCHESTER COLLEGE CHAPEL

Dating from c.1400, most of the eighteen misericords show single figures or foliage. Other carvings show a shepherd grasping a sheep under each arm, a fox making off with a goose and a kneeling beggar.

## WINDSOR, ST GEORGE'S CHAPEL

St George's Chapel boasts almost a hundred misericords, dating from 1477–84. A crowded depiction of the meeting of Edward IV and Louis XI firmly locates this royal commission, and a number of other images are appropriate to the location: military scenes, for example, and the Flight of Alexander, along with St George himself. Such celebrations of pomp and grandeur, however, are tempered by scenes from the Dance of Death and a number of threatening demons. Broad in iconographic scope –mixing saints' lives with Wild Men and anthropomorphic apes – the misericords are also significant for the influence of northern European prints upon their design, a pictorial source that was to have a significant impact upon a number of the later sets of misericords before the Reformation.

## WORCESTER CATHEDRAL

Worcester's forty-two late fourteenth-century stalls contain an unusual number of misericords depicting scenes from the Bible, including: the Temptation and Expulsion of Adam and Eve, Abraham and Isaac, Moses and the Tables of the Law, the Judgement of Solomon, Samson, Samuel, and the circumcision of Isaac. Amongst the other images of particular interest are a number of agricultural scenes probably referring to the labours of the months, a dynamically rendered scene of a joust, and a representation of the net-clad 'Clever Daughter' riding her goat.

# BIBLIOGRAPHY

Alexander, Jonathan and Paul Binski (eds). *Age of Chivalry: Art in Plantagenet England 1200–1400*. London: Weidenfeld and Nicholson, 1987.

Allen, Valerie. *On Farting: Language and Laughter in the Middle Ages*. New York: Palgrave Macmillan, 2007.

Almond, Richard. *Medieval Hunting*. Stroud: Sutton Publishing, 2003.

Anderson, J. J. (ed.). *Sir Gawain and the Green Knight, Pearl, Cleanness, Patience*. London: J. M. Dent, 1996.

Anderson, M. D. *Misericords: Medieval Life in English Woodcarving*. Harmondsworth: Penguin Books, 1954.

——. *The Choir Stalls of Lincoln Minster*. Lincoln: Friends of Lincoln Minster, 1967.

——. 'The Iconography of British Misericords'. In G. L. Remnant, *A Catalogue of Misericords in Great Britain*. London: Oxford University Press, 1969, pp. xxiii–xl.

Anonymous. *All Saints', North Street, York*, 2nd edn. York: York Civic Trust, 1989.

Aston, Margaret. 'Iconoclasm in England: Official and Clandestine'. In *Iconoclasm vs. Art and Drama*, ed. Clifford Davidson and Ann Eljenholm Nichols. Kalamazoo: Medieval Institute Publications, 1989, pp. 47–91.

Barber, Richard (ed. and trans.). *Bestiary, Being an English Version of the Bodleian Library, Oxford MS Bodley 764*. Woodbridge: Boydell Press, 1993.

——, and Anne Riches. *A Dictionary of Fabulous Beasts*. Woodbridge: Boydell, 1971.

Barney, Stephen A. 'The Plowshare of the Tongue: The Progress of a Symbol from the Bible to *Piers Plowman*'. *Mediaeval Studies* 35 (1973), 261–93.

Barnum, Priscilla Heath (ed.). *Dives and Pauper*. Vol. 1, Part 2, EETS o.s. 280. Oxford: Oxford University Press, 1980.

Barnwell, Paul, and Rosemary Horrox. Introduction to *Beverley Minster: An Illustrated History*, ed. Rosemary Horrox. Beverley: Friends of Beverley Minster, 2000, pp. 3–11.

Barr, Helen (ed.). *The Piers Plowman Tradition*. London: Everyman's Library, 1993.

Barratt, Alexandra (ed.). *Women's Writing in Middle English*. London: Longman, 1992.

Barton, Paulette E. 'Sacred Space and the Profane Image'. *Fourteenth Century England* 2 (2002), 107–29.

——. *Mercy and the Misericord in Late Medieval England: Cathedral Theology and Architecture*. Lewiston: Edwin Mellen Press, 2009.

Basford, Kathleen. *The Green Man*. Cambridge: D. S. Brewer, 1978.

Basing, Patricia. *Trades and Crafts in Medieval Manuscripts*. London: The British Library, 1990.

Baxter, Ron. *Bestiaries and their Users in the Middle Ages*. Stroud: Sutton Publishing, 1998.

Beadle, Richard, and Pamela King (eds). *York Mystery Plays: a Selection in Modern Spelling*. Oxford: Oxford University Press, 1995.

Bede. *A History of the English Church and People*, trans. Leo Sherley-Price, revised edn. Harmondsworth: Penguin, 1968.

Bell, Nicolas. *Music in Medieval Manuscripts*. London: British Library, 2001.

Bennett, H. S. *Chaucer in the Fifteenth Century*. Oxford: Clarendon Press, 1947.

Benson, C. David. *Public Piers Plowman: Modern Scholarship and Late Medieval English Culture*. University Park, PA: Pennsylvania State University Press, 2003.

Benton, Janetta Rebold. *Medieval Mischief: Wit and Humour in the Art of the Middle Ages*. Stroud: Sutton Publishing, 2004.

Bernheimer, Richard. *Wild Men in the Middle Ages: A Study in Art, Sentiment and Demonology*. Cambridge, MA: Harvard University Press, 1952.

Bestul, T. H. *Satire and Allegory in Wynnere and Wastoure*. Lincoln, NE: Nebraska University Press, 1974.

Billington, Sandra. *A Social History of the Fool*. Brighton: Harvester Press, 1984.

Blake, N. F. *The Textual Tradition of the Canterbury Tales*. London: Edward Arnold, 1985.

Blamires, Alcuin. 'The Wife of Bath and Lollardy'. *Medium Ævum* 58 (1985), 224–42.

—— (ed.). *Woman Defamed and Woman Defended.* Oxford: Clarendon Press, 1992.

Bloch, R. Howard. 'Medieval Misogyny'. *Representations* 20 (1987), 1–24.

Block, E. A. 'Chaucer's Millers and their Bagpipes'. *Speculum* 29 (1954), 239–43.

——. 'History at the Margins: Bagpipers in Medieval Manuscripts'. *History Today* 39 (1989), 42–8.

Block, Elaine C. 'Half Angel – Half Beast: Images of Women on Misericords'. *Reinardus* 5 (1992), 17–34.

——. 'A Note on Another Fight to Wear the Pants in the Family'. *The Profane Arts of the Middle Ages* 8.2 (1999), 90–9.

——. *Corpus of Medieval Misericords in France: XIII–XVI Century.* Turnhout: Brepols, 2003.

——. *Corpus of Medieval Misericords: Iberia.* Turnhout: Brepols, 2004.

——. 'The Jew on Medieval Misericords'. In *Grant Risee? The Medieval Comic Presence: Essays in Memory of Brian J. Levy*, ed. Adrian P. Tudor and Alan Hindley. Turnhout: Brepols, 2006, pp. 73–99.

——, with Frédéric Billiet. 'Musical Comedy in the Medieval Choir: England'. In *Medieval English Comedy*, ed. Sandra M. Hordis and Paul Hardwick. Turnhout: Brepols, 2007, pp. 209–30.

——, and Kenneth Varty. 'Choir-Stall Carvings of Reynard and Other Foxes'. In *Reynard the Fox: Social Engagement and Cultural Metamorphoses in the Beast Epic from the Middle Ages to the Present*, ed. Kenneth Varty. New York and Oxford: Berghahn Books, 2000, pp. 125–62.

Boenig, Robert. 'The Miller's Bagpipe: a Note on the *Canterbury Tales* A565–566'. *English Language Notes* 21 (1983), 1–6.

Bond, Francis. *Wood Carvings in English Churches 1: Misericords.* London: Oxford University Press, 1910.

Bowers, A. Joan. 'The Tree of Charity in *Piers Plowman*'. In *Literary Monographs* 6, ed. Eric Rothstein and Joseph Anthony Wittreich Jr. Madison: University of Wisconsin Press, 1975, pp. 1–34.

Bowers, John M. (ed.). *The Canterbury Tales: Fifteenth-Century Continuations and Additions.* Kalamazoo: TEAMS, 1992.

Bozon, Nicole. *Les Contes Moralisés*, ed. Lucy Toulmin Smith and Paul Meyer. Paris: Librairie De Firmin Didot, 1889.

Brant, Sebastian. *The Ship of Fools*, ed. and trans. Edwin H. Zeydel. New York: Dover Publications, 1962.

Brockwell, Charles W., Jr. *Bishop Reginald Pecock and the Lancastrian Church: Securing the Foundations of Cultural Authority.* Lewiston: Edwin Mellen Press, 1985.

Broughton, Laurel. 'Joan's Drolleries: Humour in the Margins of Fitzwilliam MS 242'. In *Medieval English Comedy*, ed. Sandra M. Hordis and Paul Hardwick. Turnhout: Brepols, 2007, pp. 125–43.

Brown, Carleton (ed.). *Religious Lyrics of the Fifteenth Century*. Oxford: Oxford University Press, 1939.

Brozyna, Martha A. (ed.). *Gender and Sexuality in the Middle Ages*. Jefferson: McFarland, 2005.

Bureau, Pierre. '"La dispute pour la culotte": variations littéraires et iconographiques d'un thème profane (XIIIe–XVIe siècle)'. *Le miroir des misericords (XIIIe–XVIIe siècle)*, Les Cahiers de Conques 2 (1996), 95–120.

Caesarius of Heisterbach. *De domino Gevardo Abbate, qui monachos in sermone dormitantes per fabulam Arcturi excitavit*, in *Dialogus Miraculorum*, ed. Joseph Strange. Cologne and Bonn: Hebeele, 1851.

Camille, Michael. *The Gothic Idol: Ideology and Image-Making in Medieval Art*. Cambridge: Cambridge University Press, 1989.

——. *Image on the Edge: The Margins of Medieval Art*. London: Reaktion, 1992.

——. *Gothic Art: Glorious Visions*. New York: Harry N. Abrams, 1996.

——. *Mirror in Parchment: The Luttrell Psalter and the Making of Medieval England*. London: Reaktion, 1998.

——. *The Medieval Art of Love: Objects and Subjects of Desire*. New York: Harry N. Abrams, 1998.

——. 'Dr Witkowski's Anus: French Doctors, German Homosexuals and the Obscene in Medieval Church Art'. In *Medieval Obscenities*, ed. Nicola McDonald. York: York Medieval Press, 2006, pp. 17–38.

Carroll, Lewis. *Through the Looking-Glass and What Alice Found There*, in *Alice's Adventures in Wonderland and Through the Looking-Glass: The Centenary Edition*, ed. Hugh Haughton. London: Penguin Books, 1998.

Cawley, A. C. (ed.). *The Wakefield Pageants in the Towneley Cycle*. Manchester: Manchester University Press, 1958.

Caxton, William. *The History of Reynard the Fox*, ed. Edward Arber. London: English Scholar's Library, 1878.

Cespedes, Frank V. 'Chaucer's Pardoner and Preaching'. *English Literary History* 44 (1977), 1–18.

Challis, M. G. *Life in Medieval England as portrayed on Church Misericords and Bench Ends*. Nettlebed, Oxfordshire: Teamband, 1998.

Chapman, Ben. *Yorkshire Misericords*. Beverley: Highgate Publications, 1996.

Chaucer, Geoffrey. *The Riverside Chaucer*, ed. Larry D. Benson. Oxford: Oxford University Press, 1988.

Cheney, C. R. 'Legislation of the Medieval English Church'. *English Historical Review* 50 (1935), 385–417.

Chrétien de Troyes. *Yvain*. In *Arthurian Romances*, trans. D. D. R. Owen. London: J. M. Dent, 1987, pp. 281–373.

Clark, Willene B. *A Medieval Book of Beasts. The Second-Family Bestiary: Commentary, Art, Text and Translation*. Woodbridge: The Boydell Press, 2006.

Cohen, Jeffrey Jerome. 'Hybrids, Monsters, Borderlands: The Bodies of Gerald of Wales'. In *The Postcolonial Middle Ages*, ed. Jeffrey Jerome Cohen. New York: Palgrave, 2001), pp. 85–104.

Coleman, Janet. *English Literature in History 1350–1400: Medieval Readers and Writers*. London: Hutchinson, 1981.

Cooper, Helen. *The Structure of the Canterbury Tales*. Athens, GA: University of Georgia Press, 1984.

——. *The Canterbury Tales*, 2nd edn, Oxford Guides to Chaucer. Oxford: Oxford University Press, 1996.

*The Danse Macabre of Women: Ms. Fr. 995 of the Bibliothèque Nationale*, ed. Ann Tukey Harrison with a chapter by Sandra L. Hindman. Kent, OH: Kent State University Press, 1994.

Davidson, Clifford (ed.). *Fools and Folly*. Kalamazoo: Medieval Institute Publications, 1996.

Dickinson, John. *Misericords of North West England: Their Nature and Significance*. Lancaster: Centre for North-West Regional Studies, 2008.

Dobson, R. B. [Barrie]. 'The Later Middle Ages: 1215–1500'. In *A History of York Minster*, ed. G. E. Aylmer and Reginald Cant. Oxford: Clarendon Press, 1977, pp. 44–109.

——. (ed). *The Peasants' Revolt of 1381*, 2nd edn. Basingstoke: Macmillan, 1983.

Doel, Fran and Geoff. *The Green Man in Britain*. Stroud: Tempus, 2001.

Dresen-Coenders, Lène. 'Witches as Devils' Concubines'. In *Saints and She-Devils: Images of Women in the 15th and 16th Centuries*, ed. Lène Dresen-Coenders. London: The Rubicon Press, 1987, pp. 59–82.

Duby, Georges. *Rural Economy and Country Life in the Medieval West*, trans. Cynthia Postan. London: Arnold, 1968.

Duffy, Eamon. *The Stripping of the Altars: Traditional Religion in England 1400–1580*. New Haven and London: Yale University Press, 1992.

Duffy, Seán. *Ireland in the Middle Ages*. London: Macmillan, 1997.

Dyas, Dee. *Pilgrimage in Medieval English Literature: 700–1500*. Cambridge: D. S. Brewer, 2001.

Edward of Norwich. *The Master of Game*, ed. William A. Baillie-Grohman and F. N. Baillie-Grohman. Philadelphia: University of Pennsylvania Press, 2005.

Enders, Jody. 'Of Miming and Signing: The Dramatic Rhetoric of Gesture'. In *Gesture in Medieval Drama and Art*, ed. Clifford Davidson. Kalamazoo: Medieval Institute Publications, 2001, pp. 1–25.

*Fasciculus morum: a Fourteenth-Century Preacher's Handbook*, ed. and trans. Siegfried Wenzel. University Park and London: Pennsylvania State University Press, 1989.

Fellows, Jennifer. 'Romance among the Choir Stalls: Middle English Romance Motifs on English Misericords'. In *Profane Images in Marginal Arts of the Middle Ages*, ed. Elaine C. Block with Frédéric Billiet, Sylvie Bethmont-Gallerand and Paul Hardwick. Turnhout: Brepols, 2008, pp.123–41.

Finucane, Ronald C. *Miracles and Pilgrims: Popular Beliefs in Medieval England*. London: J. M. Dent and Sons, 1977.

Fletcher, Alan J. Review of Siegfried Wenzel (ed.), *Fasciculus morum*, *Yearbook of Langland Studies* 4 (1990), 184–7.

——, and Susan Powell. 'The Origins of a Fifteenth-Century Sermon Collection: MSS Harley 2247 and Royal 18 B XXV'. *Leeds Studies in English* n. s. 10 (1978), 74–96.

Flynn, Tony. *The Mermaid Chair: New and Selected Poems*. Market Rasen: Dream Catcher Books, 2008.

Forrest, John. *The History of Morris Dancing: 1458–1750*. Toronto: University of Toronto Press, 1999.

Foster, Frances A. 'A Note on the *Fasciculus morum*', *Franciscan Studies* 8 (1948), 202–4.

Freitag, Barbara. *Sheela-na-gigs: Unravelling an Enigma*. London: Routledge, 2004.

Friedman, John Block. *The Monstrous Races in Medieval Art and Thought*. Syracuse: Syracuse University Press, 2000.

Froissart, John. *Chronicles of England, France, Spain and the Adjoining Countries*, trans. Thomas Johnes, 2 vols. London: William Smith, 1839.

George, Wilma, and Brunsdon Yapp. *The Naming of the Beasts: Natural History in the Medieval Bestiary*. London: Duckworth, 1991.

Gerald of Wales. *The History and Topography of Ireland*, trans. John J. O'Meara. London: Penguin, 1982.

Gibbs, Marion, and Jane Lang. *Bishops and Reform 1215–1272: with Special Reference to the Lateran Council of 1215*. London: Oxford University Press, 1934.

Gombrich, E. H. *Art and Illusion: a Study in the Psychology of Pictorial Representation*, 5th edn. Oxford: Phaidon Press, 1977.

Gower, John. *The Complete Works of John Gower*, ed. G. C. Macaulay, 4 vols. Oxford: Clarendon Press, 1899–1902.

——. *The Major Latin Works of John Gower*, trans. Eric W. Stockton. Seattle: University of Washington Press, 1962.

Gravestock, Pamela. 'Did Imaginary Animals Exist?' In *The Mark of the Beast*, ed. Debra Hassig. New York and London: Routledge, 2000, pp. 119–39.

Gray, Douglas. 'Notes on Some Medieval Mystical, Magical and Moral Cats'. In *Langland, the Mystics and the Medieval English Religious Tradition: Essays in Honour of S. S. Hussey*, ed. Helen Phillips. Cambridge: D. S. Brewer, 1990, pp. 185–202.

Grisdale, D. M. (ed.). *Three Middle English Sermons from the Worcester Chapter Manuscript F.10*. Leeds: Leeds School of English, 1939.

Grosseteste, Robert. *Epistolae*, ed. Henry Richards Luard. London: Longman, 1861.

Grössinger, Christa. 'Humour and Folly in English Misericords of the First Quarter of the Sixteenth Century'. In *Early Tudor England: Proceedings of the 1987 Harlaxton Symposium*, ed. Daniel Williams. Woodbridge: Boydell Press, 1989, pp. 73–85.

——. *Picturing Women in Late Medieval and Renaissance Art*. Manchester: Manchester University Press, 1997.

——. *The World Upside-Down: English Misericords*. London: Harvey Miller Publishers, 1997.

——. *Humour and Folly in Secular and Profane Prints of Northern Europe: 1430–1540*. London: Harvey Miller Publishers, 2002.

——. 'Tutivillus'. In *Profane Images in Marginal Arts of the Middle Ages*, ed. Elaine C. Block with Frédéric Billiet, Sylvie Bethmont-Gallerand and Paul Hardwick. Turnhout: Brepols, 2008, pp. 47–62.

——. 'The Foolishness of Old Age'. In *The Playful Middle Ages: Meanings of Play and Plays of Meaning. Essays in Memory of Elaine C. Block*, ed. Paul Hardwick. Turnhout: Brepols, forthcoming.

Hardwick, Oz. *Carrying Fire*. Bristol: bluechrome, 2006.

Hardwick, Paul. 'The Monkeys' Funeral in the Pilgrimage Window, York Minster'. *Art History* 23 (2000), 290–9.

——. 'Breaking the Rules that "ben not written": Reginald Pecock and the Vernacular'. *Parergon* n.s. 19.2 (2002), 101–18.

——. 'Through a Glass, Darkly: Interpreting Animal Physicians'. *Reinardus* 15 (2002), 63–70.

——. 'Foxing Daun Russell: Moral Lessons of Poultry on Misericords and in Literature'. *Reinardus* 17 (2004), 85–94.

——. 'The Merchant, the Monkeys and the Lure of Money'. *Reinardus* 19 (2006), 83–90.

——. 'Making Light of Devotion: The Pilgrimage Window in York Minster'. In *Medieval English Comedy*, ed. Sandra M. Hordis and Paul Hardwick. Turnhout: Brepols, 2007, pp. 61–82.

——. '"Hares on the Hearthstones" in Medieval England'. *Reinardus* 20 (2007–08), 29–39.

——. 'Talking Dirty: Vernacular Language and the Lower Body'. In *The Playful Middle Ages: Meanings of Play and Plays of Meaning. Essays in Memory of Elaine C. Block*, ed. Paul Hardwick. Turnhout: Brepols, forthcoming.

Harris, Mary Dormer. 'The Misericords of Coventry'. *Transactions and Proceedings of the Birmingham Archaeological Society* 52 (1927), 246–66.

Harrison, Hugh. 'Technical Aspects of the Misericord'. In *Profane Images in Marginal Arts of the Middle Ages*, ed. Elaine C. Block with Frédéric Billiet, Sylvie Bethmont-Gallerand and Paul Hardwick. Turnhout: Brepols, 2008, pp. xix–xlii.

Haydn, J. A. *Misericords in St Mary's Cathedral Limerick*. Revised by M. J. Talbot. Limerick: Treaty Press, 1994.

Henisch, Bridget Ann. *The Medieval Calendar Year*. University Park, PA: Pennsylvania State University Press, 1999.

Holbein, Hans the Younger. *The Dance of Death: A Complete Facsimile of the Original 1538 Edition of Les simulachres et historiees faces de la mort*. New York: Dover Publications, 1971.

Hourihane, Colum. *Gothic Art in Ireland 1169–1550: Enduring Vitality*. New Haven and London: Yale University Press, 2003.

Houwen, Luuk. 'Sex, Songs and Sirens: A New Score for an Old Song'. *The Profane Arts of the Middle Ages* 5.1 (1996), 103–21.

——. 'Bestiaries in Wood? Misericords, Animal Imagery and the Bestiary Tradition'. In *The Playful Middle Ages: Meanings of Play and Plays of Meaning. Essays in Memory of Elaine C. Block*, ed. Paul Hardwick. Turnhout: Brepols, forthcoming.

Hudson, Anne. 'A Lollard Sect Vocabulary?' In *Lollards and their Books*, ed. Anne Hudson. London: Hambledon Press, 1985, pp. 141–64.

——. 'Epilogue: The Legacy of *Piers Plowman*'. In *A Companion to Piers Plowman*, ed. John A. Alford. Berkeley: University of California Press, 1988, pp. 251–66.

——. *The Premature Reformation: Wycliffite Texts and Lollard History*. Oxford: Oxford University Press, 1988.

——. '*Piers Plowman* and the Peasants' Revolt: a Problem Revisited'. *Yearbook of Langland Studies* 8 (1994), 85–106.

Hudson, H. A. *The Medieval Woodwork in Manchester Cathedral.* Manchester: Sherratt and Hughes, 1924.

Humphrey, Chris. *The Politics of Carnival: Festive Misrule in Medieval England.* Manchester: Manchester University Press, 2001.

Hunt, John. 'The Limerick Cathedral Misericords'. *Ireland of the Welcomes* 20.3 (1971), 12–16.

Jacobus de Voragine. *The Golden Legend: Readings on the Saints*, trans. William Granger Ryan, 2 vols. Princeton: Princeton University Press, 1993.

Jacques de Vitry. *The Exempla or Illustrative Stories from the 'Sermones vulgares' of Jacques de Vitry*, ed. and trans. Thomas F. Crane. London: Nutt, 1890.

James, M. R. '*Pictor in carmine*'. *Archaeologia* 94 (1951), 141–66.

Janson, H. W. *Apes and Ape Lore in the Middle Ages and the Renaissance.* London: Warburg Institute, 1952.

Jones, Malcolm. 'The Misericords of Beverley Minster: a Corpus of Folkloric Imagery and its Cultural Milieu, with special reference to the influence of Northern European Iconography on Late-medieval and Early Modern English Woodwork'. Unpublished PhD thesis. Polytechnic of the South West, 1991.

——. 'The Secular Badges'. In *Heilig en Profaan*, Rotterdam Papers 8, ed. H. J. E. van Beuningen and A. M. Koldeweij. Cothen: Stichting Middeleeuwse Religieuze en Profane Insignes, 1993, pp. 99–109.

——. 'The Misericords'. In *Beverley Minster: An Illustrated History*, ed. Rosemary Horrox. Beverley: Friends of Beverley Minster, 2000, pp. 157–74.

——. 'The Sexual and the Secular Badges'. In *Heilig en Profaan* 2, Rotterdam Papers 12, ed. H. J. E. van Beuningen, A. M. Koldeweij and D. Kicken. Cothen: Stichting Middeleeuwse Religieuze en Profane Insignes, 2001, pp. 196–206.

——. 'German and Flemish Prints as Design-Sources for the Misericords in St George's Chapel, Windsor (1477×84)'. In *Windsor: Medieval Archaeology, Art and Architecture of the Thames Valley*, ed. Laurence Keen and Eileen Scarff. *The British Archaeological Association Conference Transactions* 25 (2002), 155–65.

——. *The Secret Middle Ages: Discovering the Real Medieval World.* Stroud: Sutton Publishing, 2002.

——. Review of Ruth Mellinkoff, *Averting Demons*. In *Profane Images in the Marginal Arts of the Middle Ages*, ed. Elaine C. Block, with Frédéric Billiet, Sylvie Bethmont-Gallerand and Paul Hardwick. Turnhout: Brepols, 2008, pp. 339–63.

——. 'Metal-Cut Border Ornaments in Parisian Printed Books of Hours as Design Sources for Sixteenth-Century Works of Art'. In *Publishing the Fine and Applied Arts, 1500–2000*, ed. Giles Mandelbrote. Forthcoming.

Kaske, R. E. 'The Knight's Interruption of the Monk's Tale'. *ELH* 24 (1957), 249–68.

Kauffmann, C. M. *Biblical Imagery in Medieval England 700–1550*. London: Harvey Miller Publishers, 2003.

Kempe, Margery. *The Book of Margery Kempe*, ed. Sanford Brown Meech and Hope Emily Allen, EETS o. s. 212. Oxford: Oxford University Press, 1886.

Kirk, Elizabeth D. 'Langland's Plowman and the Recreation of Fourteenth-Century Religious Metaphor'. *Yearbook of Langland Studies* 2 (1988), 1–21.

Knapp, Peggy. *Chaucer and the Social Contest*. London: Routledge, 1990.

Koldeweij, A. M. 'A Barefaced *Roman de la Rose* (Paris, B.N., ms. fr. 25526) and some Late Medieval Mass-Produced Badges of a Sexual Nature'. In *Flanders in a European Perspective: Manuscript Illumination around 1400 in Flanders and Abroad*, eds. Maurits Smeyers and Bert Cardon. Leuven: Uitgeverij Peeters, 1995, pp. 499–516.

Kraus, Dorothy and Henry. *The Hidden World of Misericords*. London: Michael Joseph, 1976.

Laird, Marshall. *English Misericords*. London: John Murray, 1986.

Lamond, Elizabeth (ed. and trans). *Walter of Henley's Husbandry, together with an Anonymous Husbandry, Seneschaucie and Robert Grosseteste's Rules*. London: Longmans, Green and Co., 1890.

Langland, William. *The Vision of Piers Plowman: a Complete Edition of the B-Text*, ed. A. V. C. Schmidt. London: Dent, 1995.

Laver, James. *Costume and Fashion: A Concise History*, revised edn. London: Thames and Hudson, 1995.

Lavezzo, Kathy. *Angels on the Edge of the World: Geography, Literature, and English Community, 1000–1534*. Ithaca: Cornell University Press, 2006.

Lawton, David. 'Lollardy and the *Piers Plowman* Tradition'. *Modern Language Review* 76 (1981), 780–93.

——. 'The Unity of Middle English Alliterative Poetry'. *Speculum* 58 (1983), 72–94.

Leclercq-Marx, Jacqueline. *La Sirène dans la pensée et dans l'art de l'Antiquité et du Moyen Âge: Du mythe païen au symbole Chrétien*. Brussels: Académie Royale de Belgique, 1997.

Lenihan, Maurice. *Limerick: Its History and Antiquities, Ecclesiastical, Civil, and Military, from the Earliest Ages*. Repr. Cork: The Mercier Press, 1967.

Lester, G. A. (ed.). *Three Late Medieval Morality Plays*. London: A. C. Black, 1990.

Lomas, Roy. *Grasmere Sports: The First 150 Years*. Kendal: MTP, 2002.

Lumiansky, R. M., and David Mills (eds). *The Chester Mystery Cycle*, EETS s.s. 3. London: Oxford University Press, 1994.

McAlpine, Monica E. 'The Pardoner's Homosexuality and How It Matters'. *PMLA* 95 (1980), 8–22.

Mandeville, John. *The Travels of Sir John Mandeville*, ed. A. W. Pollard. London: Macmillan, 1900; repr. Mineola: Dover Publications, 1964.

Mannyng, Robert, of Brunne. *Handlyng Synne*, ed. Idelle Sullens. Binghamton, NY: Medieval and Renaissance Texts and Studies, 1983.

Marks, Richard. *Image and Devotion in Late Medieval England*. Stroud: Sutton Publishing, 2004.

Matthew, F. D. (ed.). *The English Works of Wyclif, Hitherto Unprinted*, EETS o.s. 74, rev. edn. London: Kegan Paul, 1902.

Mellinkoff, Ruth. *Averting Demons: The Protective Power of Medieval Visual Motifs and Themes*, 2 vols. Los Angeles: Ruth Mellinkoff Publications, 2004.

Merceron, Jacques E. *Dictionnaire des Saints Imaginaires et Facétieux*. Paris: Seuil, 2002.

Mirk, John. *Festial*, ed. Theodore Erbe, EETS e.s. 96. London: K. Paul, Trench, Trübner and Co., 1905.

——. *Instructions for Parish Priests*, ed. Gillis Kristensson. Lund: CWK Gleerup, 1974.

Mittman, Asa Simon. 'The Other Close at Hand: Gerald of Wales and the "Marvels of the West"'. In *The Monstrous Middle Ages*, ed. Bettina Bildhauer and Robert Mills. Cardiff: University of Wales Press, 2003, pp. 97–112.

——. *Maps and Monsters in Medieval England*. London: Routledge, 2006.

Montagu, Jeremy and Gwen. *Minstrels and Angels: Carvings of Musicians in Medieval English Churches*. Berkeley: Fallen Leaf Press, 1998.

Murray, Hilda M. R. (ed.). *Erthe upon Erthe, Printed from Twenty-Four Manuscripts*, EETS o.s. 141. London: Oxford University Press, 1911.

Nelson, Alan H. *The Medieval English Stage: Corpus Christi Pageants and Plays*. Chicago and London: Chicago University Press, 1974.

Nichols, Ann Eljenholm. *Seeable Signs: The Iconography of the Seven Sacraments 1350–1544*. Woodbridge: Boydell Press, 1994.

O'Connor, David, and Jeremy Haselock. 'The Stained and Painted Glass'. In *A History of York Minster*, ed. G. E. Aylmer and Reginald Cant. Oxford: Clarendon Press, 1977, pp. 313–93.

O'Connor, Terry. 'Thinking about Beastly Bodies'. In *Breaking and Shaping Beastly Bodies: Animals as Material Culture in the Middle Ages*, ed. Aleksander Pluskowski. Oxford: Oxbow Books, 2007, pp. 1–10.

Owst, G. R. *Literature and Pulpit in Medieval England: a Neglected Chapter in the History of English Letters and of the English People*, 2nd edn. Oxford: Blackwell, 1961.

Pantin, W. A. *The English Church in the Fourteenth Century*. Cambridge: Cambridge University Press, 1955.

Paré, Ambroise. *On Monsters and Marvels*, trans. Janis L. Pallister. Chicago: University of Chicago Press, 1982.

Pearsall, Derek. *The Life of Geoffrey Chaucer*. Oxford: Blackwell, 1992.

——. *The Canterbury Tales*. London: Routledge, 1993.

Pearson, Terry. 'The Mermaid in the Church'. In. *Profane Images in Marginal Arts of the Middle Ages*, ed. Elaine C. Block with Frédéric Billiet, Sylvie Bethmont-Gallerand and Paul Hardwick. Turnhout: Brepols, 2008, pp. 105–22.

Pecock, Reginald. *The Repressor of Over Much Blaming of Clergy*, ed. Churchill Babington, 2 vols. London: Longman, Green, Longman and Roberts, 1860.

——. *Reginald Pecock's Book of Faith*, ed. J. L. Morison. Glasgow: J. Maclehose and Sons, 1909.

——. *The Reule of Crysten Religioun*, ed. William Cabell Greet, EETS o.s. 171. London: Oxford University Press, 1927.

Phillips, Helen. *An Introduction to the Canterbury Tales*. London: Macmillan, 2000.

Phipson, Emma. *Choir Stalls and their Carvings: Examples of Misericords from English Cathedrals and Churches*. London: B. T. Batsford, 1896.

Piponnier, Françoise, and Perrine Mane. *Dress in the Middle Ages*, trans. Caroline Beamish. New Haven and London: Yale University Press, 1997.

*The Plowman's Tale: The c.1532 and 1606 Editions of a Spurious Canterbury Tale*, ed. Mary Rhinelander McCarl. New York and London: Garland, 1997.

Powell, Susan. 'A Critical Edition of the *Temporale* Sermons of MSS Harley 2247 and Royal B XXV'. Unpublished D.Phil thesis, University of London, 1980.

—— (ed.). *The Advent and Nativity Sermons from a Fifteenth-Century Revision of John Mirk's Festial, edited from B. L. MSS Harley 2247, Royal 18 B XXV and Gloucester Cathedral Library 22*. Heidelberg: C. Winter, 1981.

——. 'John Mirk's *Festial* and the Pastoral Programme'. *Leeds Studies in English* n. s. 22 (1991), 85–102.

Pudney, John. *Lewis Carroll and His World*. London: Thames and Hudson, 1976.

Purvis, J. S. 'The Ripon Carvers and the Lost Choir-Stalls of Bridlington Priory'. *Yorkshire Archaeological Journal* 29 (1929), 157–201.

——. 'The Use of Continental Woodcuts and Prints by the "Ripon School" of Woodcarvers in the Early Sixteenth Century'. *Archaeologia* 85 (1935), 107–28.

Rawcliffe, Carole. *Medicine and Society in Later Medieval Europe*. Stroud: Sutton Publishing, 1995.

Reeves, Compton. *Pleasures and Pastimes in Medieval England*. Stroud: Sutton Publishing, 1995.

Remnant, G. L. *A Catalogue of Misericords in Great Britain*. London: Oxford University Press, 1969.

Riches, Samantha. *St George: Hero, Martyr and Myth*. Stroud: Sutton Publishing, 2005.

Robbins, Rossell Hope. 'Levation Prayers in Middle English Verse'. *Modern Philology* 40 (1942), 131–46.

—— (ed.). *Historical Poems of the XIVth and XVth Centuries*. New York: Columbia University Press, 1959.

Rogers, Katharine M. *Cat*. London: Reaktion Books, 2006.

Ross, Woodburn O. *Middle English Sermons edited from British Museum MS. Royal 18 b. xxiii*, EETS o.s. 209. London: Oxford University Press, 1940.

Rothwell, Harry (ed.). *English Historical Documents 1189–1327*. London: Eyre and Spottiswoode, 1975.

Rowland, Beryl. *Blind Beasts: Chaucer's Animal World*. Kent, OH: Kent State University Press, 1971.

——. *Animals with Human Faces: A Guide to Animal Symbolism*. London: George Allen and Unwin, 1974.

Rubin, Miri. *Corpus Christi: The Eucharist in Late Medieval Culture*. Cambridge: Cambridge University Press, 1991.

Salisbury, Joyce E. *The Beast Within: Animals in the Middle Ages*. London: Routledge, 1994.

Scase, Wendy. 'Reginald Pecock'. In *Authors of the Middle Ages* 3, ed. M. C. Seymour. Aldershot: Variorum, 1996, pp. 75–146.

Scott, Kathleen L. 'Sow and Bagpipe Imagery in the Miller's Portrait'. *Review of English Studies* 18 (1967), 287–90.

Shallers, A. P. '*The Nun's Priest's Tale*: an Ironic Exemplum'. *ELH* 42 (1975), 319–37.

Siefker, Phyllis. *Santa Claus, Last of the Wild Men: The Origins and Evolution of Saint Nicholas, Spanning 50,000 Years*. Jefferson: McFarland, 1997.

Simmons, Thomas Frederick (ed.). *The Lay Folks Mass Book*, EETS o.s. 71. London: Oxford University Press, 1879.

*The Simonie: A Parallel-Text Edition*, ed. D. Embree and E. Urquhart. Heidelberg: Carl Winter Universitätsverlag, 1991.

Southworth, John. *Fools and Jesters at the English Court*. Stroud: Sutton Publishing, 1998.

Speake, Jennifer (ed.). *The Oxford Dictionary of Proverbs*, 4th edn. Oxford: Oxford University Press, 2003.

Spencer, Helen Leith. *English Preaching in the Late Middle Ages*. Oxford: Oxford University Press, 1993.

Sprunger, David A. 'Parodic Animal Physicians from the Margins of Medieval Manuscripts'. In *Animals in the Middle Ages*, ed. Nona C. Flores. New York and London: Routledge, 1996, pp. 67–81.

Sturges, Robert S. *Chaucer's Pardoner and Gender Theory: Bodies of Discourse*. London: Macmillan, 2000.

Syme, Alison. 'Taboos and the Holy in Bodley 764'. In *The Mark of the Beast*, ed. Debra Hassig. New York and London: Routledge, 2000, pp. 163–84.

Tentler, Thomas N. *Sin and Confession on the Eve of the Reformation*. Princeton: Princeton University Press, 1977.

Tisdall, M. W. *God's Beasts: Identify and Understand Animals in Church Carvings*. Plymouth: Charlesfort Press, 1998.

Tracy, Charles. *English Gothic Choir-Stalls 1200–1400*. Woodbridge: Boydell Press, 1987.

——. *English Gothic Choir-Stalls 1400–1540*. Woodbridge: Boydell Press, 1990.

——. 'Dating the Misericords from the Thirteenth-Century Choir Stalls at Exeter Cathedral'. In *Medieval Art and Architecture at Exeter Cathedral*, ed. Francis Kelly. Leeds: Maney, 1991, pp. 180–7.

——. *Continental Church Furniture in England: A Traffic in Piety*. Woodbridge: Antique Collectors' Club, 2001.

——. 'Misericords as an Interpretative Tool in the Study of Choir Stalls'. In *Profane Images in Marginal Arts of the Middle Ages*, ed. Elaine C. Block with Frédéric Billiet, Sylvie Bethmont-Gallerand and Paul Hardwick. Turnhout: Brepols, 2008, pp. 3–20.

*Les Très Riches Heures du Duc de Berry*. With an introduction by Jean Longnon and Raymond Cazelles. London: Thames and Hudson, 1969.

Trevisa, John. *On the Properties of Things: John Trevisa's translation of Bartholomæus Anglicus De Proprietatibus Rerum, A Critical Text*, ed. M. C. Seymour *et al.*, 2 vols. Oxford: Clarendon Press, 1975.

Trubshaw, Bob. *Explore Folklore*. Loughborough: Heart of Albion Press, 2002.

Turville-Petre, Thorlac (ed.). *Alliterative Poetry of the Later Middle Ages: An Anthology*. London: Routledge, 1989.

Twycross, Meg, and Sarah Carpenter. *Masks and Masking in Medieval and Early Tudor England*. Aldershot: Ashgate, 2002.

Varty, Kenneth. 'Reynard the Fox and the Smithfield Decretals'. *Journal of the Warburg and Courtauld Institutes* 26 (1963), 348–54.

——. *Reynard the Fox: A Study of the Fox in Medieval English Art.* Leicester: Leicester University Press, 1967.

——. *Reynard, Renart, Reinaert and Other Foxes in Medieval England: The Iconographic Evidence.* Amsterdam: Amsterdam University Press, 1999.

Waddell, Helen. *Beasts and Saints*, new edn. London: Darton, Longman and Todd, 1995.

Walker Bynum, Caroline. *Fragmentation and Redemption: Essays on Gender and the Human Body in Medieval Religion.* New York: Zone, 1991.

Walter, D. Alleyne. 'Ancient Woodwork IV: The Misericords in the Cathedral Church of Limerick'. *The Reliquary*, n. s. 7 (July 1893), 129–31.

*The Wars of Alexander: an Alliterative Romance, Translated Chiefly from the Historia Alexandri Magni De Preliis*, ed. Walter W. Skeat, EETS e.s. 47. London: N. Trübner and Co., 1886.

Watson, Nicholas. 'Censorship and Cultural Change in Late-Medieval England: Vernacular Theology, the Oxford Translation Debate, and Arundel's Constitutions of 1409'. *Speculum* 70 (1995), 822–64.

Wawn, Andrew N. 'The Genesis of *The Plowman's Tale*'. *Yearbook of English Studies* 2 (1972), 21–40.

Weir, Anthony, and James Jerman. *Images of Lust: Sexual Carvings on Medieval Churches.* London: B. T. Batsford, 1986.

Wenzel, Siegfried. 'Chaucer and the Language of Contemporary Preaching'. *Studies in Philology* 73 (1976), 138–61.

——. *Verses in Sermons: Fasciculus morum and its Middle English Poems.* Cambridge, MA: Medieval Society of America Publications, 1978.

——. Review of Helen Leith Spencer, *English Preaching in the Late Middle Ages. Yearbook of Langland Studies* 9 (1995), 197–203.

Westwood, Jennifer, and Jacqueline Simpson. *The Lore of the Land: A Guide to England's Legends, from Spring-Heeled Jack to the Witches of Warboys.* London: Penguin Books, 2005.

White, Lynn, Jr. *Medieval Technology and Social Change.* Oxford: Oxford University Press, 1962.

Wildridge, T. Tindall. *The Misereres of Beverley Minster: A Complete Series of Drawings of the Seat Carvings in the Choir of St John's, Beverley, Yorkshire; with Notes on the Plates and Subject.* Hull: J. Plaxton, 1879.

Wilkins, David (ed.). *Concilia Magnae Britanniae et Hiberniae*, 4 vols. 1373: repr. Brussels, 1964.

Winternitz, Emanuel. *Musical Instruments and their Symbolism in Western Art*, 2nd edn. London: Yale University Press, 1979.

# INDEX

www.ingramcontent.com/pod-product-compliance
Ingram Content Group UK Ltd.
Pitfield, Milton Keynes, MK11 3LW, UK
UKHW020324280225
455670UK00009B/128